Greg Whitlock

Returning to Sils-Maria

A Commentary to Nietzsche's "Also sprach Zarathustra"

PETER LANG
New York • Bern • Frankfurt am Main • Paris

Library of Congress Cataloging-in-Publication Data

B
3313
, A44
W55
1990

Whitlock, Greg
   Returning to Sils-Maria : a commentary to
Nietzsche's "Also sprach Zarathustra" / Greg Whitlock.
     p. cm. — (American university studies. Series V,
Philosophy ; vol. 87)
     Includes bibliographical references.
     1. Nietzsche, Friedrich Wilhelm, 1844-1900. Also
sprach Zarathustra. 2. Philosophy. I. Nietzsche,
Friedrich Wilhelm, 1844-1900. Also sprach Zarathustra.
II. Title. III. Series.
   B3313.A44W55   1990   193 — dc20   89-27809
   ISBN 0-8204-1198-1   CIP
   ISSN 0739-6392

CIP-Titelaufnahme der Deutschen Bibliothek

Whitlock, Greg:
Returning to Sils-Maria : a commentary to
Nietzsche's "Also sprach Zarathustra" / Greg
Whitlock. — New York; Bern; Frankfurt am
Main; Paris: Lang, 1990.
   (American University Studies: Ser. 5,
   Philosophy; Vol. 87)
   ISBN 0-8204-1198-1

NE: American University Studies / 05

Printed by Weihert-Druck GmbH, Darmstadt, West Germany

Returning to Sils-Maria

American University Studies

Series V
Philosophy
Vol. 87

PETER LANG
New York • Bern • Frankfurt am Main • Paris

Dedicated to

JOHN H. ZAMMITO,

LEONARD G. SCHULZE

and

RICHARD L. SCHACHT

Acknowledgments

As is appropriate upon the completion of such a task, I would like to acknowledge those who were the primary sources of aid, inspiration and encouragement to me in the production of this manuscript. My foremost gratitude is toward my parents for my education and for their encouragement over the years. Second only to my parents in my gratitude are my educators, most notably John H. Zammito, Richard L. Schacht and Leonard G.Schulze. This project is unthinkable without the help of the Fulbright-Hayes Commission and the University of Heidelberg. I would like to thank the Goethe-Schiller Archives in Weimar, East Germany, and Nietzsche-Haus in Sils-Maria, Switzerland, for valuable research opportunities. Dr. Klaus Kaehler, my primary German reader, also deserves my deep gratitude for his comments concerning Feuerbach and Nietzsche. This acknowledgment would be unacceptably incomplete without an expression of my heartfelt gratitude to Alfred and Elfriede Fischer of Weimar, East Germany and especially to Wulf and Gisela Datow of Heidelberg, West Germany, for encouragement, professional guidance in Germanistics and for magnificent hospitality and friendship.

Finally, I would like to express my heartfelt thanks and love to Allison Hawkins, whose encouragement empowered me to bring this long project to completion.

Table of Contents

Preface

One hundred years have passed since Friedrich Nietzsche penned the last words of *Also sprach Zarathustra*. And yet the significance to mankind of both author and book has continued to grow steadily. Indeed, *Zarathustra* is a book whose significance could not have been recognized immediately: its conception was a supernova whose emissions only now begin to reach us. *Zarathustra* is for this reason Nietzsche's most untimely meditation. *Zarathustra* is a book whose time is yet to come, a book whose meaning unfolds only over generations and therefore a book whose ultimate value will be judged by its effects on *millenia*, not on a mere lifetime or generation. When such a work arises on mankind's spiritual horizons, it inspires a multitude of studies, both lyrical and scholarly. *Zarathustra* is a book so (relatively) recent that few detailed studies exist, though its richness assures that over time countless secondary sources will be written.

Nietzsche's *Zarathustra*, I would argue, is a book of man's *future*, not of his past or present. Man's past is an endless procession of tradition and unchallenged social moralities. Looking over man's past, Zarathustra concludes that mankind has hitherto lacked a *goal*. Zarathustra's project is to give humanity a goal it may strive after. And he commands that every resource must be allocated in the service of this goal. Humanity has been led by standards of "good and evil," "right and wrong" according to the whims of the ages. Only when mankind has a goal, or purpose for its existence, based on the values of "body and earth" rather than the "soul" and the "hereafter," will basic standards of right and wrong, etc., make sense for the first time.

Man's history is not unlike a directionless flow of countless waves that rise and fall. Humanity has been countless experiments, trials and failures, concerning every aspect of its existence.

Humanity, for Zarathustra, is not a changeless, eternal species: the very idea of one single continuous species is itself a mere abstraction. Mankind is pure self-overcoming, i.e., the species is in constant, if gradual, change. But this change is not aimless motion. Human spirit is self-creative: it is that which determines what it is by *becoming* what it is. As a goal, humanity strives to achieve something over and beyond itself. Mankind's goal, however, cannot be measured by the average specimen, but only by its highest types.

Opportunistic leaders have used the great masses of humanity to further their own finite projects. But so far only the worst have led mankind; those with brute power or the narcotic attraction of religion, or both. Such leaders have only contributed to the dangers faced by man as he attempts to search for a meaningful goal in life. They have organized society in all cases to produce only the minimally human specimen, hardly an individual at all. Yet it is only the creation of higher types that allows for such a goal to be created. All too many humans are superfluous, simply leading out standardized lives. Mankind's destiny, though, rests with the exemplars of the species, not with its masses and herd-types. Until the proper leaders arise, mankind must aimlessly flail under the abuses of jesters and tyrants. Thus Zarathustra asks the terrifying question, how might man sacrifice himself that a higher type may arise? To this end mankind is only a means: the "overcoming" of the species is more important than its preservation. Humanity in its historical circumstances, as Zarathustra says repeatedly, is "something that must be overcome." Like all great works, then, *Zarathustra* does not find the limit of its message in the faiths, ideologies and mass movements of a bygone era.

Nor does *Zarathustra's* message limit itself to the narrow confines of some "present day." Nietzsche was, if anything, the philosopher who discerned that the "present day" for Europe would be an era of commercialism, spiritual shallowness and petty politics (i.e., class and national interests). Ideas in the modern age could mean only the threadbare ideologies of capitalism, socialism and democracy. But *Zarathustra* is not a book whose purpose is either offensive or defensive in the struggles of contemporary man.

Although nineteenth and twentieth-century experience has centered on the legitimation, or illegitimation, of all authority, *Zarathustra* is not a partisan on the cause of nihilism (and *a fortiori* not on behalf of a social morality). For its author *presumes* the foundationlessness of all values hitherto. Unlike the reactive nihilists (Ludwig Feuerbach, Max Stirner, Bruno Bauer, David Friedrich Strauss, et al.), who tasked themselves a critique of the highest values (and so arrived at a nihilistic conclusion), Nietzsche begins with the presumption of nihilism, to arrive at a type, however idiosyncratic, of optimism. Many would-be critics of Nietzsche from both the right and left-wing have erred in identifying him with partisan battles being fought in the nineteenth and twentieth-centuries. But it must be concluded after searching his texts for any sustained commentary on european events whatsoever, that Nietzsche laid no importance on the victory of one recognizable, politically organized group or country over any other, and that the entire panorama of european power politics held no more romantic delight for him than the carnage of Woerth. Nietzsche's thought in *Zarathustra* is "untimely" to its own historical setting and has far more to do with man's future beyond nihilism.

Indeed, *Zarathustra* is a book for future man. To this end, Nietzsche has built a *soothsaying* faculty into his main character. Zarathustra can foresee outlines of the future of mankind, and indeed at one point "flies into the future." It is upon his vision of man's destiny that the riddles of overman, eternal return, will to power and the death of god find a ground for unification. And if the solutions to these riddles are harbingers of man's fate, as I would suggest, then it must be possible to explicate what Zarathustra's vision of the future holds.

In Zarathustra's vision of the future, mankind as a species suffers a general demise (*Untergang*). Human life as known hitherto would cease to exist. It is Nietzsche's odd sort of optimism that some life-form would overcome these conditions to begin aright at what the spiritual leaders of mankind hitherto (i.e., the founders and proponents of religions) had failed. As I interpret his teaching, Zarathustra envisions a future of great wars, nihilism, more wars, and more nihilism, until these wars result in a catastrophe so great as to cause a general and deep loss of belief in God. (One possible precedent here is the increased secularization of judaism after the holocaust.) This period, cryptically called "the Great Noon," ushers in a *post-christian era*. In this era the human species dirempts into two distinct sub-species; the last man and the overman. The overman is one who is able to accept, affirm and live by the doctrine of eternal return of the same. He interprets the universe and himself in terms of will to power. He is filled by a superabundant health and well-being. To these overmen, christianity and its related monotheisms would be no more believable than ancient mythologies. In their relation to their own *body and earth*, these new types would discover a health and well-being unimaginable in the age of poisoned foods, radiation, pollution and bio-engineered diseases. On the other hand, the last man is one who escapes the terrible nihilism of God's death by forfeiting the ability to esteem anything at all. These two types represent the *two primary fates open to future man*.

Both Zarathustra and Nietzsche look upon christianity in terms of the lifespan of its god. Christianity's God begins life as the jewish Yahweh (Jehova): in mid-life he became Jesus, God of the christians: in his senility, God aged to become "old grimbeard," the God of Pietism and Deism. The christian God has been alive scarcely two millenia: but over the entire long history of mankind, two thousand years is a mere moment. And if it were to take another two millenia for christianity to expire, what then? That too is a mere moment in the life of mankind. Nietzsche's visions are measured in millenia, not mere generations or centuries. To discern the unfolding destiny of mankind is a task still to be delegated to the "philosophers of the future." As a "firstling" of such philosophers, though, Nietzsche sees beyond the age of man and his God to the age of the overman.

It is in this idea of a *post-christian era* that Zarathustra achieves his identity, terribleness and greatness. Zarathustra demands a future in which churches lie in ruin, grass and poppies growing up through their broken walls and rooves. For the overman to live, belief in God must become impossible, i.e., Yahweh must die. Zarathustra is the one who would kill God that a *future man* might come to be. Christianity, judaism, islam, and all other monotheisms based on belief in Yahweh, would have to be crushed for the zarathustran future to be actualized. This alone shows the necessity of *millenia* for the zarathustran project to be judged by adequate standards.

It can be no coincidence that Zarathustra's most central doctrines are simultaneously clarified in his vision of the future. Zarathustra himself says repeatedly that while he is still full of wisdom about Yesterday and Today, his real concern and center of focus is Tomorrow. His image of the future thus serves as a standard of Zarathustra interpretations: only interpretations capable of resolving the teachings with Zarathustra's visions of man's destiny are plausible.

It is also no coincidence that Zarathustra's vision of the future has strong resonances in Nietzsche's other writings. Nietzsche interpreted the present and near-future of mankind to be an inevitable movement toward nihilism. Great conflicts between the last true believers in absolute values would create the conditions for a decline of civilization into wars and chaos. Nietzsche envisioned an era of great wars and unprecedented destruction and suffering. As a result of this devastation a great and deep nihilism would flood over mankind. Those whose values originated in the very motor of this cycle of nihilism and annihilation, i.e., christianity, could offer only the ancient myths of Yahweh to a species looking for new values to pull them up from nihilism. Once the ultimate aim of christianity is exposed—apocalypse—human spirit should not be deluded again. Zarathustra's "overman" would be the value to aid the "overcoming of man."

In *Zarathustra* the demise of christianity is envisioned as a *self-destruction*. Nietzsche's militant atheism at that time still fell short of advocating the violent destruction of religion from without. Encouragements to militancy in one section (e.g., IV.13) are taken away by others (e.g., II.4). But it is clearly Zarathustra's unshaken belief that, left to its own laws of degeneration, christianity will die a thousand deaths of disbelief. The higher man can afford to "pass by" the priest, because the latter is symptomatic of a type whose path is degeneration. These preachers of death lead the herds of mankind into anti-naturalism of body and spirit. Thus the "all-too-many," "rabble" et al., degenerate in the unfolding of their own innermost destinies. But what this means is that innermost thanatological impulses express themselves in a cycle of nihilism and self-annihilation. The Church leads mankind into the apocalypse as a sort of grand scale self-fulfilling prophecy. For to look at the judeo-christian image of man's fate as apocalypse is to foresee what christianity would will as the inevitable, final and irreversible future of man: death, pestilence, war and disease. As consolation, it offers the illusory "soul," "redemption" and "reward." On an historical and personal level, then, christianity is the force of nihilism which has successfully taken direction over human spirit and which leads spirit to its own self-destruction: man's greatest struggle must therefore be against this "greatest enemy of all man's future."

It is crucial to recognize that, when I argue that *Zarathustra* is a book of the future, I do not mean to say that either Nietzsche or his character foretell future events with any specificity. Nor do I mean to say that any vision of the future Nietzsche may have had has any bearing on the validity of his ideas. Humanity has already experienced two wars on a scale unprecedented in Nietzsche's time: thus the only prophecy he made of any specificity whatsoever has already been actualized. Yet this means nothing to Nietzsche's vision, for all wars, small or large, are examples of what Nietzsche calls "great events," i.e., world historical happenings affecting masses of people, but nonetheless giving no higher direction to humanity. Nietzsche and Zarathustra are unconcerned about great events and "men of great events." They look instead to "the stillest hours," when values are created and destroyed. The one and only important event in Nietzsche's vision of the future is one such "stillest hour," which he calls the "death of god." Regardless of whatever else Nietzsche says about the future, the only significant question raised by it is whether or not mankind will experience a post-christian era, and if so, whether man's response to the death

of god will be to seek the value of "last man" or "overman." Without
the death of god, mankind will have no future other than drifting
aimlessly through nihilism. Once the death of god is an accomplished fact, mankind will be faced with the choice between overman and last man. This highlights the floundering point of the
zarathustran vision: if mankind returns to christianity, or never
leaves it, no genuine advance, or metamorphosis, of the human
spirit is possible.

No contemporary or past event, therefore, could invalidate
Zarathustra's vision of man's destiny. Its conditions for verification
or falsification are met only when man's fate is completed. Thus
only the future will demonstrate the real meaning of Nietzsche and
his works. "The time for me hasn't come yet: some are born
posthumously." Indeed, the book is intended for a future man—
"everyone and no one"—and not for the human of his christian
Today. The real meaning of the book awaits the distant future, and
so only slowly unfolds. To read a book so full of destiny is also to
participate in its destiny. Each reader directly influences the
gradually unfolding meaning of the book *for man*. Ultimately, then,
the meaning of *Zarathustra* for man will become whatever man determines it to be.

Zarathustra is, on my interpretation, a set of riddles on man and
his fate, whose idealized and abstract characters nonetheless are to
be found shadowed in nineteenth and twentieth-century experience, e.g., the "man of great events" and Adolf Hitler. For
Zarathustra, the entire march of human history is the replication of
higher and lower types. He attempts to identify recurring types:
the "afterworldly," "scholars," "famous wise men," "warriors," "flies
of the marketplace," and many others. They are abstract, stylized,
shadowy figures whose bizarre pronouncements nonetheless
achieve starkly realistic meaning when associated with events of
past and present: for within the landscape of modern human experience we find harbingers of the fanatics, leaders, followers,
prophets, men of action and men of passionlessness that populate
the pages of *Zarathustra*.

If *Zarathustra* is a riddle of man's fate, as I have suggested, then individuals interested in commenting on their own times will find in it a voice of timeless experience and wisdom. With each age there arises new generations of "the afterworldly," "despisers of the body," "men of great events," "flies of the marketplace," and all the others. As each generation passes, so every generation will profit from a multiplicity of perspectives on this oblique and fateful book.

But if the very meaning of *Zarathustra* is so intimately connected to human future, then there must indeed be many, if not indefinitely many, possible meanings of the text. Just as *Zarathustra* is a book of infinite possible meanings, so it is a book of indefinitely many possible commentaries. There are of course an unlimited number of philosophical commentaries conceivable (—between the time the text at hand was written and its publication several years later, one other *Zarathustra* commentary has appeared along with several secondary sources on the theme.) But there are also musical commentaries: such as Richard Strauss' symphonic Opus 30; or Delius' oparatic "Eine Messe des Lebens." Sculptural commentaries such as Hermann Gysin's masterpiece "Also sprach Zarathustra" from wrought iron are rare but may achieve the depth of any other medium. Indeed, *every* medium should be capable of yielding *Zarathustra* interpretations of vast variety and depth.

But aside from the limitless possibilities of interpretation, the message of man's fate in *Zarathustra* is such a powerful, terrifying and credible vision that it alone should compel us to return once again to Sils-Maria and her brightest sun, Zarathustra. Scarcely one hundred years after the completion of *Zarathustra*, we already live in an age of nuclear weapons, biological-chemical-genetic warfare and strategies of mutual self-destruction. We have seen in events such as the holocaust how even the modern military state can transform, however temporarily, into a machine of death. We have also seen how such events lead to increased secularization in even the oldest and most venerable of faiths. And if we can raise ourselves to such a dizzying perspective, we can also look from Today into a distant Yesterday and witness the rise and fall of countless peoples, mythologies and gods. Thus even within the finite present, Zarathustra's possibility of a post-christian era does not seem so far-fetched. Indeed, one may ask whether the "going under" of mankind, the death of God and birth of the overman will require a millenium.

Even more pressing, though, is the question, given the almost inconceivable destructive power of nuclear weaponry and consequent radiation poisoning, whether lifeforms *of any type whatsoever* will survive man's next great folly. A planet as devoid of life as our moon is a different image than Zarathustra's beloved earth. Where there is no life whatsoever, there is no self-overcoming and no overman. Nietzsche's "optimism" is based on the assumption that humanity and earth are in early, if highly unstable, stages of development: it is not part of his vision, as I interpret it, that he foresees the total destruction of life on earth. Although Nietzsche noted that he had read of the theoretical possibility of "molecular explosions," he could not have envisioned the power of nuclear weaponry at mankind's disposal. Even less could he have envisioned that man would wreak such catastrophes on the earth as threatened destruction of the very ozone layer in a mere century's time. But if lifeforms of some type were miraculously to survive, they would be presented with a "body and earth" almost inconceivable to Homo Sapiens. One must imagine minimally that any lifeform surviving a nuclear war, upon discovering the last surviving copy of *Zarathustra*, would relate to it like an ape discovering a great black obelisk left by space travellers. But by my interpretation of Zarathustra's prophetic visions, mankind will suffer a "going under," or general decline, short of total annihilation. Rather than become extinct, Homo Sapiens would diverge into two successor subspecies. These two types are not distinguished genetically, racially or biologically in any sense. There is no reason to believe that Nietzsche envisioned the "overman" as possessing a bodily constitution radically different from modern man, except in terms of health. Biological evolution alone does not guarantee the "overcoming" of mankind. This is in fact precisely the fundamental problem with man: he is only minimally advanced above the ape spiritually, despite his biological advantages. But if he meant his message to be for man in *this* Homo Sapien bodily constitution, in *this* atmosphere of oxygen and nitrogen, surrounded by the species of *this* earth, then only time will tell whether Friedrich Nietzsche was, in his relation to mankind and its destiny, "untimely" or simply "too late."

Greg Whitlock
Austin, Texas
November, 1989

Introductory Essay

I. Introduction

All readers of *Zarathustra* will want to know the answers to several basic questions: who was Friedrich Nietzsche? who was the historical Zarathustra? Who is Nietzsche's Zarathustra? What is the history of the text? As an initial answer to these questions and others, Part II of this Introductory Essay gives the necessary historical context for approaching *Zarathustra*.

Once the reader has a context in which to place the text, a natural follow-up question would be, what are the basic tenets of zarathustran philosophy? Although limited in length by necessity, Part III of this Introductory Essay attempts to give a *summary of the interpretation at hand*. Zarathustra's four central teachings are summarized as presented in the commentator's perspective. The overman, will to power, eternal return of the same and the death of god are presented as interconnected and interdependent riddles whose solutions must be discovered simultaneously or not at all. A statement of my simultaneous solution may be found at the end of the summary.

II. An Overview of Nietzsche's Life and Intellectual Development

Early personal history

Friedrich Wilhelm Nietzsche was born October 15, 1844, in the village of Roecken (by Luetzen) as the first son of the hamlet's ill-fated pastor, Karl Ludwig Nietzsche. Franziska Oehler Nietzsche, the pastor's pious lutheran wife, was widowed with three children—Friedrich (5 years), Elizabeth (3 years) and Joseph

(newborn)—when the young pastor suddenly died of brain soften-
ing in 1849. The children were to be raised with the help of the wi-
dow's two spinster sisters and mother. Shortly after his father's
death, Joseph also died suddenly, leaving his brother as the sole
male family member.

As a youth, Nietzsche attended Schulphorta, a famous school for
gifted children in Naumburg. Having come from a long clerical tradition on both sides of parentage, Nietzsche was expected to study
theology upon entering the university, in preparation for a clerical
career. Whether Nietzsche was ever a christian in any serious
sense, though, is doubtful.[1] By the age of sixteen, he had come
into contact with the atheistic ideas of Ludwig Feuerbach and
David Friedrich Strauss. And his poem "To An Unknown God," far
from a confirmation of faith, is a departure from orthodox
lutheranism. However early his doubt may have risen, it became
clear to Nietzsche before his third semester at Bonn University
that he must reject theological studies in favor of classical studies
with Friedrich Wilhelm Ritschl at Leipzig University.

Reading Strauss' *Das Leben Jesu, kritisch bearbeitet* and Ludwig
Feuerbach's *Das Wesen des Christentums* and *Tod und Un-
sterblichkeit* seems to have been a watershed in Nietzsche's disen-
franchisement from christianity, but his atheism was satisfied only
when he discovered the philosophy of Arthur Schopenhauer.[2] The
twenty-two year old philology student discovered Schopenhauer's
Die Welt als Wille und Vorstellung (1818) in late 1865. Its appeal
was unambiguously stated in *Ecce Homo*: "It was atheism that led
me to Schopenhauer."[3] It was Schopenhauer's presumption of an
atheist universe that distinguished him from the reactive atheists
(Feuerbach, Strauss, Stirner). His interest in Schopenhauer continued unabated as Nietzsche was offered a professorship at Basel
University in January, 1869. (Since this offer was given without ex-
amination—Nietzsche did not yet have his doctorate—his name became an overnight sensation within academic circles.)

While a young professor, Nietzsche made the fateful ac-
quaintance of musician, and fellow Schopenhauer enthusiast,
Richard Wagner in May, 1869. Frequent visits and vacations were

spent with the Wagners at Tribschen in the same year. Nietzsche spent August and September of 1870 *as a medical orderly* in the Franco-Prussian War (he had already rejected his German citizenship and became Swiss in April, 1869).

He remained in close friendship with Wagner throughout 1871-73, though the latter exerted considerable pressure on Nietzsche to propagandize for the Bayreuther Festspiele. Nietzsche's first book, *Die Geburt der Tragoedie*, was in part an endorsement of wagnerian music resulting from this pressure. In 1874-5, Nietzsche wrote *Schopenhauer als Erzieher* and *Richard Wagner in Bayreuth*, evidencing the undiminished influence of the two figures upon his thought. But Nietzsche became disillusioned with Wagner in July and August of 1876, at the opening of the Festspiele. Once shaken from the spell of the flattering Wagner, Nietzsche realized that Wagner embodied everything he had already rejected: opportunism, theatricality, nationalism, anti-semitism, Germanism et al.. Wagner had achieved popularity and mystique by exploiting the reactionary tide led by Otto von Bismarck.

> What did I never forgive Wagner? That he condescended to the Germans—that he became *reichsdeutsch.*[4]

Once opened, the schism broke absolutely: between Nietzsche and Wagner now laid the abyss separating disbelief and faith. Nietzsche left the Bayreuther Festspiele abruptly, went into isolation and produced the anti-wagnerian *Menschliches, Allzumenschliches*, which he sent to Wagner directly.

> When the book was finally finished and in my hands . . . I also sent two copies, among others, to Bayreuth. By a miraculously meaningful coincidence, I received at the very same time a beautiful copy of the text of Parsifal, with Wagner's inscription for me, "for his dear friend, Friedrich Nietzsche, Richard Wagner, Church Councilor" . . . . Around that time I understood for what it was high time.—Incredible! Wagner had become pious.[5]

Wagner received *Menschliches, Allzumenschliches*, in May, 1878, marking the absolute and final break with Nietzsche.

When Nietzsche rejected Wagner, he discovered his own intellectual orientation for the first time. The post-wagnerian Nietzsche is, among other things, a harsh critic of christianity. Christian moral sentiments became the targets of *Menschliches, Allzumenschliches, Morgenroete* and *Froehliche Wissenschaft*. In *Also sprach Zarathustra*, Nietzsche parodies the Bible, committing countless blasphemies *en passant*: yet many passages evidence a residual respect for the faculty of religious esteem. In consequent works, even this minimal regard is lost, as he takes on an increasingly militant stance to christianity, until, at the end of the *Antichrist*, he delivers a "declaration of war to the death" against christianity.[6]

Nietzsche's intellectual resources and inspirations ranged well beyond the classics, romanticism and Schopenhauer. At his death, Nietzsche's library contained almost eight hundred volumes. Classical studies accounted for only a minority of the collection, other subjects including modern philosophy, psychology, religion, theology, mythology, education, natural sciences, mathematics, medicine, history, geography, politics, economics, law, aesthetics, art history and music. His collection of literature included German, French, English, American, Italian, Scandanavian, Russian, Hungarian and Polish authors. In addition to being well-read, Nietzsche was also well-travelled. The magnificently rich inner life which this education and experience afforded Nietzsche, allowed him, despite grave physical ailments, to affirm that life's joys are indeed deeper than its woes.

Nietzsche's personal circumstances

During the "Zarathustra period," Nietzsche suffered acutely from a wide range of physical ailments accumulated over many illnesses in young adulthood. A gradual blindness, probably a symptom of progressive syphillis, had already claimed a large portion of his vision. Severe headaches plagued him and robbed him of sleep: the narcotics prescribed against insomnia took their own toll. A permanent stomach condition required close attention constantly, as did sensitivity to humidity and altitude. This overall physical discomfort from waking to sleep would occasionally escalate to debilitating seizures in which Nietzsche could do little more than dictate and swoon.

Nietzsche's friends

Nietzsche's friends could not provide the sort of comradery for which Nietzsche had always longed: though they were all very exceptional individuals in their own right, Nietzsche's friends were not his peers. And so they were in a position of close proximity to one of the great minds of the century and yet were inadequate to his fraternal and social needs. Thus most of his friends stood in silent awe before his work, unable to fully evaluate its worth. Others were progressively repulsed by his militant atheism. As his rhetoric grew shriller, and the message more urgent, fewer and fewer of his acquaintances could, or would, continue to tolerate his ideas.

Two friends in particular, Lou von Salomé, a Russian general's daughter, who would traverse many important intellectual circles, and Paul Reé, a psychologist of moral sentiments and author of several books, were dear to Nietzsche, and the three may have even maintained a triadic relation for a short while. Lou eventually shifted her alliance to Reé and both became estranged from Nietzsche in a complex, if not eternally muddled, disenchantment. This personal catastrophe is one which he never fully overcame.

Nietzsche's later familial relations

If Nietzsche's friends were inadequate to his needs, his family was a misfortune of tragic proportion. Elizabeth, his sister, meddled in his personal affairs, attempting to affect a break between Nietzsche and Lou, as well as influenced her mother's actions. Elizabeth's choice of husbands, an anti-semitic racial colonist who would later take his own life, infuriated Nietzsche. His mother, predictably aghast at her son's atheism, sought Elizabeth for support, and so played into a dastardly plot to associate Nietzsche with anti-semitism on the thin pretense of bourgeois morality. At the time of *Zarathustra's* creation, Nietzsche had not yet completely broken with his family. He would later, though, denounce mother and sister as *canaille* in a section intended for *Ecce Homo*, but which was suppressed at the last moment by Elizabeth herself.

The historical Zarathustra

The historical Zarathustra (alternately Zoroaster in English and Greek) was a religious visionary and prophet of ancient Persia. His approximate year of birth was 630 B.C. and approximate date of death 550 B.C.. His area of activity was Chorassan, an area in northeast Iran of mountainous and desertous geography. Zarathustra's main teaching appears to have been the cosmic battle between good (represented as Ormuzd the eagle) and evil (symbolized as Ahriman the dragon). Worship of fire and the importance of certain animals were central features of the religion, as it has survived through the hymns and teachings of the holy scripture *Avesta*. As with Buddha, Confusius and certain pre-socratics, little accurate evidence concerning this enigmatic figure survives.

Nietzsche's Zarathustra

The name "Zarathustra" (the germanization of "Zoroaster") appears in Nietzsche's notes from 1870 and 1874, but without any direct relation to any (planned) work. It is rather in *Froehliche Wissenschaft*, aphorism 342, where Zarathustra makes his first appearance in Nietzsche's published works. Therein we find a very close forerunner to section 1 of *Zarathustra's* Prologue. However, there exists a still earlier note (dated August 1881) which clearly anticipates the opening line of both *Froehliche Wissenschaft 342* and the Prologue:

> Zarathustra, born on Lake Urmi, left his home in his thirtieth year, went into the province of Arya and reveled in his solitude for ten years in the mountainside of Zend-Avesta.[7]

Here Nietzsche demonstrates his knowledge of the historical Zarathustra. But aside from allowing arabesque imagery, the selection of Zarathustra as a character is arbitrary. What does interest Nietzsche is the unique historical position Zarathustra's cosmological doctrine enjoys.

I have not been asked, as I should have been asked, what the name of Zarathustra means in my mouth, the mouth of the first immoralist: *for what constitutes the tremendous historical uniqueness of that Persian is just the opposite of this*. [My emphasis.] Zarathustra was the first to consider the fight of good and evil the very wheel in the machinery of things: the transposition of morality in the metaphysical realm, as a force, cause, and end in itself, is his work. But this question itself is at bottom its own answer. Zarathustra created this most calamitous error, morality; consequently, he must also be the first to recognize it. Not only has he more experience in this matter, for a longer time, than any other thinker—after all, the whole history is the refutation by experience of the principle of the so-called "moral world order"—what is more important is that Zarathustra is more truthful than any other thinker. His doctrine, and his alone, posits truthfulness as the highest virtue; this means the opposite of the cowardice of the "idealist" who flees from reality; Zarathustra has more intestinal fortitude than all other thinkers taken together. To speak the truth and to shoot with arrows, that is self-overcoming of morality, out of truthfulness; the self-overcoming of the moralist, into his opposite—into me—that is what the name Zarathustra means in my mouth.[8]

It is precisely the concepts good, evil, moral order, guilt, bad conscience et al., then, which Nietzsche's Zarathustra overthrows. What little else in the book relating to the historical Zarathustra is limited to idiosynchratic moments of ancient persian imagery.

Creation of "Zarathustra"

The creation of *Also sprach Zarathustra* involved a series of poetic inspirational experiences beginning in August, 1881, and lasting until the summer of 1883. Nietzsche's general method of inspiration during the creative period of *Zarathustra* (as with the remainder of his most productive years) began with day-long walks through the mountains and valleys of Switzerland and northern Italy. During these extended walks, Nietzsche's mind would become like swollen thunderclouds finally triggered by lightning. As the torrent of ideas and images fell, he would record them in a small notebook. Later, as he returned to his modest boarding house rooms, he would transfer the quick notes to a larger notebook, which would form the basic materials for rough drafts of the various sections and Parts. When satisfied that he had enough material to begin writing, Nietzsche would arrange and rework the notes into handwritten rough drafts. His primitive typewriter was often broken, and whenever his health worsened, he was forced to dictate to hired secretaries or friends. These drafts were further reworked and rearranged according to evolving tables of contents, until a printer's draft emerged. As soon as the presses allowed, Nietzsche ordered the publication of each Part, always at his own expense, since no publisher would extend credit to an independent writer whose reading public was small and shadowy at best. Part IV was not publicly circulated until Nietzsche's death in 1900. From beginning until end, the creation process of *Also sprach Zarathustra* was that of a lone individual reaching for his star in a void of public indifference.

Nietzsche's creativity is documented in his autobiography, letters and the accounts of his contemporaries. Despite his rejection of the romantic notion of inspiration, Nietzsche's own account of his creative moments are filled with stories of poetic revelation. Nietzsche's own account of the first Zarathustra-related experience is given in *Ecce Homo* ("Warum ich solche gute Buecher schreibe" *AsZ* section 1):

> Now I shall relate the history of Zarathustra. The fundamental conception of this work, the idea of the eternal recurrence, this highest formula of affirmation that is attainable, belongs in August 1881: it was penned on a sheet with the notation underneath, "6000 feet beyond man and time." That day I was walking through the woods along the lake of Silvaplana; at a powerful pyramidal rock not far from Surlei I stopped. It was then that this idea came to me.

Thereafter, the Ober-Engadine, Switzerland, became the "holy spot" where the lightning of Zarathustra first had flashed for him. Section 3 of "Warum ich solche gute Buecher schreibe" details this experience.

> A rapture whose tremendous tension occasionally discharges itself in a flood of tears—now the pace quickens involuntarily, now it becomes slow; one is altogether beside oneself, with the distinct consciousness of subtle shudders and of one's skin creeping down to one's toes; a depth of happiness in which even what is most painful and gloomy does not seem something opposite but rather conditioned, provoked, a *necessary* color in such a superabundance of light; an instinct for rhythmic relationships that arches over wide spaces of

forms—length, the need for a rhythm with wide arches, is almost the measure of the force of inspiration, a kind of compensation for its pressure and tension. . . . The involuntariness of image and metaphor is strangest of all; one no longer has any notion of what is an image or a metaphor: everything offers itself as the nearest, most obvious, simplest expression.[10]

After this astounding first experience, Nietzsche convalesced from an illness presumably brought on by the stress of such an occasion. He then settled down to write Part I (including the Prologue). Even during writing, long walks were maintained.

The following winter I stayed in that charming quiet bay of Rapallo which, not far from Genoa, is cut out between Chiari and the foothills of Portofino. . . . Mornings I would walk in a southerly direction on the splendid road to Zoagli, going up pines with a magnificent view of the sea; in the afternoon, whenever my health permitted it, I walked around the whole bay from Santa Margherita all the way to Portofino. —It was on these two walks that the whole of *Zarathustra* I occured to me, and especially Zarathustra himself as a type: rather, he *overtook me.*[11]

Parts II and III were created over the next several seasons with the now familiar technique of long walks. During these creative periods, Nietzsche's physical would peak.

Often one could have seen me dance; in those days I could walk in the mountains for seven or eight hours without a trace of weariness. I slept well, I laughed much—my vigor and patience were perfect.[12]

After such peaks, declines in health were inevitable and permanent.

Except for these ten-day works, the years during and above all *after* my *Zarathustra* were marked by distress without equal.[13]

Once Nietzsche had barely completed his autobiography the distress would devolve into mental collapse and the solar brilliance of his creativity finally set. It may rightfully be said that *Zarathustra* was created when his genius was at its zenith.

Characters in "Zarathustra"

The other characters of *Zarathustra* embody complexes of ideas which, while ranging over wide variations, may be said to be representative of some major figure in Nietzsche's personal intellectual history. And indeed, it is the set of figures cited earlier as formative to his atheism who reappear here: the schopenhauerian Soothsayer, the wagnerian Magician, the straussian Ugliest Man, the feuerbachian Last Pope et al.. Such identifications, while speculative, highlight the personal nature of the book and suggest in what context one should interpret passages. With minor exceptions, the only proper name mentioned in the work, other than Zarathustra himself, is Jesus Christ: while Christ does not make a personal appearance in *Zarathustra*, he nonetheless is the absolute antipode facing Zarathustra. It may be said with some reason that all characters of *Zarathustra* are masks of either the Anti-christ or Christ.

Reaction to "Zarathustra"

Expecting a great public outcry upon publication of the first three Parts, Nietzsche was stunned by the prolonged silence greeting their arrival. As evidenced by a letter to von Sedlitz in 1888, one may infer that Nietzsche felt the same hurt years later.[14]

> In Germany, though I am in my forty-fifth year and have published about fifteen books (including a non plus ultra, *Zarathustra*), there has not yet been a single even moderately reputable review of any one of my books. People help themselves out now with the phrases "eccentric," "pathological," "psychiatric." There are plenty of bad and slanderous gestures in my direction: an unrestrainedly hostile tone is paramount in the periodicals—learned and unlearned—but how is it that nobody protests against this?

Many in his audience had progressively distanced themselves from Nietzsche's anti-christianity, others from his anti-socialism, still others from his anti-parlimentarianism, and so on. Those who were like-minded were dazzled by his stylistics and/or were uncertain as to the ultimate meanings of the notions expounded in his writings.

The oxen among my acquaintances—mere Germans, if I may say so—suggest that one cannot always agree with my opinions, but at times—This I have been told even about *Zarathustra*.[15]

His friends, absurdly silent about *Zarathustra*, were finally publically assailed in *Ecce Homo*:

I tell every one of my friends to his face that he has never considered it worthwhile to study any of my writings: I infer from the smallest signs that they do not even know what is in them. As for my *Zarathustra*: who among my friends saw more in it than an impermissible but fortunately utterly inconsequential presumption?[16]

Not even the anticipated moral indignation of the "good and just" Philistines materialized. Taking its promotion upon himself, Nietzsche set out to draw attention to *Zarathustra* by writing a series of new Prefaces to his previous works, which were to be released in a new edition. Each Preface would draw attention to the recent book. His next two books, *Zur Genealogie der Moral and Jenseits von Gut und Boese*, also expounded on the themes of *Zarathustra* in an attempt to make them more accessible. Further, in *Ecce Homo* Nietzsche devotes a significant portion of the book to reflections on *Zarathustra*. It was destined, however, that *Zarathustra's* fame would not spread within Nietzsche's own lifetime.

Misuse of "Zarathustra"

If the public reaction to *Zarathustra* during Nietzsche's lifetime was a stunned silence, it seems preferable now to the abuse given it at the hands of the Nazis and their precursors after his death in 1900. Nietzsche's own sister, Elizabeth, tampered with manuscripts and even forged whole spurious letters in her official capacity as curator of Nietzsche's literary estate. By systematic falsification and misediting, she prepared the way for the Nazi appropriation of Nietzsche's thought and went so far as to have herself photographed greeting Adolf Hitler at the doorstep of Silberblick (Nietzsche's Weimar residence where he spent the last eleven years of his life).[17]

Promotion of *Zarathustra* coincided with the militarization of Germany leading to World War One. On its battlefields, *Zarathustra* was often found in the backpacks of German soldiers, who took consolation in Zarathustra's words to "warriors." When the humiliated veterans of that war prepared the grounds of the next, the political abuse of *Zarathustra* entered into a new phase. Official Nazi editions of Nietzsche's works appeared (by Kroener Press), were circulated to universities, and Nietzsche soon became a fashionable topic for the half-educated.[18] Of course the real "philosophical" foundations of Nazism reside in the thoughts of Artur Gobineau and Houston Stewart Chamberlain,[19] but one irony emerged: Nietzsche's first notariety resulted from a misidentification of himself with his opposite. The irony is bitter indeed when Nietzsche's plea to his own sister is considered:

> . . . I understand how precisely you, out of your incapacity to see the things in whose midst I live, have had to take refuge in almost the opposite of what I am . . . . This last I wish for your own sake; above all, I ask you fervently not to let yourself be seduced by any friendly and, in this case, actually dangerous curiosity into reading the writings I am at present publishing. . . .[20]

This entire history may, ironically again, be seen within the terms of *Zarathustra* itself. The Nazi "rabble," driven out of revenge, comes to a position of power over the masses by an act of violence, all the while supported by the "good and just" man. Zarathustra's "Ape"—the bilious imitator of Zarathustra's style–is Nietzsche's own sister Elizabeth in the historical scenario. The Nazis' "new idol"—the facist state—proves itself "the coldest of monsters" in a series of bloodthirsty wars. As "justification" for pernicious political machiavellianism, the state hitches a "famous wise man" before their processional cart, the unfortunate here being Nietzsche himself. Although the rabble and their man of the masses almost proved to be the downfall of man, the latter survived to "fight step by step with the giant, accident."

None of this speaks against the book of course, for, as Zarathustra says, "where the rabble drinks, all wells are poisoned."[21] Admittedly, the book is seductive and invites abuse in a sense. But its seductiveness is a quality *Zarathustra* shares with many great books including the scriptures of every faith. But for all its presumptuousness, *Zarathustra* is not a book for fanatics.

> Yet for all that, there is nothing in me of a founder of religion—religions are affairs of the rabble; I find it necessary to wash my hands after I have come into contact with religious people.—I want no "believers"; I think I am too malicious to believe in myself; I never speak to masses.[22]

Any mass movement attempting to claim Nietzsche as its ideologue must therefore necessarily expose itself as opportunistic and desperate.

Though fanatics may approach *Zarathustra* and defile it, the book is a classic of free thinking and human liberation. True, Nietzsche knows the fanatic—his ressentiment, nihilism and bad conscience—but this knowledge is that of a diagnostician. And it is fanaticism itself which Nietzsche attempts to cure.

Nietzsche and Germany

In the 1800's, Germany was a loose confederation of states based on a rapidly industrializing economy. Following the Franco-Prussian War of 1870/1, nationalism was rampant and the question, What is German? had already become a public issue. In the spiritual sphere, christianity—pietism, deism, lutheranism or catholicism—held absolute power. But it was Bismarck and his Junker class who held secular power in Germany. As time wore on, the Junkers grew more militant, anti-semitic and aristocratic. Meanwhile, civil society threatened to divide into two great economic classes, as industrialization, urbanization, commercialization and monetarization of life split the populace into the rich and poor. Urbanization and industrialization, along with unemployment, also gave rise to a criminal class with rightist tendencies, who struggled against the socialists and Jews at the bottom of the social ladder. Education in Germany had long become the assembly-line preparatory station before entry into the partly feudal, partly industrial economy. In such a swamp of desperate conditions, there could lurk only subterranean monsters and Nietzsche knew this well.

Though Nietzsche had served briefly in the Franco-Prussian War, he had done so only as a field nurse. Far from a romanticizer of combat, the Battle of Woerth had caused Nietzsche terrifying memories and dreams. Soon after the war, he forfeited his German citizenship and wrote numerous addresses to the Germans aimed at discrediting their false pride.[23]

> There is no more malignant misunderstanding than to believe that the great military success of the Germans proved anything in favor of this "culture"—or, of all things, its triumph over France.

But cultural critics were not given serious attention in Germany and so his anti-militarism was a lost cry in the night.

Thus it is doubly ironic when *Zarathustra* is associated with German militarism. What Nietzsche said in 1887 had long been true; " . . . for this present day Germany, bristling stiff with weapons though it may be, I no longer have any respect."[24] And again: "The madness of nationalism and fatherland foolishness have no magic for me: "Deutschland, Deutschland ueber Alles" is painful to my ears . . . "[25] Though Zarathustra often spoke to warriors of knowledge, he never spoke to soldiers, who are, after all, merely the cannon fodder which the state assembles from the rabble. Nor were nationalistic and class wars glorified by Zarathustra: he twice advises civil disobedience above military duty.[26] Wars spell the dormancy of culture, according to Nietzsche, for straightforward economics reasons of tradeoff.[27]

> If we could dispense with wars, so much the better. I can imagine more profitable uses for the twelve billion now paid annually for the armed peace we have in Europe; there are other means of winning respect for physiology than field hospitals.

Nietzsche had already gleaned many hard-earned lessons from "life's school of war": ignoring his message, though, Germany learned its lessons firsthand only later.

His forfeiture of German citizenship was symbolic of a deeprooted opposition to all things German.

To think German, to feel German—I can do anything, but not that.[28]

In *Ecce Homo* Nietzsche even denied his German heritage altogether, disowning the Oehler (i.e. maternal) lineage, and claimed to be of noble Polish lineage instead. True or not, this is the ultimate symbolic rejection of Germany and Germans.

Nietzsche and anti-semitism

Anti-semitism was a spiritual illness that Nietzsche confronted in many relationships but one that never infected him personally.[29] During his friendship with Wagner, Nietzsche became fatefully acquainted with a number of anti-semites who would later play uniformly negative roles in his life. Just as a quaranteen from this disease seemed guaranteed by his break with Wagner, Elizabeth became involved with an anti-semite,

> Foerster: long legs, blue eyes, blond (straw head!), a "racial German" who with poison and gall attacks everything that guarantees spirit and future: Judaism, vivisection, etc-[30]

Elizabeth even attempted to break Nietzsche from his jewish acquaintances, while her husband circulated petitions for the seizure of jewish businesses. Totally beyond control, Elizabeth and Foerster married, moved to Paraguay and formed a short-lived racial colony. These momentous personal calamities occured during the *Zarathustra* period, i.e., when Nietzsche felt himself at the helm of man's destiny.

> And from what did all great obstructions, all calamities in my life emanate? Always from Germans. The damnable German anti-semitism, this poisonous boil of *nevrose nationale*, has intruded into my existence almost ruinously during that decisive time when not my destiny but the destiny of humanity was at issue. And I owe it to the same element that my *Zarathustra* entered this world as indecent literature—its publisher being an anti-semite.[31]

It was such exasperation with "anti-semitic canaille" and "that anti-semitic goose," Elizabeth, which is echoed in a note from 1885: "Formerly I wished I had not written my *Zarathustra* in German."[32]

By many machinations, the anti-semites in Nietzsche's life attempted to make common cause with him. Finally driven to public
self-defense, Nietzsche wrote *Ecce Homo* "to prevent people from
doing mischief with me."[33] And yet such mischief was almost a *fait
accompli*; for Nietzsche's "revaluation of all values" offered the
ocassion for all types of irrationalism and extremism. Many passages openly acknowledge his own special seductiveness and his
willful lack of "responsibility." But Nietzsche's brand of extremism
and irrationality did not encompass narrow-minded anti-semitism.
While Nietzsche's extreme notions of writer's responsibilities are
worthy of serious debate, there is no evidence of anti-semitic sentiment anywhere in Nietzsche's authentic works.

Nietzsche's last years and death
    In early 1889, Nietzsche suffered a mental collapse which spelled
the end to his creative life. A shadow of his former self, Nietzsche
remained for eleven years under the care of his sister and mother,
who shamelessly took him to church services in his disability. On
August 25, 1900, Nietzsche died in Weimar and was later laid to
rest next to his brother and father in the parsonage at Roecken;
the entry in the parsonage death records lists his religious affilia-
tion as "anti-christian," twice underlined.[34] In his circuitous secular
journey, the pastor's son never compromised his "war to the death"
against christianity. Nietzsche was, and remains, the atheist's atheist, the anti-christian's anti-christian.

III. Summary of Interpretation At Hand

First Riddle: the Overman
    The first of Zarathustra's teachings to appear in the book is the
often-discussed, much maligned but generally misunderstood notion of the overman (Ger. *Uebermensch*). Already in Prologue 3
Zarathustra inaugurates his speeches to mankind with the oblique
challenge,

I teach you the overman. Man is something that shall be overcome. What have you done to overcome him? All beings so far have created something beyond themselves; and do you want to be the ebb of this great flood, and even go back to the beasts rather than overcome man?[35]

As the remainder of the ninety or so speeches reveals, Zarathustra himself puts forth a variety of apparently unrelated, if not contradictory, interpretations concerning this "overman."[36] But each perspective on the overman returns to the idea that mankind, as with all species, creates, by means of species-activity, a type which exceeds the common estimations and determinations of the species. Zarathustra envisions the human species as a herd pulled in two directions. In its species-activity, mankind dirempts itself in two polar directions: the "overman" and his opposite type, "the last man." Each polar type represents something other than the normal "herd" type. The greater this diremptive force, the greater is the species' "self-overcoming." The human herd is destroyed, or "overcome," as its members separate into two great camps.[37]

   Zarathustra's notion must be sharply contrasted to any idea of evolution. To put the matter most bluntly, man does not evolve as a species into a more adapted, more survivable species. Any species, for Zarathustra, breaks down into *two new species* which are different from each other and different from the parent species. The creation of an overman out of mankind cannot be said to be an evolution of *one self-same species*. And if one insists on calling Zarathustra's diremption "evolution," then the diremption of the last man must also be called a "devolution": and no forward advance of the species as a whole may be inferred. Various teachers of evolution portray species as attempting to increase adaptation as a means to survival: Zarathustra teaches that each species attempts to complete its activity with ever greater efficiency in power. When the goals of species-activity are met with greater efficiency, energy becomes available for the creation of a surplus—a luxury beyond the necessities of existence. Increased efficiency in meeting necessities requires increased exploitation of the normal type. That in turn creates a greater luxury surplus of totally non-ordinary types, or a plurality of "overmen."[38]

But if the overman is central to uniquely zarathustran philosophy, it must be said that the notion of the "higher man" is a limiting
boundary to this center. For the diremption of the overman from
the herd first requires the production of many *higher types*. These
higher types are not the overman, but a collection of individuals
who ascend over man and yet are still recognizably human, all-too-
human. It must be said that, relative to the overman, *all* previous
and present types of human life are *failures*. Even the highest examples of humanity only foreshadow a metamorphosis of spirit
which leads to totally unknown possibilities. All spiritual leaders
have so far been only "preachers of death," "the afterworldly,"
"despisers of the body," etc.. Even the higher men of Part IV are
mere "soothsayers," "voluntary beggars," "magicians," etc., whose
lifeforms are flawed in some fundamental way. A "higher man" is
indeed metamorphosed from mankind in the zarathustran scenario,
but this type represents only partial success and partial failure. A
wholly successful creation—the overman—would therefore find its
existence neither in the past nor the present, but rather in the *future*.

This "future" is described primarily in terms of absence: it is a distant age in which the "state," "marketplace," "great men" and
"great events" no longer exist. All institutions and power structures
of the modern world have been destroyed in civil and nationalist
wars, the proportions of which defies the finite imagination. This
self-destruction of civilization is called the "going under" (Ger.
Untergang) of man.[39] This future also postdates the judeo-christian
era: with the decline of civilization occurs widespread loss of faith
in the religious fabric of western society. Churches, empires and
individuals lie tattered at Zarathustra's feet as he envisions the destruction of civilization and the metamorphosis of spirit necessary
for his post-christian overman.[40]

Amid the rubble of the past, future man will by necessity create
new values to fill the vacuum of nihilism. Of these creators
Zarathustra has little definite to say. One might well note that his
descriptions are always of a type combining active will and affirmative force: there is no hint of reactive will or negative force in

the superhuman type. Zarathustra allows himself only metaphors; lightness, dancing, music, laughter. By an exceptionally complex set of symbols, Zarathustra depicts as his foreseen overman a type one might well call *dionysian*.[41] This type is marked by "superhuman" health, sensibilities (enhanced senses), wholeness, refinement, subtlety, elevation, courage and willpower. He embodies life force itself and achieves great power with maximally efficient force. Zarathustra goes off on a great many seemingly unrelated tangents in describing the dionysian type, and we need not enumerate all particulars at this point.

One may well ask what it is that accounts for superhuman abundance of any quality. The answer, according to the perspective elaborated in this commentary, begins with the idea of the *liberated will*. While the idea of will itself shall be considered at length only later, its liberation may already be preliminarily sketched. According to Zarathustra, if an individual or group is to "cross over" to the overman, human will must be liberated from *ressentiment*. Only once will is liberated from *ressentiment* is the superhuman type possible.

> For *that man be delivered from revenge*, that is for me the bridge to the highest hope, and a rainbow after long storms.[42]

Creation of the overman then is the liberation of the will from the power of *ressentiment* or revenge.

Zarathustra's idea of *ressentiment* is not that of a subjective or momentary mental state. It is rather a *stance toward the passage of time*. The man of *ressentiment* is unable to overcome his own powerlessness before the facticity (i.e., irreversibility and unalterability) of the past. The passage of time creates events which are eternally beyond any act of will. But will often desires that the past be different than its actuality.

> Willing liberates; but what is it that puts even the liberator himself in fetters? "It was"—that is the name of the will's gnashing of teeth and most secret melancholy. Powerless against what has been done, he is an angry spectator of all that is past.[43]

The resentful will does not outwardly revolt, but internalizes its anger and frustration. *Revenge on the present* is the path taken by resentful will; but not an overt, active revenge. Rather, revenge becomes a system of internalized beliefs and values: thus *ressentiment* is not a momentary act of revenge but is expressed in the covert disguise of value systems such as socialism, democracy, feminism, nationalism, racism, etc.. Negative will is allied with reactive force in these disparate, but profoundly related, expressions of revenge.[44]

A man of *ressentiment* subordinates his will to a memory of past events which terrorize him in their unalterability. Resentful man suspends his will and does not act at all. Any perceived harm is internalized and reinforces the structure of repression. Action itself is internalized as the negative will and reactive force are played out in the imagination: all external action has been undermined by the repressive force of *ressentiment.*

Zarathustra's speech "On Redemption" draws to a close as he observes that the will shall be a prisoner to the past, "until the creative will says to it, "But thus I willed it."" Zarathustra unwittingly continues however:

> And who taught him [will] reconciliation with time and something higher than any reconciliation? For that will which is the will to power must will something higher than any reconciliation; but how shall this be brought about? Who could teach him also to will backwards?

This unguarded question prompts a challenge from a listener for Zarathustra to answer his own question, thus revealing Zarathustra's inability to teach the doctrine of the overman. This creates in Zarathustra a crisis of confidence ending in Part III with the discovery of *the directional relativity of time* and with it the solution to the riddle of eternal return. The intimate connection between the teachings unfolds with each Part of the work.

Second Riddle: Valuation as the Will to Power

Zarathustra delivers only three speeches giving verbal mention of the doctrine of "will to power," and yet the central importance of these sections, and the theoretical role this doctrine plays in the speeches in which there is no verbal mention, leaves little doubt that this idea is one of the principle teachings of zarathustran philosophy.

Man's distinguishing drive, according to Zarathustra, is his will to find value in things. In contrast to all other species, man has various notions of "good" or "evil." And he does so as a basic necessity, for it is a condition of conscious life that some or another canopy of values and meaning be spread over the sorrows and tribulations of human existence. The various tribes, clans, nations, or "peoples," of the earth find their inner identity and uniqueness in shared value systems, and without a shared set of beliefs about "good and evil," no people could retain its identity and existence.

Every people thus raises above itself a code of values which it affirms as objective absolute truth: no question arises whether such a tablet of values is valid for all men and for all time or whether values are limited to specific times, places and believers.

In an important speech entitled "On the Thousand and One Goals,"[45] Zarathustra dissects all such tablets of values from a perspective of ethical relativism. From his vast travels and insights, Zarathustra has learned that there are a great many such tablets and that all judgments of good and evil are contradicted within some other set of values. Whatever is "good" to one man will be found "evil" by another. It is a fundamental revolutionary doctrine of zarathustran philosophy that objective good and evil do not exist: *all* valuations are man-made and valid only within limited populations, times and places. Valuations are made along two broad dimensions: *positively,* "good" is considered to be that in which a people excels above all other groups, i.e., their unique talent; *negatively*, "good" is considered to be whatever a people is unable to do, or what they find beyond their willpower, i.e., what they would achieve, if only they could. Valuations, then, are determined by the specifics of a people and their circumstances: nonspecific, indeterminant, unlimited or otherwise "absolute" values simply do not exist.

Valuation is a voluntaristic creation of man: without the force of human will, neither "good" nor "evil" would exist. Zarathustra seeks to name the force of human will underlying all valuation and comes to denominate it "the will to power."

> A tablet of the good hangs over every people. Behold, it is the tablet of their overcomings; behold, it is the voice of their will to power.[46]

Indeed, if the inner force of will necessary and sufficient for human activity may be termed "will to power," then precisely valuation, the drive to esteem or reject something as good or evil, is the greatest expression of will to power. Man's greatest power is not brute physical force, but the force of esteeming, for it adds all meaning to life itself.

> Through esteeming alone is there value: and without esteeming, the nut of existence would be hollow. Hear this, you creators![47]

So long as man esteems, human life will have meaning and hope. Without values, life itself is meaningless and mankind doomed.

In another important speech, entitled "On Self-Overcoming,"[48] Zarathustra repeats the insights of "On the Thousand and One Goals," but attempts to go one step further in broadening the notion of will to power. Will to power has been described as the inner force of will within all human activity. But now this notion takes on a much broader definition and is described as "the unexhausted procreative will of life," expanding the idea to capture *all* lifeforms.

> Where I found the living, there I found will to power . . . . And life itself confided this secret to me: "Behold," it said, "I am *that which must always overcome itself*. Indeed, you call it a will to procreate or a drive to something higher, farther, more manifold: but this is all one, and one secret."

Valuation, then, is only one expression of a procreative will of life within one species; but all forms of life and all forms of activity are also this will. As the Prologue announced, *all beings* have sought to create "something higher" than themselves: this is the universal dynamic within the species. Man, too, must create "something higher, farther, more manifold," namely, the "overman." Since life is *"that which must overcome itself,"* man is "something that shall be overcome." Zarathustra's inaugural statement in Prologue 2, that "man is something that shall be overcome" is therefore perfectly identical to the later admonition that "the overman shall live." This inevitable creation of an overman is none other than the dynamic of species-change which I have previously called, for lack of a more adequate term, "diremption."

By investigating valuation as will to power, then, we are led back to the teaching of the overman and are left with the following interconnections. Due to an inner dynamic of species-change, mankind strives to dirempt itself into a successor "overman." The natural drive to create an overman, to overcome itself, is the will to power. Valuation is the most powerful expression of this will. In order to create an overman, the will to power must be "liberated" from *ressentiment*. This liberation requires that the will overcome its *ressentiment* to the passage of time. Only the power possible in valuation is adequate to alter the psychology of mankind to the degree of total otherness: the overman breaks with human psychology by means of a *valuation*. We have seen already that such a valuation must allow the will to "will backwards." But what is this act of esteeming which alone certifies creation of an overman? This problem is solved only with the discovery of eternal return, the third zarathustran riddle.

Third Riddle: Eternal Return of the Self-Same Moment

By the end of Part II, Zarathustra is in a crisis: he has discovered the teachings of the overman and will to power, but these themselves remain only riddles so long as it remains unclear how the will can be liberated by "willing backwards." The overman is created only once man can overcome the all-pervasive psychological structure of *ressentiment*, and only an act of valuation as will to power can secure this victory. This much is symbolized in the hallucinatory section, "On the Vision and the Riddle."[49] But the exact nature of the required valuation is uncertain and lies subconscious within Zarathustra for the majority of Part III. Zarathustra's inability to arrive at the crucial valuation comes to a climax in "The Convalescent," as he succumbs to a long and deep comatose state. During this apparent breakdown, Zarathustra subconsciously solves the riddle of the overman's will. But upon regaining consciousness, it is his *animals* who deliver the doctrine of eternal return; that is, Zarathustra himself has not yet delivered the necessary idea, relying on an *external* source for a representation of the notion.

For several sections after "The Convalescent,"[50] Zarathustra experiences a superhuman bliss as the notion of eternal recurrence rises up through the various levels of consciousness. In "The Other Dancing Song," Zarathustra whispers the basic notion of eternal return into the ear of life itself, personified as an irrational but most desirable female. In the final sub-section of "The Other Dancing Song," Zarathustra delivers a song which certifies beyond all doubt that he himself knows, is able to formulate, and *wants* to express the mysterious notion of eternal return.

Zarathustra earns "the seven seals" of affirmation by singing the "Yes and Amen Song" in the last section of Part III. Great joy, as exclaimed in the prior section, "wants deep, deep eternity," and now Zarathustra sings seven times, "For I love you, O eternity!" *Desiring eternity*, however, is the very key to the notion of eternal return. For the notion is not a matter of intellection, analysis or any type of thought; rather, the notion is a *will* or desire. To accept the notion is not a passive, conscious reception: it is an active *will* or desire for something that has been affirmed, or valued.

The one who discovers eternal return of the same gives a double affirmation, that of *being* and *becoming*. Being and becoming, eternity and the passage of time, can be affirmed together only in the *being of becoming* and the *becoming of being*. Together these necessitate the eternal return of the self-same moment. One can affirm, or will, the passage of time only if one desires eternal being for it. This may be called affirming the being of becoming. But if one desires eternity, and yet time passes, one must desire the repetition of that passage: if time is eternal, it must repeat itself, bending back on itself such that the "last" moment gives way once again to the "first" moment of time. Were time to have such a circular configuration, being and becoming would be joined together (Zarathustra says "wed") in a coexistence in which all points of time would be simultaneously past, present and future. Since past, present and future are a repeated series, each moment could be said to exist "eternally," for it would exist an *infinite number of times regardless of the direction of time.* Time itself would be infinite in all directions and each moment would be at once beginning, midpoint and end of all time. Thus a sort of einsteinian relativity is attributed to time in this act of will.

Herein lies the solution to the riddles of the overman and valuation as will to power. The overman is *the one who affirms the eternal return of the same by an act of valuation as will to power.* By willing the eternal return of any moment one wills the eternal return of all moments, and so wills "backwards" as well as "forwards." Such an act of willpower is the greatest act of will,   totally affirmative and active, and the path by which man "crosses over" to the overman. Desire for eternity destroys structured *ressentiment* by sheer force: inactivity and reaction are inferior forces relative to positive, active will. Anybody with a desire for eternity could in no way resent the past or plot revenge. Such an overman would *value* something, anything, so as to desire its eternity, meaning its eternal *return.* Since all events are seen as totally interdependent and self-generating, to value something, anything, in this way is to value *everything* unto eternity.

It cannot be stressed enough that the overman's valuation is an *act of will to power.* To will the eternal return, to desire eternity along with the passage of time, the overman must exert himself in superhuman fashion, like a young god who sets the entire universe rolling with one great kick. Such an exertion of will is impossible unless *ressentiment* is totally absent, and with it all human psychology. If the notion of eternal return is connected to *ideas* or the *intellect* whatsoever, it is as a *superhuman psychological structure*: but more accurately it should be said that it is the configuration of will that replaces the previous configuration, *ressentiment.*

These two structures delineate the opposite directions into which mankind is dirempted. By species-activity—actions of superhuman will—the species "overcomes itself" and dirempts into over-man and human, all-too-human, beings. *Only by the greatest act of will shall the overman be created, but this act of will to power is acceptance of the eternal return of the self-same moment.*

It should be remembered that the notion of eternal return has two primary interpretations. First, as a solution to the riddles of overman and will to power; this interpretation views the notion voluntaristically, i.e., as one concerning the will. Second, it is also interpreted as a metaphysical doctrine, i.e., one concerning the ultimate nature and inner workings of the universe. As a metaphysical teaching about the nature of space and time, the notion is defended by two proofs. Given infinite time, finite force, random ordering of events and a finite number of power relations between forces, there must be a repeating series of random but definitely ordered events. This could be called the repeating series proof.[51] Also, given the directional relativity of time and definite ordering of moments, there must be a sempeternity of self-same moments. This may be termed the sempeternity proof.[52] But both proofs are offered by Zarathustra's animals: they are not his own, active formulations. And while they are grand visions deserving a place in the pantheon of ideas, they are at odds with Zarathustra's suspicions of metaphysics and scientific will to truth. Thus the commentary at hand retains the metaphysical interpretation for completeness, but gives a dominant role to the voluntaristic interpretation.

Fourth Riddle: the Death of God

Throughout *Zarathustra* one finds the notion that man projects his own image into the image of a god. In the image of his god, we always find the man. The "afterworldly" philosophers represent god as a tortured god seeking entertainment and diversion from suffering; but it is they who suffer, and therefore create a divine diversion.[53] The "great man" of the masses would believe only in a "god who makes great noises."[54] The morbid gravediggers of Prologue 8 imagine a punishing and cruel god. The "despisers of the body" imagine a spritual god who rewards deprivation of the body and material goods.[55] The virtuous represent god as a rewarder of the good and punisher of the vicious.[56] The "pious" imagine a god of grandfatherly demeanor who has his senile and puritanical lapses.[57] The "rabble" envision a god of the masses who plots revenge and exercises negative force. The "apostates" imagine a god of violent unstable emotional changes who loves and then consumes the beloved.[59] It is, in short, very much as Zarathustra says in "On the Afterworldly," reporting on his own brush with religion:

> Alas, my brothers, this god whom I created was man-made and madness, like all gods! Man he was, and only a poor specimen of man and ego; out of my own ashes and fire this ghost came to me, and, verily, it did not come from beyond.

God lives only so long as such a self-deceptive projection lasts. Once belief in a god can no longer be sustained, "God is dead."

In the first nine sections of Part IV, Zarathustra stumbles upon a scattered collection of individuals who seek refuge from the herd of mankind: in their union they form "the higher man," who seeks to "cross over" to the overman but is ultimately unable. Each in his own way has experienced the death of god. All of them, even the last pope, has lost any semblance of belief in the idols of the tribe. And yet they have their own idols in various forms.

Like the apostates of earlier sections, the higher men eventually revert in "The Ass Festival" to adoration of an ass, which simultaneously reflects democratic, socialist, anarchic and christian overtones.[60] When berated for such asinine apostasy, the higher men offer a variety of dialectical, theatrical, deceptive and pitiful alibis, all of which yield no satisfaction to Zarathustra the questioner. To higher man, "the death of god" is an empty phrase whose meaning depends merely on the force which appropriates it.

In the mouth of Zarathustra, the death of god means that man reverses the inverted imagine of god over man. All religious and spiritual entities are projections of a subject. Even the various phantasms of atheism—the "species-being," "objective spirit," "ego," etc.—are projections in the imagination of a unique subject. The various atheisms represented in the higher man are all, in some fashion or another, negative, reactive and passive. And they project negativity, reaction and passivity into the new idols of democracy, socialism and anarchy. Their project is in essence still one of *ressentiment* and revenge, and not an end to projective will.

But Zarathustra knows already in "The Wanderer"[61] that "in the end, one experiences only oneself." In a later description of the overman, Zarathustra portrays

> the most comprehensive soul, which can run and stray and roam farthest within itself; the most necessary soul, which out of sheer joy plunges itself into chance; the soul which, having being, dives into becoming; the soul which *has, wants* to want and will; the soul which flees itself and catches up with itself in the widest circle . . . .

This same inner being is heralded still later as the will.

> O thou my will! . . . Thou destination of my soul, which I call destiny! Thou in-me! Over me!

Over and in Zarathustra is the overman's will to power. Zarathustra's destiny is to teach the eternal return of the self-same moment: achieving this destiny formed the plot of the first three Parts. It has only been by the greatest exertions of will to power that Zarathustra has won the subconscious and conscious battles to achieve command over the notion. Yet he has no real chance to fulfill his destiny by actively teaching the notion to others, e.g., the higher man, until the very last sections of Part IV. Once this is accomplished, the necessary Parts of the work are complete and *Zarathustra* comes to a close, though much could have conceivably followed.

Notes

1. *Basic Writings*, translated and edited by Walter Kaufmann (New York: Modern Library, 1968), p.692: Giorgi Colli and Masino Montinari, *Kritische Studienausgabe* (Berlin:De Gruyter, 1980), Band VI page 278.

2. For Nietzsche's relation to Strauss, Feuerbach and other "Young Hegelians," see Kamenka's *The Young Hegelians* and Karl Loewith's *From Hegel to Nietzsche* (New York: Anchor Books, 1964).

3. *Basic Writings* p.735: *KSA* VI 318.

4. *Basic Writings* p.704: *KSA* VI 289.

5. *Basic Writings* p.744: *KSA* VI 327.

6. *KSA* VI 254. (My translation.)

7. *KSA* IX 519. (My translation.)

8. *Basic Writings* pp.783-4: *KSA* VI 367.

9. *Basic Writings* p.750: *KSA* VI 335.

10. *Basic Writings* p.756: *KSA* VI 339-340.

11. *Basic Writings* p.753: *KSA* VI 336-337.

12. *Basic Writings* pp.758-59: *KSA* VI 341.

13. *Basic Writings* p.759: *KSA* VI 341-342.

14. Christopher Middleton, translator and editor, *Selected Letters of Friedrich Nietzsche*. (Chicago: University of Chicago Preess, 1969), page 284.

15. *Basic Writings* p.720: *KSA* VI 303.

16. *Basic Writings* p.780: *KSA* VI 363.

17. While visiting Silberblick (Nietzsche's residence) in Weimar, East Germany, I discovered that the Goethe-Schiller Nationale Forschungs- und Gedenkstaetten der klassischen deutschen Literatur in Weimar plans to display an enlarged copy of this photograph in the front hall of the house (now a museum), to reinforce notions of the alleged Nazism of Nietzsche.

18. Kroener Press in Germany continues to publish the Baeumler edition of *Der Wille zur Macht* to this day.

19. See Ernst Cassirer, *The Myth of the State* (New Haven: Yale University Press, 1946), Chapter XVI.

20. Middleton, p.339.

21. From Friedrich Nietzsche's *Thus Spoke Zarathustra*, translated by Walter Kaufmann (New York: Viking Press, 1966), "On the Rabble."

22. *Basic Writings* p.782: *KSA* VI 365.

23. *Basic Writings* p.732: *KSA* VI 316.

24. Middleton, p.262.

25. *KSA* XII 70. (My translation.)

26. See *Zarathustra* IV.12.

27. *Basic Writings* p.800: *KSA* XIII 646.

28. *Basic Writings* p.719: *KSA* VI 301.

29. Nietzsche's anti-semitic acquaintances were: Elizabeth Foerster-Nietzsche, Bernd Foerster, Richard Wagner, Max Heinze, E.W. Fritsch, Adolf Schmeitzner, et al..

30. *Basic Writings* p.798.

31. *Basic Writings* p. 798.

32. *Will to Power*, translated and edited by Walter Kaufmann, (New York: Vintage Books, 1968), page xxiii. This fragment may be found in Musarian's edition, XIV 373.

33. *Basic Writings* p.782: *KSA* VI 365.

34. In 1984 I had the honor of speaking with the Parson of the Roecken church where Nietzsche's family resided. He showed me the *Kirchenbuch* registering Nietzsche's death. I photographed the death registration, though the photos remain unpublished.

35. See *Zarathustra* Prologue 1.

36. For a complete list of sections overtly discussing the overman, see Appendix IV.

37. A very interesting note from the *Zarathustra* period may be found at *KSA* XIII 191. Other important sources are *Will to Power* 866, 881, 953, *Goetzen-daemmerung* 33 and *Antichrist* 3 and 4.

38. See *Will to Power* 866.

39. See my comments to Prologue 1.

40. See *Zarathustra* II.20, III.7 and III 16(2).

41. For a list of sections dealing specifically with the dionysian, see Appendix VII. Also, footnote 145 of Part I of this commentary is important.

42. See *Zarathustra* II.7.

43. See *Zarathustra* II.20.

44. Giles Deleuze gives the concept of *ressentiment* a central place in his book *Nietzsche and Philosophy*, translated by Hugh Tomlinson, (New York: Columbia University Press, 1983), first published in French in 1962. He is the primary influence in Nietzsche-interpretation throughout this commentary. Thus the centrality of *ressentiment* here.

45. See *Zarathustra* I.15.

46. Ibid.

47. Ibid.

48. See *Zarathustra* II.12.

49. See *Zarathustra* III.2.

50. See *Zarathustra* III.13.

51. See *Zarathustra* III.2 and III.13.

52. See *Zarathustra* III.2 and III.13.

53. See *Zarathustra* I.3.

54. See *Zarathustra* II.18.

55. See *Zarathustra* I.4.

56. See *Zarathustra* II.5.

57. See *Zarathustra* III.8.

58. See *Zarathustra* II.6.

59. See *Zarathustra* III.8.

60. See *Zarathustra* IV.18.

61. See *Zarathustra* III.1.

Prefatory Remarks to Prologue and Part I

The Prologue and Part I of Zarathustra were written in their entirety in February of 1883 in Rapallo, Italy, and were published almost immediately upon their completion.

Following upon the arabesque Prologue, Part I has the task of couching the Prologue's imagistic messages into more conceptual formulations. In particular, Part I concerns itself with the dangers of the higher man as he "crosses over." Man's spirit must pass through three stages of development on its path to the overman, but each stage contains a danger as he "crosses over."

Though there is no mechanical pattern, each section of Part I instantiates either the camel, lion or child images of the important "On the Three Metamorphoses." The fundamental distinction of the Prologue—the overman versus the last man—is maintained throughout Part I: the overman is explicitly mentioned in half the sections and occupies the background, in greater or lesser presence, in all remaining sections. Of special import are sections I.1, I.15, I.7, I.19 and I.22.

After reading the Prologue, one is struck by the abrupt and oblique beginning of Part I. The Prologue, though bizarre, was written in a coherent, sparkling, even brilliant, narrative style. Part I opens directly and abruptly with a speech. Only at the end of the speech is it even mentioned that the setting of the speech is the "Motley Cow," a town not far from Zarathustra's mountains, where he sojourns. This is presumably the town whose Market Place was the setting of the Prologue, sections 3 -8. All speeches of Part I take place in the Motley Cow, with minor variance in exact location. Thus there seems to be little, if any, plot structure to Part I. Its apparent flatness is due to its task: that of rendering a first formulation of Zarathustra's ideas in their depth and breadth. Though additions and refinements occur later, the formulations of Part I must constitute the referent for many later allusions, discussions and reflections.

Nietzsche supplied introductory quotations to Parts II, III and IV, but did not do so for the first Part. I take the liberty of doing so, supplying a favorite passage from I.22, which, I believe, encapsulates in one image the urgent message communicated in the Prologue and Part I. From such a treasure chest as *Zarathustra*, of course, the selection of an introductory quotation is happily arbitrary.

Commentary to Prologue and Part I

Not only the reason of millenia, but
their madness too, breaks out in us.
It is dangerous to be an heir. Still
we fight step by step with the giant,
accident; and over the whole of humanity there has ruled so far only nonsense—no sense.

(Part I, sec.22)

Prologue and Part I

Prologue: On the Overman and the Last Man[1]

Sub-section 1. Nietzsche's Zarathustra presents himself in the initial scene as being in a state of transfiguration already achieved. The single piece of biographical information given the reader is that, at the beginning of his self-imposed hermitage, Zarathustra was thirty years old, a fact intending to allude to the hermitage of Jesus Christ at the same age.[2] And indeed, the imagery and language of the entire first section suggests a sort of transfiguration of the spirit. After ten years of solitude, Zarathustra's heart transformed itself (*verwandelte sich*), suggesting a metamorphosis of the sort accredited to the great religious figures of history. Zarathustra speaks the first words of the book at dawn, the period of transformation from night to day.

The sun itself is the audience for the first spoken words of the Prologue, and appropriately so, for its motion, as Zarathustra describes it, becomes the primary image for the remainder of the book. With a sort of pre-copernican figure of speech, the sun is said to climb up to Zarathustra's cave, and then descend once again under the sea. Thus the sun's motion forms a circle of sunrise (*Aufgang*), noon (*Mittag*), descent (*Untergang*) and midnight (*Mitternacht*). The ascent to, and descent from, Zarathustra's cave circumscribes Zarathustra's non-verbal action throughout the book.

The vertical relation of over/under (*ueber/unter*) will allow many word plays in both Zarathustra's speeches and Nietzsche's narrative. In the first section of the Prologue alone, the relation is used nine times: the radiance of the sun is an overflow (*Ueberfluss*); Zarathustra is weary (*ueberdruessig*) of his wisdom; he wants cyclically to go among men (*unter die Menschen gehen*); the sun brings light to the underworld (*Unterwelt*); the sun is an overrich star (*ein ueberreiches Gestirn*); Zarathustra must go under (*unter gehen*); the sun and Zarathustra, by design, are compared to a cup that wants to overflow (*ueberfliessen*) and carry its contents everywhere (*ueberallhin*); and Zarathustra at the end of this section begins his descent (*Untergang*). Many such word plays are impossible to capture in English and there is no one rule which captures Nietzsche's use of the *ueber*/*unter* relation in the German.

Of the greatest importance is the word *Untergang*, or "going under," which means (1) *descent* or *setting* when applied to stars or the sun, (2) *decline*, when applied to a group or civilization, (3) *end*, or *destruction*, when applied to the world, and (4) *downfall, ruin* or *perishing*, when applied to an individual. The word *Untergang*, "going under," is the substantive noun of *unter gehen*, or "to go under." But in German, *unter gehen* means not only to go under, but also to go among a group of people. Thus when Zarathustra begins his descent (*Untergang*), he also goes among his fellow man (*unter die Menschen gehen*). Nietzsche intends to play on these multiple meanings to the fullest extent. In Zarathustra's apocalyptic figures of speech, this fourfold meaning is preserved and deepened.

In addition to semantical acrobatics with certain prepositions, Nietzsche builds into the *ueber*/*unter* relation a qualitative dimension. With great regularity, the prefix *ueber* implies an excess (Ger. *Uebermass*) of a quality, while the prefix *unter* implies a deficiency of the same.[3] The adjectival form of *ueber*, e.g., *ueberdruessig*, implies an excess of a quality; that is, the state of exceeding or overstepping, a standard or mean (*Mass*), which for Nietzsche has a positive connotation. Thus, in this section, Zarathustra describes himself and the sun in terms of excess. The negative evaluative sense of *Untergang* is preserved in the qualitative dimension, as well. When Zarathustra begins his descent (*Untergang*), he goes among his fellow man (*unter die Menschen gehen*); that is, he goes among those who do not exceed the standard, or essence, of man. There is, then, an evaluative dimension drawn between sub-standard man and the standard man (and later, the superstandard man) which reflects the non-evaluative, merely spatial, meaning of the prepositions *ueber-unter*.[4]

The vertical dimension of the narrative space-time supports two motifs in *Zarathustra*, each of which are evidenced in this initial section. First, the motif of solitude versus brotherly community finds expression in this section, in the form of Zarathustra's hermitage and in his resolve to seek out his fellow man. Like Jesus, Zarathustra went into self-isolation: but unlike Jesus, who remained in the desert for forty days, Zarathustra maintained his hermitage for ten years. Thus the latter's capacity for self-seeking is intentionally held to dwarf that of the former. Yet Zarathustra wills to give his overflowing wisdom to his fellow man. The upper limit of the vertical dimension of the narrative is thus Zarathustra's cave, where only the sun visits him; while the lower limit is his existence among fellow man (Ger. *Mitmenschen*). The wanderings back and forth between these poles constitutes the major form of non-verbal action in the narrative.

The second motif introduced here is that of giving and receiving. Like the sun, Zarathustra is one who gives: by nature he wants to give away his overflowing wisdom. Those who receive without giving back are the poor in spirit, and while Zarathustra appreciates those to whom he may give his wisdom, he does not bless the spiritually poor, as did Jesus, but rather regards them with the pathos of distance between almsgiver and beggar. This motif becomes particularly important in Part II.

Sub-section 2. In this section, Zarathustra meets the first of a number of hermits scattered throughout the book. Like Zarathustra, the old hermit lives alone by choice and has done so for some time, since he remembers Zarathustra's original ascent to the cave. The Hermit greets him and asks,

> At that time you carried your ashes to the mountains; would you now carry your fire into the valleys?

This ash image occurs later several times in the narrative,[5] and a comparison shows that the ashes carried by Zarathustra are a symbol for his extinguished love of man. This misanthropy, or "disgust" with man, becomes a major theme in the most central notion of the book, i.e., the eternal return of the same. But the Hermit notes that the disgust with man has left Zarathustra and that he once again has a burning enthusiasm in an ideal. In this way, the Hermit and Zarathustra are alike; both have turned away from man because he is too imperfect a thing and sympathy for man in his imperfection too great a burden to bear.[6]

But the Hermit turns away from man toward God, for he has no will to stay among them and improve them. Instead, he prefers to sing and hum and cry and laugh in praise of the Perfect Being. And he admonishes Zarathustra to go among the animals rather than among men. The Hermit contents himself to be a bear among bears (*ein Baer unter den Baeren*). Zarathustra, however, wants once again to go among men and bring them his fire, his enthusiasm and inspiration about a higher ideal. This fire is not the Hermit's god, but, as will be seen in the next section, an image of a man over all men. The Hermit created his god as a result of his overwhelming sympathy for mankind:[7] Zarathustra, however, overcomes the imperfection of man and creates a new burning ideal, not out of love for man, but out of a sense of expectation and will to complete, not abandon, the imperfect. For Zarathustra, the Hermit's god is long dead, and has died out of his sympathy for mankind:[8] now Zarathustra wants the completed man to live. And although Zarathustra has the will to teach his new value, he passes the Hermit by, and leaves him in his naive beliefs.

Sub-section 3. Zarathustra at last arrives in the town at the edge of the forest, and enters the Market Place, where he delivers the doctrine of his new ideal to the people assembled and waiting for a tightrope walker (Ger. *Seiltaenzer*: lit. rope dancer). The doctrine of the overman (*Uebermensch*) is that man is something that ought be overcome (*ueberwunden*). By "overcoming" (*Ueberwindung*), one is to understand the overstepping of a standard, an excelling beyond previous limits.[9] The overman is that which exceeds the standards of mankind, i.e., that which goes beyond the common estimations and determinations of man. He is the one who excells mankind, and so is the excellent man: he is that which man can, and should, become. Consequently, the overman is above (*ueber*) the common man, and to the same extent as man stands over the other animals, though Nietzsche does not mean the overman to be a matter of biological evolution.[10] Man is still the minimal man; he has just enough special characteristics to be differentiated from the merely simian,[11] and yet he lies barely over this border. Zarathustra bids the crowd to become more than an advanced ape, more than a loose confederation of plant and ghost. The vegetative, motive and spiritual qualities are found in the rest of nature to a greater extent than the vanity of man recognizes. Zarathustra bids man to put an ideal over himself, to create something beyond, above and higher than himself, and to will to become that higher being.

To understand the great difference between what man can become and what he has been so far, one must rid oneself of pride in the alleged "highest goods" at man's disposal—happiness, reason, virtue, but especially education (*Bildung*). The hour in which one becomes disgusted by these smallnesses is the hour in which the overman is made possible. Not sin, but mediocrity, is the great shortcoming of man.

Zarathustra does not want, however, for man to become happier, more virtuous, more reasonable, etc.: the qualities considered highest by mankind, even in great measure, are meager, for these qualities seek the comfort and stasis of man. Rather than setting man at odds with himself, that he might overcome himself, these "goods" allow the mediocre man to be at peace with himself. In all values hitherto, prudence has been a decisive moral prejudice.

The overman achieves his greatness by qualities which are considered "evil" by the upholders of traditional values—the so-called "good and just" members of philistine bourgeois culture, especially the christian.[12] Only out of great evil will man go beyond himself to something higher: he cannot seek happiness, the resolution of conflict, rational agreement, nor can he have sympathy for his fellow man and still strive to complete and improve himself. Zarathustra claims that for man to become something higher, he must strive against himself and others, producing a great unhappiness. And he claims further that man must commit great "injustices" in violation of rational agreement to go beyond the meanness of modern man. To overcome (*ueberwinden*) means to surmount difficulties and barriers, not to avoid them; and to become great means to overcome great barriers. And so the greatest man will be the one who overcomes the greatest barriers.[13] This however requires great passion, self-seeking and will to command—drives which the christian deems "evil," and so the overman is the ideal diametrically opposed to the christian god.

The overman however is not a platonic ideal, not an abstract *idée fixe*: he shall be of flesh and blood, living on this earth. He is not a transcendent superhuman, as in the god/man of christianity: he is all that man shall become in this life.[14] Thus Zarathustra bids man to remain true to the earth.[15] In christianity, nature and the body are the contaminations of man and the source of his downfall. Zarathustra, on the contrary, wills that man become great by means of the body and earth. He also sees christianity as the source of man's shortcomings and bids that man's downfall (in the christian sense) become greater. The sin of seeking pleasure in the goods of the earth and body becomes a virtue for Zarathustra, and the greatest offense for him is consequently a turning away from earthly and bodily things. (He later denominates this anti-naturalist stance "the turning disease.")

In language meant to parody the Bible, Zarathustra says, "Not your sin but your thrift cries to heaven; your meanness even in your sin cries to heaven."[16] Even in the "original sin" there is great pettiness. The christian is petty and mediocre in his goodness and in his evil.[17] The overman is the one who is great in his goodness and his evil.

Sub-section 4. As Zarathustra extends his rope analogy, the audience's initial confusion about his meaning grows. In this section, Zarathustra delivers a parody of the beatitudes, each beatitude delivering the same message, that "what is great in man is that he is a bridge and not an end: what can be loved in man is that he is an overture (*Uebergang*) and a going under (*Untergang*)." Man cannot be loved as an end because in his present condition he is still all-too-human: but as a means to a higher being, man finds his purpose and his worth. Thus Zarathustra's teaching of the overman is a teleology in the extreme,[18] for man has no value whatsoever in himself (=not an end).

The condition of man is "A dangerous across (*Hinueber*), a dangerous on-the-way, a dangerous looking-back, a dangerous shuddering and stopping" because man is as yet without a purpose, but is on the way to his destiny, which is the overman. He is tempted to look back to where he has been, i.e., his simian past, as if he has already arrived at his destination. But should he look down from his dangerous path and stop to shudder, he may become a victim of vertigo and topple. Man is indeed on his way to his destiny, for he is no longer merely animal. But the completion of his destiny in the arrival of the overman is by no means a certainty, much less an accomplished fact.

Nietzsche employs an extremely elegant image to symbolize the human condition. Above Zarathustra is a tightrope (*Seil*) suspended over the Market Place, on which a tightrope walker (*Seiltaenzer*) is about to perform. Zarathustra describes man as "a rope tied between beast and overman—a rope over an abyss." Thus the two towers holding the rope represent man's merely animal origins and his superhuman destiny. As man walks across (*hinueber*) the rope, he finds himself over an abyss, for a fall is entirely possible, and would mean a real end to his venture. Looking back or down confuses the walker and cause a fall, for the only real way is forward: but for this man needs to keep a purpose, the tower of the overman, in sight.

The purport of Zarathustra's beatitudes is a praise of those who "cross over" (*hinuebergehen*) to the goal of the overman. Such men by nature live by "going under" (*untergehen*). As previously noted,[19] *untergehen* implies a perishing, and so such men are those who by nature live dangerously. They are the "great despisers" because they are nauseated by the static present, and wish to accomplish more, like arrows that arch for a target. But Zarathustra praises only those who aim for an earthly target, and do not seek an oth-

erworldly goal—something "behind the stars." He rather lauds those
who shoot for the sun (called "the great star" in section 1), which
represents *what is over man in this world.* The knowledge sought by
such men is constrained only by the ultimate goal of the overman.
The "great attempters" command nature for the purpose of advancing mankind and so continue the upward path from plant to
animal to man to overman. Virtue for such a man does not consist
in attention to deontological proscriptions, but is rather the over-
riding desire to reach a *telos.* He does not attempt to preserve his
energy for the sake of his own comfort or happiness, but spends
himself entirely in the service of surpassing himself and the species.
(Thus the later theme of self-overcoming is introduced here as a
parallel motif to the overcoming of man as a species.) This surpassing becomes his addiction which he does not attempt to cure,
but which he presses to its full catastrophic conclusion.[20] Like the
addict, the great attempter pursues one addiction, that he be entirely in its service, though it surely proves to be the noose which
breaks his neck.[21] Such men do not seek praise and give none, but
they nonetheless unerringly serve a purpose which spells the sur-
mounting, but not the preservation, of themselves. The undergoer
promises great things in flowing language, but does not rest even
with his accomplishments and goes yet further. The trials and errors of the past are redeemed in him as necessary tests, for he im-
proves mankind beyond its present lot. Such a spirit finds his god
within himself and criticizes this spirit out of deep reverence for its
worth as a means to something higher (=he chastens his god). For
the drive to what is highest will spell his own annihilation (=he
must perish of the wrath of his god), in that the drive to go beyond
himself implies the loss of his present self. The self-criticism of him
who "crosses over" means that failure in even the smallest test
wounds him greatly: such willingness to suffer trials and tribulations
is a mark of one who gladly crosses the bridge over the minimally
human to strive for the superhuman. The spirit of the hyper-critical, hyper-sensitive man is centered in his heart rather than his reason, but his heart is hard in that it has no room for pity, but only for
love of the ultimate goal.[22] Such men are heralds of the overman:

they are signs of the self-overcoming of man: they are the dark cloud that "hangs over man" though they are not the lightning itself, i.e., not yet the overman.

The language of this section, as with all of *Zarathustra*, is extremely biblical, but the content is a complete inversion of christian dogma. For example, the statement that

> I love him who does not hold back one drop of spirit for himself, but wants to be entirely the spirit of his virtue; thus he strides over the bridge as spirit

is an inversion of Luke 17:33,.[23] And the statement

> I love him who chastens his god because he loves his god: for he must perish of the wrath of his god

is an inversion of Hebrews 12:6.[24] The parodical language of this and other sections serves two general purposes. First, it highlights the contrast between nietzschean and christian ethics in the most dramatic way possible, and secondly, it repels the pious, whom Nietzsche wishes to exclude from his audience.

Sub-section 5. At the end of the third sub-section, it became clear that the crowd had confused the message of the overman with that of the Tightrope Walker they had expected to perform over the crowd. In the fourth section, the confusion grew as Zarathustra drew the extended metaphor of man as a rope and of the beloved as "the one who crosses over." The crowd believes Zarathustra to be a barker announcing the Tightrope Walker in a buffoon-like fashion. By the end of section 4, they have begun to deride him. As with Jesus, it has become clear to Zarathustra that he is "not the mouth for these ears."[25] The crowd assumes that Zarathustra is no more than a showman announcing the next act for their entertainment, by presenting the two extreme options facing mankind—the overman or the last man.[26]

The last man is the overape,[27] or minimal man: he has enough specific differences from the merely simian to be called "man," but he has done nothing to surpass himself. He knows nothing of love, creativity, longing for the stars, etc., but instead blinks in animalic

contentment. All things about him become small, and his overcomings are as the leaps of a flea,[28] for he has found happiness and
seeks to preserve his contentment. He has sought the end of strife
with his fellow man, and seeks them only for the creature comforts
they provide (=warmth). The last man has become petty in his relations to others (=one proceeds carefully), petty in his pleasures
(=a little poison), petty in his sufferings (=seeks a fast and painless
death). He seeks only entertainment, but is petty even therein, so
that it might not overexert him. The ideal for him is that there be
"No shepherd and one herd": i.e., that all men become the same
and undifferentiated, that man return to the herd-like state of the
merely animal. His cry "No shepherd and one herd," alluding to
John 10:16, is one step furtheer than the christian "One shepherd
and one herd" in the movement toward the total demeaning of
man. *The last man is the logical conclusion of christianity: it is the
herd when belief in the Shepherd is no longer possible.* Those who
dare to be different are only considered mad. And indeed, since the
world about him has shrunk to the narrow limits of his own needs
and satisfactions, the ego of the last man becomes the endpoint
and meaning of history in his own mind, for all knowledge and
value is already contained in his immediate monadic consciousness.

The last man is the most disgusting man for Zarathustra because
he is the one who can no longer become disgusted with himself.
With the advent of the last man, no new values will be created
(=no new stars born), for the last man is incapable of looking and
longing beyond himself. There is no longer the chaos in him necessary to form "a dancing star" (i.e., a living, vital ideal: it is here that
the theme of dancing, and of the dancing god Dionysus, is first anticipated). In his creature comforts, the last man loses the vital tension for struggle and self-overcoming. Moreover, he loses the ability to become nauseated with himself and his fellow man. And so
the last man closes the possibility of an hour in which the overman
is created.[29]

Zarathustra thus presents the clear choice between overman and
last man to the crowd. With the desire only to be entertained,
though, they shout for the last man, as the crowd in Jerusalem

chose Barabus over Christ. And in their derision was the ice that would attempt to distinguish Zarathustra's burning love of the overman.[30]

Sub-section 6. The heavily symbolic action in this sub-section is to be analyzed by resolving its imagery into five components: the rope image; the figure of the Tightrope Walker; the figure of the Jester; the separate images of going over (*uebergehen*), going under (*untergehen*) and jumping over (*ueberspringen*); and the position and reaction of the crowd.

We have already analyzed the elegant metaphor of the rope as a symbol for the human condition.[31] Man is a tension between his merely animalic origins and his superhuman destiny. The rope image in this section performs the same symbolic function as before.

The Tightrope Walker is the man praised in section 4 as "the one who wills to cross over" (*der Hinuebergehende*); i.e., he lives dangerously by attempting the transition from man to overman. He is not the overman but he is a herald of the overman's advent. Later epithets for the same figure include "the higher man," "the great despiser," "the great attempter" et al.. He is closely associated with the sailors of Part III and other characters who live dangerously, e.g. the Shadow of Part IV.

The Jester is a new figure whose complex symbolic meaning unfolds throughout the book. The initial description Nietzsche gives is that of "a fellow in motley clothes, looking like a jester" (*ein bunter Gesell, einem Possenreiser gleich*). The adjective "motley" (*bunte*) occurs throughout the book as a sign of the ununified, purposeless patchwork nature of modern man, and in particular, of his education. The fellow (*Gesell*) is a member of the community (Ger.: *Gesellschaft*) of the Motley Cow (*die Bunte Kuh*) and so he operates at one level as a symbol for the anonymous undifferentiated modern man. He has no real purpose for his actions; that is, he does not wish to "cross over" to the overman, but attempts to overtake the Tightrope Walker only to overthrow one who places himself above the crowd.[32] And so he merely defends the common against him who would cross over the mean (—he appears from the tower as the Tightrope Walker is at the exact middle of the wire). That one so highly praised, as in section 4, may fall to the absurdities of the reckless and purposeless actions of this representative of the crowd is lamented in the next section: "Human existence is uncanny and still without meaning: a jester can become man's fatality." And so at one level the Jester is a symbol for the dangers facing the higher man on his path over man.

Another aspect of the Jester is that he is mistaken for the devil as he jumps over the performer. That fear of the devil and hell was a long-standing complex with the Tightrope Walker is confirmed in his brief words with Zarathustra. As the Jester springs over the performer, he lets out a devilish cry, and is (mis)taken to be the devil, though belief in the devil and hell is simply a naive production of *das Volk*. But the Tightrope Walker is not physically knocked from the wire; rather, he "lost his head and the rope" when he thought the devil had overtaken him. The mistake of the performer was to take what was over him (i.e., the springing Jester) to be something "beyond the stars," in the language of section 4. Yet the Tightrope Walker has indeed willed to live dangerously, and so Zarathustra praises him, performing a sort of inverted last rites, ridding him of belief in the supernatural, and biding him to fear no more.

But what is the core symbolic meaning of the Jester's actions? To answer this we must consider the action of jumping over (*ueberspringen*). The Tightrope Walker undertook his "crossing over" (*Uebergang*) with great care: he walked in measured steps and used a pole. In contrast, the Jester catches up to the Tightrope Walker with fast steps, lets out a wild cry and recklessly springs over the Walker. The meaning of his actions, in contrast to the Tightrope Walker, is that the Jester believes man can be overcome by a single leap.[33] This is confirmed much later (III.12);

> There are many ways of overcoming: see to that yourself! But only a jester thinks: "Man can also be skipped over."

That is, the Jester believes that man can be overcome, for whatever reason, without going through many trials and tribulations. To extend the rope metaphor, he believes that some steps along the overcoming can be skipped. But Zarathustra teaches that one must advance through each and every metamorphosis of the spirit: a qualitative leap occurs only after the long accumulation of quantitative increments. In the language of I.1, the Jester does not see the necessity of the camel in the metamorphosis of the spirit, but instead wants to leap to the lion stage and say "No!" to existing values. Such recklessness, however, only causes the downfall (*Untergang*) of the other who wills to "cross over."

Finally, the placement and action of the crowd has symbolic import. Along the vertical dimension they are placed below the Ropewalker in a teeming undifferentiated mass. With the downfall of the performer, "the Market Place became as the sea when a tempest pierces it: the people rushed apart and over one another . . . ," alluding to III.3:

> Where the storms plunge down into the sea . . . there everyone shall once have his day and night watches for his testing and knowledge.

And so in the Market Place the people were found to be still all-too-human, but the Tightrope Walker also was found to be not yet the overman.

Sub-section 7. Like Christ, Zarathustra is a fisherman who casts his nets after human disciples.[34] But those who would come out of isolation to gather believers must expect disappointment. In "On the Apostates" Zarathustra exclaims, "Whoever is of my kind will also encounter the experiences of my kind: so his first companions will have to be corpses." The very project of one so enlightened to go among the unenlightened is suspect: the teacher runs the risk of being taken as a fool or a leader of the dependent. For first followers of a doctrine are always the nonserious and frivolous (=jesters), or the dependent looking for a leader, since they cannot move under their own power (=corpse).[35] Since Zarathustra is surrounded by the ingenuine, he is therefore "still the mean between a fool and a corpse" to mankind. The Hermit of section two is one who prefers to remain isolated rather than suffer the imperfections of such others. This problem of followers and believers is a theme throughout the entire book.

The enlightened one speaks in words totally alien to the uninitiated. Thus Zarathustra says, "My sense (*Sinn*: "meaning") does not speak to their senses (*Sinnen*: "senses")." Like the "godless one" of Proverbs 4:19, the ways of Zarathustra are dark. But here darkness does not mean "without the light of God," who does not exist; rather, the ultimate motives and destiny of Zarathustra spring from deep spiritual origins, obscured from those who are not of his kind. And so he goes his way through the night as the man of common consciousness enjoys good sleep.

Sub-section 8. The Jester Scene.[36] The events in the Market Place have a different meaning to the Jester, the crowd and Zarathustra.

In the mind of the Jester, the rope performance is a bid for the attention of the crowd. His only concern is that the people do not give consideration to another performer. He is thus in the position of the political figure who must always vie for the attention of the masses, however foolish and compromising he must make himself. The Ropewalker had attempted to place himself above the crowd, but by a merciless act of violence, he was desposed by the Jester, to the terror and astonishment of the crowd. As the Jester reports the reactions of the crowd, Zarathustra is considered the enemy of the "good and just" man, i.e., the believer of the true faith; in short, Zarathustra is "the danger of the multitude," an epithet they do not apply to the Jester. The Jester, whose motley clothes reflect the nature of the crowd, is thus a man of the people, while the Ropewalker and Zarathustra are men outside of the people.[37]

To the crowd, the rope performance is merely another form of their highest good, i.e., entertainment. Nothing is taken seriously in the Market Place, as was evidenced in their initial reaction to Zarathustra's speech. Zarathustra's action of stooping to pick up the fallen performer, like his speech, was difficult to take seriously, but those among them whose smallness includes pride in goodness, justice and a little faith, now feel threatened. And so in the aftermath of the Market Place scene, the man of the people comes to threaten Zarathustra.

But to Zarathustra, the rope performance, as a symbol of political contest for popular support, is inessential to the overcoming of man.[38] It is becoming clear to him that to win the attention of the crowd he would have to become a jester himself. Individuals, not crowds, is what he must seek, and so he leaves the city without defiance of the Jester's threat.

The Gravediggers Scene. The image of the gravediggers occurs only two other times in the book and these other occurences must be used as the key to unlocking this otherwise oblique scene.[39] In III.9 Zarathustra reflects on the various types he has met among men. At one point he comments on the scholars of the species:

> Their gravediggers—I called them researchers and testers; thus I learned to change words. The gravediggers dig themselves sick; under old rubbish lie noxious odors. One should not stir up the morass.

The phrase "researchers and testers" refers here to the average scholar who buries himself in his books and removes himself from life. In section II.14 Zarathustra clearly associates the scholar with the gravedigger: "You are half-open gates at which the gravediggers wait. And this is *your* reality: Everything *deserves* to perish." The combined images of perishing, gravity and scholarship are used in *Froehliche Wissenschaft* as well.[40] Scholars do not concern themselves about the health of the body, nor do they have healthy instincts (=they dig themselves sick).[41] Instead, they use and abuse their bodies as tools for the purpose of draining research, and so develop morbid tendencies toward life. And rather than living their own lives, and being and feeling truly vital, scholars dig through the remains of the dead and of dead cultures.

Zarathustra has already attacked the education of modern man and the escatological sense of history held by the last man in a speech the gravediggers are familiar with.[42] And so the gravediggers want nothing to do with the ropewalker or Zarathustra, just as the philologists of his time wanted nothing to do with Nietzsche. Gravediggers concern themselves only with dead history: Zarathustra and his companions represent vitality and the unfolding of human destiny. The only words spoken by the gravediggers show a great delight in the imagery of dismemberment and pain in the afterworld—another sign of their morbidity.

Zarathustra, however, passes by without a word, for the events of the day have given him the unconscious impression that he must choose his audience with greater care, and instruct only those who have ears for his words. Zarathustra returns to the scholars of today in II.14, III.9 and II.16, where Zarathustra is allegorically shed of his title "scholar." Scholarship in modern education is not a sign of higher spiritual development. The action of putting their heads together and laughing as Zarathustra passes by invites a comparison between the gravedigger/scholar and "the last man."

Hermit Scene. The key to this scene is the maxim, "He who feeds the hungry refreshes his own soul: thus speaks wisdom."[43] To give satisfies the spirit's desire to overflow, to give of its wisdom. Zarathustra was giving his wisdom, feeding the poor in spirit, and so was satisfied: but now, like the wolves, he is hungry and seeks wisdom. The Hermit feeds animal and man, but they are not refreshed, because the food he gives is for the body but not for the spirit. His spiritual poverty causes him bad sleep, as the wolves suffer, but he does not understand the nature of his disturbance. Thus he offers the corpse food as well: he has no understanding of the needs of the spirit in contrast to those of the body. So while the Hermit has the gift-giving virtue, it is wisdom without critical faculty (—the condition of Zarathustra before the hard-earned lessons of the Market Place). And while Zarathustra's spiritual hunger is not at all satisfied by the Hermit, he nonetheless sleeps well, for at least he understands the nature of his desire.

Zarathustra walked for two hours from the city before arriving at the Hermit's cottage, and walks another two hours thereafter, until he arrives at the spot where he will meet his companions: thus the Hermit is halfway between the crowd and the enlightened Zarathustra: while he is an individual of virtue, he is unable to recognize worthy companions, since he does not fully understand himself.[44]

Sub-section 9. In general, the notions of Zarathustra follow a developmental path.[45] The notion is first seen as a perceptual—experienced—thing without conscious symbolic meaning. Next, a symbolic vision or event comes *to* Zarathustra in a dream, image or incarnate symbol. Finally, the doctrine comes to a fully conscious level when the notion becomes a teaching—i.e., a self-professed, self-formulated idea. Zarathustra then has full command over the meaning of his visions and perceptions.

The notion of *proper companions* follows such a developmental path. The experience of the previous day was a painful learning experience for Zarathustra, which remained at the level of *living through* the events of the Market Place. The relationship of himself to the crowd is immediate and as yet not understood. In an unconscious manner Zarathustra passes the gravediggers by: he does not speak to them or to himself, though the events of the day have made a deep impression on him. The scene in the Hermit's cottage is a densely symbolic experience which will prove to be a catalyst to consciousness of the notion. *The Hermit is Zarathustra's error incarnate.* Once in contact with the thing overrich in symbolism, full consciousness results upon awakening. This is the meaning of the light in the Hermit's cottage. He sheds light on Zarathustra's error without being conscious of it himself (i.e., he doesn't explicate the error himself). Next morning, Zarathustra says "Ein Licht ging mir auf": that is, he has seen the light!

The lessons of the previous day now occur to Zarathustra in a completely conscious way. His choice of audience has been a great mistake: like the Hermit of section 8, he has spoken to those who are dead to the meaning of his words; that is, he has addressed the corpse, the crowd and its leaders, and the "good and just." Now he must seek companions who are living and lively to his meanings, who are able to move under their own power, rather than having to be dragged along like a corpse. Zarathustra resolves to seek those of his kind—the creators, harvestors and cultivators—that is, those who are morally autonomous,[46] who would gather together the best of the human species, and who rejoice in the life of *this* earth and the pleasures of *this* body.

Once the notion is conscious, Zarathustra returns to the level of symbol. In complete command of his revelation, he teaches (in a

monologue) the difference between those he seeks and those
whom he passes by, in terms of the symbolism of *animal species*.[47]
Throughout his works and notebooks, Nietzsche makes extensive
use of animal imagery in defining and analyzing man. But the animal metaphors are meant literally, as other notions about the nature of man and his origins are illusions. Zarathustra wishes first to
reveal the animal nature of man, and second to urge man to re-
trieve this nature. Nietzsche's imagery always points toward the
animal, primitive, instinctual and violent nature and origin of man.
But this is all to be restored, since it is by the competitive instinct of
the animal that it overcomes itself. Thus, as in section 3 of the
Prologue, the overman, while overcoming man, affirms his natural,
animal origins, in contrast to the spiritual, divine nature and origin
of man as conceived by christianity. All cultural, intellectual and
physical enhancement of man has come when he has pitted himself
against his environment, his fellow man, or himself, in a life or
death struggle that reflects not just the nature of the animal world,
but of plant and inorganic matter as well.

Zarathustra chooses the image of the herd and shepherd. The
herd member is the mean, or average, specimen of any species. All
species possess specific characteristics which are distributed in random fashion. The vast majority of the members of any species have
the traits in mean quantity, and so are average. The exceptional is
in the minority by nature, and so falls outside the herd. The shepherd is he whose task is to watch over, safeguard and *preserve* the
herd. In the symbolism of christianity, Christ is the shepherd of the
human herd. Zarathustra has come to realize that he ought not
seek the herd-like, average man. The undifferentiated mass of the
crowd wants no more than to be entertained and satisfied by creature comforts. Nor ought Zarathustra assume the role of the shepherd, for to do so one must become the Jester, the entertainer of
the masses. What he needs then is companions who are likewise
exceptional men, who have gone beyond, overcome, the mean and
the average. They cannot be followers but must be other leaders.
Together they will harvest the higher specimens of man, will create
new values and will break old standards. The image of breaking

tablets alludes of course to Exodus 32:19. But Zarathustra is an inverted Moses: Moses broke the tablets of Yahweh's commandments without negating their spirit and without replacing them with his own tablets; Zarathustra breaks the tablets of old values, but teaches the *Uebermensch*.[48] Rather than seeking to preserve the species, like the shepherd, he and his follower/leaders will seek to *overcome* mankind.

With this revelation, Zarathustra gives a warning: that those he must overcome shall suffer a going under. This is a necessary part of the dynamics of overcoming: *an overcoming must have an object; some static object must undergo a change of elevation in order and rank.* This is symbolized clearly in the scene with the Ropewalker. The Ropewalker was a relatively static object whose overcoming meant a reciprocal going under. "Over those who hesitate and lag behind I shall leap. Thus let my going over be their going under."[49] One man's overcoming (*Uebergang*) is another's going under (*Untergang*). To surpass something is a relational action: man cannot be overcome without *going under*.[50] Given the denotations of *untergehen* explained previously, this becomes a very striking revelation, indeed.

Sub-section 10. The concluding sub-section of the Prologue, while relatively simple in its action, is nonetheless heavily symbolic in its imagery. In this section we find symbols for the three major notions of the book: the overman, the eternal return of the same and the will to power.

The first step in unpacking the imagery is to resolve it along the vertical dimension. At the lowest extreme of the image is Zarathustra and the corpse. The corpse is a vivid symbol of the literal meaning of going under (*untergehen*): as of this section, Zarathustra begins his going under in a more figurative sense; that of overcoming himself. As Zarathustra will later say, life is that which cuts into itself; that is, the nature of existence is overcoming (advancing, enhancing life) and going under (dissolution of former structures, death). But this life which cuts into itself is the will to power.[51]

Above Zarathustra and the corpse fly the animals. That the animals fly in circles anticipates the notion of the eternal return, though in a completely unconscious, as yet merely perceived, manner.

Both animals are "under the sun." The sun, which stands at its highest point (=noon), is a symbol of the overman, as it is from the very first sub-section of the Prologue until the book's end: it symbolizes that which is *over man in this world*. But the full significance of the overman is not yet conscious. *Only at the Great Noon will the full meaning of these three notions become fully conscious.* While it is noon in this section, it is not yet the "Great Noon," when the knowledge of man stands at its highest. It is the ultimate test of any *Zarathustra*-interpretation to be able to explain these three notions together as a unity. But just as the Jester cannot overcome man with a single leap, so we cannot leap to our conclusions without first working through the developmental paths of the notions.

While we must defer discussion of the major notions until later, we should give an explanation of the serpent and eagle image without further ado. The animals are projections of two traits of man—his pride and wisdom—separated, purified, raised to superabundance, incarnate and animated. The eagle is the symbol of pride, nobility, aspiration, elevation and height of spirit, conquest of fear, and conquest of gravity.[52] While there are many birds in *Zarathustra*, there is only one eagle. In contrast, there are many snake images. In "On the Adder's Bite," a snake represents the spirit of malevolence, against which Zarathustra recommends not revenge, but the turning of harm into advantage. The Pale Criminal is described as "a ball of wild snakes, which rarely enjoy rest from each other," representing once again deep motives of malevolence. In "On Human Prudence" the smallness of modern man's evil is symbolized by the rattlesnake which rattles but does not bite. "The Vision and the Riddle" contains the well-known vision of the shepherd in whose throat a great black snake has crawled: this operates as a symbol for the terrifying and nauseating notion of eternal return. A snake within the mask of a god, in "On Immaculate Perception," symbolizes the dark, slimy, reptilian motives of those who would create gods. In "The Ugliest Man" Zarathustra enters a valley devoid of trees and grass, which all animals avoid, except a type of ugly thick green snake which crawls there in old age to die. Thus the image of the snake in general symbolizes the notion of the subterranean, dark, malevolent and disgusting in man's nature.

But the image of the snake and eagle *together* symbolizes a notion other than those taken separately. In Babylonian, Indian, Oriental, Norse and Greek mythology, among others, the snake and eagle are depicted as enemies, locked in mortal combat of cosmic significance. The cosmology of the historical Zarathustra (Zoroaster) is based on the cosmic struggle between Ormuzd the eagle (=goodness and light) and Ahriman the dragon (=evil and darkness). In Nietzsche's *Zarathustra*, however, there is an inversion of this symbolic form: eagle and serpent are harmoniously matched in the service of Zarathustra. They are the great opposites of good and evil brought together not as either/or but as both/and; and they are each opposite to its highest degree. Thus they are intimately linked symbolically to the overman. Yet they are also linked with the eternal return: in this section they give the first anticipation of the notion; they help Zarathustra convalesce after receiving the vision symbolizing the notion; they give Zarathustra the notion as a conscious doctrine; and they are in his cave when he actively teaches the notion, thus fulfilling his destiny. In section IV.13, the animals are clearly revealed as *emblematic signs* of the very essence of Zarathustra:

> But courage and adventure and pleasure in the uncertain, in the undared—
> *courage* seems to me man's whole prehistory. He envied the wildest, most
> courageous animals and robbed all their virtues: only thus did he become
> man. *This* courage finally refined, spiritualized, spiritual, this human courage
> with eagles' wings and serpents' wisdom—that, it seems to me, is today
> called—"Zarathustra!" all who were sitting together cried as with one mouth,
> and they raised a great laughter that rose above them like a heavy cloud.

Thus the vertical dimension of this scene is resolved: man (=Zarathustra) becomes the complete human, or overman (=sun), only by going through animal nature (=eagle and serpent). That is, man becomes great only by rejuvenating his animal nature, for good *and* evil, each to their highest degree. Thus we come full circle to the first section of the Prologue, and its *horizontal* dimension of the sun (=overman) at its highest point where man (=Zarathustra) and his animal nature (=eagle and serpent) are united and fulfilled to their greatest degree.[53]

Part I: On the Dangers of "Crossing Over"

1. On the Three Metamorphoses

Zarathustra teaches the three metamorphoses (*Verwandlungen*) of the spirit as his first speech in the Motley Cow. As has been previously stated,[54] the entire *Zarathustra* concerns metamorphosis: its images, notions and characters are not static fixed ciphers; rather, they lead a life of transformation and transfiguration of the wildest sort, crossing all manners of category and fixed boundary, so that a notion which first appears as an animal next is personified as human, or represented as some type of inorganic matter, and may reappear without warning later as, for example, the motion of some object. Metamorphosis is evident in the very beginning of the Prologue, when Zarathustra is described as undergoing a change (*sich verwandeln*). But in this section appears for the first time a word which will appear frequently hereafter; namely, *spirit* (*Geist*).[55] The spirit Nietzsche speaks of, which will be considered later in depth, begins its metamorphosis by becoming a camel, or rather like a camel. Nothing is said of spirit in itself, or spirit prior to its metamorphosis.

What is the distinguishing characteristic of the camel? The spirit is said to resemble a camel because it "kneels down, wishing to be well-laden." This is its natural activity, and the natural goal of this activity is said to be exaltation in its own strength; that is, it derives a feeling of *power* in its actions. The camel assumes its burden *wilfully* in an exalting, voluntary, natural manner. Spirit as camel is laden with various burdens it finds difficult to bear: humility, self-mockery, suffering, sickness, nausea of the truth, and love for its detractors. These are the things the camel finds *hardest to do*: they cost him the greatest of his will power. The spirit that wishes the greatest overcoming must tackle the greatest barriers: the camel is thus the first necessary moment of the spirit that wills the *Ueber-mensch*. So laden, the camel rushes in the desert. The word rendered in English as "speeds" (*eilen*) means alternatively to rush, to make haste, to be in a hurry, to waste no time. Nietzsche chooses a verb indicating that the camel does not trod along under its burden: rather, it lifts tremendous weight and makes haste. *Why* it does so will be said later.

Now of course the image of the camel is connected to many other figures in *Zarathustra* (we have seen an anticipation of the camel in the image of Zarathustra carrying the corpse). But it is most certain that Nietzsche alludes to a figure external to his own text. Here is meant the figure of Jesus and his temptations in the desert.[56] But while Nietzsche wants us to think of Jesus when we think of the camel, our associations should not be limited to him alone.

Selection of the desert is crucial here, whereas the choice of the camel is not. Nietzsche might have chosen any number of beasts of burden for his imagery. The image of the camel is bizarre and arabesque to his German readers, but it is really of secondary importance. The desert is a more primary symbol than the camel. Why so? What does the desert represent?

As a hint, we are told that the desert belongs to the camel and not vice-versa. The camel hastens to a desert of its own making (*seine Wueste*). Just as the camel creates its own burden, so it creates its own desert. Christ, by wilfully taking up the ministry, thereby wilfully created a desert to test them in. As soon as Christ is baptized and ordained he goes into the desert.

The desert is by nature a wilfull creation of spirit as camel. It is also by nature *lonely*. Nietzsche writes that the camel races to "the loneliest desert." Voluntarily assuming a burden creates an *individual self*; that is, it *individuates* the burdened from all others. The desert, then, is a trope for the self's isolation from all others, and the camel is the trope for of spirit that has differentiated itself from all other spirit by assuming a burden. The spirit kneeling down is spirit as camel, giving simultaneous occasion to a self, the "others," and a distance between the self and others.

In this self-created and self-creating distance occurs the second metamorphosis. Now the self wants to become complete master of the desert. The last limit that controls the shifting and expanding sands of the annihilating desert must be fought by the camel. This last limit to the mastering type and its desert is named "Thou Shalt." The invisible line checking expansion of the distance between an individual and others is the moral constraint "Thou Shalt." So long as "Thou Shalt" lives in the desert of the camel, as god or some other moral master, the camel will not be alone, but rather it will be in check, because "Thou Shalt" lies in his way. To fight and destroy Thou Shalt, the camel must first become a lion. The lion opposes his "I will" to "Thou Shalt." "Thou Shalt" says there must be no more "I will": "I will" says there must be no more "Thou Shalt."

The lion says "I will": in German it says "Ich will." There is an ambiguity in the English "I will" not present in the German "Ich will." "I will" may be a transitive verb of volition requiring an intentional object: "I will such and such to be the case . . . . " Or it may be a promissory verb of future action: "I will do it . . . . " But the German "Ich will" can here only mean the former sense. The lion thus wills that something be the case. What is the intentional object of the lion's will? The lion wants absolute, ultimate victory over "Thou Shalt." He wills absolute negative freedom from all constraint. (By "negative freedom" I mean freedom *from* something or someone. "Positive freedom" is freedom *to do some action or another*. This distinction was made famous by Kant.) Understood in terms of the desert metaphor, the lion wills the ultimate absolute expansion of his own desert: he wills that no god or master bind him.

This dragon named "Thou Shalt" is representative of all values hitherto. "All values of all things shine on me. All value has long been created, and I am all created value . . . . Thus speaks the dragon." The lion, then, is the destroyer of all previous values, and the institutions which embody them. He is anti-everything.

Note that this is a substantial change of spirit from the camel. The camel was a change of spirit into the self-distinguishing ethical agent. It voluntarily created a self, the "others" and a distance between them. But this is in no way incommensurate with a pre-formed, pre-existing social morality. It is precisely traditional virtues, accepted standards and conventional ways which the camel assumes as a burden. The lion, though, wills that *all* preformed, pre-existing values be destroyed and that spirit become all-encompassing. This difference is substantial. If the camel is for something, the lion is against everything: if one possible camel is Christ, one possible lion is the Anti-christ.

The camel, further, changes spirit without a sense of sacrilege because it is born *into* a tradition of spirit. But Zarathustra clearly associates a sense of sacrilege with the lion. "To assume the right to new values—that is the most terrifying assumption for a reverent spirit who would bear much." The spirit who would bear much is the camel: it is terrified of the pride and audacity of the lion. The camel is a traditional, *reverent* spirit. Christ is the moral camel *par excellence*: he bears much but never challenges his master, his god, his Thou Shalt, his law-giving dragon named Moses.

Zarathustra continues, "Verily, to him it is preying and a matter for a beast of prey." The beast of burden is *repulsed* by the beast of prey. The lion is a symbol of what eats christians, just as a lion might eat a camel. The camel, says Zarathustra, "once loved Thou Shalt as most sacred": to the lion, nothing is sacred. The lion is the nihilist *par excellence*. "Nihilism" is a psychological, cultural phenomenon which Nietzsche spent a great deal of time considering. As a rough definition, we might say that nihilism is a total loss of values. A note from the Spring-Fall 1887, number 3 of *Will to Power*, fits well with my analysis of the three metamorphoses: "*Radical nihilism* is the conviction of an absolute untenability of existence when it comes to the highest values one recognizes; plus the realization that we lack the least right to posit a beyond or an in-itself of things that might be "divine" or morality incarnate. This realization is a consequence of the cultivation of "truthfulness"—thus itself a consequence of the faith in morality."

The cultivation of truth and morality is the camel: he who assumes the right to posit higher values is the child: the nihilist is squarely between them.

The shift of spirit from camel to lion therefore is substantial and absolute. Spirit, in this metamorphosis, is strung in high-tension between two poles. It may remain the camel indefinitely, constrained, and the slave of Thou Shalt. Or it may alter into the lion and purge the desert of all Thou Shalts, but it may not indefinitely waiver between camel and lion. To do both is to kill what one regards as sacred, to be repulsed at the nihilism one's own self has created. For absolute negative freedom, then, the lion is needed.[57]

But now a new bind is generated: the spirit-now-lion has mastered the desert created by the camel. The desert has been overthrown of all masters and gods. The camel brought his god into the desert with him; the lion has nothing at all. Now enters the bind.

Either the spirit must remain impoverished by its own isolation, or it may create its own world by creating new values for itself. Granted, Zarathustra says that the lion *must* become the child, seemingly leaving no choice. But the lion *may* remain in its own nihilism, a beast of prey without prey. But this is a powerless state. By this very act of self-isolation, spirit has become *der Weltverlorene*. This means in English the lonely, the isolated, the solitary: one who has been cut off from the world. Kaufmann translates this literally as "he who had been lost to the world." The lion seeks the feeling of power, but cannot tolerate the old: thus he must have power over the new.

But this is a substantial change of spirit once again. For hitherto spirit was reactive: as a camel the spirit reacted to some natural tendency toward kneeling down and testing itself. That is why the camel *rushes* into the desert. And as lion, the spirit reacted to Thou Shalts the way a lion reacts to tender little lambs. It says a sacred No and wills annihilation.

But the child is entirely active—it says a sacred Yes and wills an absolute positive freedom. It "now wills his own will." The child wills a new world, a new geography of the spirit. But this entails putting limits on the shifting and expanding sands of the desert, and that introduces a bind. The lion sought complete victory over any limit. Now the spirit wants mastery over its own sands—it wants its own transfiguration. But the lion doesn't distinguish between self-imposed and external limits. It simply destroys all limit.

Once again, then, the spirit is a high-tension wire between two poles. It may remain a No-saying lion or it may become a Yes-saying child. But it cannot do both, for eventually it will either say No to its Yes or Yes to its Yes. Either way it has relieved the tension.

But what of the "necessity" of these metamorphoses of the spirit? Why are they necessary? It is surely not the case that Nietzsche is giving us a set of sufficient conditions for becoming the value-creator symbolized by the child. Rather, Nietzsche is describing a logical sequence that is non-temporal, though his narrative is in temporal language.[58] This logical structure is seen when we run through the speech "backwards." Suppose spirit is a child, a creator. What does creativity presuppose? Real creativity requires going beyond standard reproduction: it is the creation of *new values*. But what does this creation of new values presuppose? It supposes that previous values have in some sense been overcome. This is the essence of the lion: it overcomes previous values. So the child presupposes the lion. What in turn does overcoming of values require? It requires that one willingly take the pre-existing values seriously. It requires a familiarity with values of some sort, with a mastery of them adequate to allow one to improve or alter the values at all. To overcome, go beyond, or excell previous values, is Nietzsche's preferred mode of overcoming. For the spirit to *start* by creating new values is incoherent. It requires an exulting attitude toward standards and their responsibilities. But this is just what the camel represents. Thus the lion presupposes the camel.

Nietzsche, then, is describing a logical structure of necessary conditions for the creator. It is the developmental path of a certain type of spirit; namely, the higher man, the immoralist, the atheist, Zarathustra. In the Prologue Zarathustra is described as metamorphozed into the child[59]: his spirit has already followed the developmental path, and he now instructs us on its necessary sequence. There is no doubt in Zarathustra's mind about the goal of the project—it is the overman.[60] There is no doubt about the importance of the project—it is the very meaning of the earth. There are no metaphysical or epistemological issues unresolved: philosophy stands at the service of the overman, not vice-versa. There remains only the psychological and rhetorical problem of how one convinces and motivates the audience to become higher men.[61] The first Part of *Zarathustra* concerns itself with these psychological problems: gravity v. seriousness, the loneliness of going into the desert, the sacrilege which keeps the camel from becoming the lion, and the single-minded nihilism which keeps the lion from becoming the child.

2. On the Teachers of Virtue

In a note to this section Nietzsche writes, "Previously I called it "christianity"—today I call it "the means to good sleep."[62] And indeed, this section is a parody of christian virtues, continuing the contrast between the overman and the last man begun in the third section of the Prologue. The first speech of *Zarathustra* in the Motley Cow taught the tension of the spirit and the will to overcome, to "metamorphose," to become the creator of the overman. The teachings of the "sage" in this section preach the will to release tension in the spirit. The good-in-itself for the sage is good sleep; that is, loss of cares, sorrows and the desire for anything higher. Self-overcoming is a means to this end. But the sage preaches an overcoming in small things only to make one tired, and an overcoming that must be resolved before bedtime. The sage teaches not the overman but rather the last man: he offers sleep-like peace requiring smallness in good and evil and obedience to the powerful. To bring sleep on, urged to chew the cud (think only of the immediate) and hope for green pastures.[63] Waking life itself is merely a means to sleep.

This section closely relates to the two Hermits of the Prologue. The first Hermit asked, "Zarathustra has changed, Zarathustra has become a child, Zarathustra is an awakened one; what do you now want among the sleepers? And what if at night, in their beds, they hear a man walk by long before the sun has risen—they probably ask themselves, Where is the thief going?"[64] This anticipatory remark is now fulfilled: Zarathustra has found the sleepers, and they fear above all else those who go through the night (=night watchmen). The second Hermit, who suffered of bad sleep, anticipated this section as well. "Ten truths a day you must find; else you will still be seeking truth by night, and your soul will remain hungry."[65]

The second Hermit had the virtue of solitude, but like the sage he sought only good sleep. Just as the first Hermit caused Zarathustra to have a revelation about true companions, so the sage gives to him a revelation about christian virtues. (In both instances Zarathustra says "Ein Licht ging mir auf," i.e., "I've seen the light!")

> Now I understand clearly what was once sought above all when teachers of virtue were sought. Good sleep was sought, opiate virtues for it. For all these much praised sages who were teachers of virtue, wisdom was the sleep without dreams; they knew no better meaning of life.

Thus the secret of such virtue is laid bare: the "virtuous" seek virtue not for its own sake, but as a means to release of an inner tension, as the opium smoker seeks to escape life.[66]

3. On the Afterworldly

The notion that man creates the gods in his own image, rather than conversely, is a perennial possession of philosophy dating back at least to Xenophanes. Nietzsche's treatment of the afterworldly here bears strong resemblance to another German philosopher of the nineteenth-century, Ludwig Feuerbach,[67] whose great contribution was extensive investigation of this notion. Prior to his isolation, Zarathustra underwent a great disgust with humanity, and when he was unable to bear his suffering further, he carried his extinguished love for man (=ashes) to the mountain. The love he had felt for man was then transferred to a god (=out of my ashes and fire), who was nonetheless nothing other than a human invention and illusion. The image of man, abstracted from

the flesh and blood of human existence, as a *holy ghost*, is projected
by man into a realm of the imagination, which is taken to be in fact
beyond this world: this is the creation process of all superhumans.[68]
Man also takes the objects of this world, of nature or "the earth,"
and duplicates them in a supernatural form in the realm of the
imagination: this is the creation of *afterworlds*, e.g., the christian
heaven.[69] Man, in this theogeny, projects his entire being into the
superhuman, not merely his rationality (=head): thus the superhumans of the imagination evidence animal drives as well.[70]

Zarathustra repeatedly states that the afterworldly realm of the
imagination is a product of the *body*. The import of this is that the
spiritual life of man is a result of the *physical*: the spiritual life of
man *depends* upon the physical. As a metaphysical doctrine, this
viewpoint endorses a materialism (the primacy of body before
spirit) and naturalism (the rejection of supernaturalism).[71]

When one attempts to imagine that which is beyond this world,
one must always project the human and the natural: for the imagination is constrained by human perspective, which cannot be
shaken off. The dehumanized world seen from outside the human
perspective, the thing-in-itself, is nothing at all—a qualityless, in-
definite non-being.[72] Man is the measure and valuation of all
things: being is that which can enter into man's perspective.[73] And
that which man can take to exist with the greatest certainty is the
self (*das Ich*),[74] but the self is in turn grounded in the body and its
senses. Man, in his wildest flights of fantasy and poetry, can only
speak of the body and its senses. The range of the senses is nature,
the sensual world, *the earth*. All things supernatural are imagined
duplications of the natural in the superlative: all superhuman beings are fanciful creations employing the image of man raised to its
highest grade of thinkability.[75]

Zarathustra attributes all attempts to create the supernatural
and superhuman to weariness: that is, weakness of will and inability
to cope with the sorrows of *this* world.[76] The religious consciousness can no longer bear the sorrows of this world, and in an attempt to escape them, jumps to an afterworld without such sorrows. Thus in the world religions and theology one finds the notion

that the Creator produces the universe as an object of contemplation. And to the gods he attributes those things which he takes
from himself, including the drive to escape from sorrow.[77] Thus for
the religious consciousness the world is an illusion, a smokey hallu-
cination of the deity, who is more opium smoker than benevolent
father. But man is in fact beholder of the pipedream, which is none
other than his imagination of another world. Zarathustra's belief in
a suffering god refers to Nietzsche's adoption of the schopenhauerian philosophy in his youth, which takes the world to be a sense-
less, painful eternal "will" and its veil of projections, or "representa-
tions."

Before his "great disgust," Zarathustra's love for mankind was a
fire; his extinguished love thereafter is his "ashes." When he went
to the mountains he created a god out of ashes (—the period of
disillusionment during the affinity with Schopenhauer's pessimism).
But when he found his true self (=invented a new flame) he found
his love recreated in his love of the overman and simultaneously his
god disappeared.[78] The birth of the overman thus spells the demise
of the gods; and his renewed concern and love for the earth and
body spells the end of the afterworld.[79] Zarathustra now sees
clearly that seeking the afterworldly is a sickness and weariness of
the body, and that every age in which sickness is rampant, unbelief,
which is true health, is taken to be sin, and orthodoxy to be godliness. But the inversion is the truth: afterworldliness denies the
body only to reconstruct it in the form of a personal god.[80] The religious consciousness would like to crawl out of its skin, but the
ghosts[81] of its creation themselves are imagined as bodily. The very
image of the blood of Christ is but a ghostly reflection of the flesh
and blood nature of man.[82] Zarathustra wants above all for the
earth to become a site of recovery for man, where the sickness of
the afterworldly is cured, and where man speaks of the healthy
body and its senses. This is the period of the so-called
"philosophers of the future." Feuerbach used this phrase consistently in reference to himself. (The phrase may come from Feuerbach to Nietzsche through the influence of one-time feuerbachian
Richard Wagner.) Healthy human senses (*Sinne*) for such philoso-

phers are the meaning (*Sinn*) of the earth—and that is the *over-man*. Nietzsche calls the hour of god's death and the overman's birth "the Great Noon": Feuerbach calls this the "turning point of world history." For both, it is the highest (and lowest) point of mankind, when man knows himself as the creator of god, and moreover, knows himself as divine. Feuerbach however locates the divinity of man in the *species-being* (i.e., in the species of man collectively), while Nietzsche locates godliness, if anywhere, in the dionysian, superhuman metamorphosis of spirit.

4. On the Despisers of the Body

The despisers of the body are those religious teachers and moralists who profess that the body and its senses are something of negative moral value, a source of spiritual pollution, an unnecessary, unclean and undesirable fetter of the spirit; i.e., a despicable limitation that is best abstained from in this world and one which will not exist in the next world. (Such a doctrine was held, for example, by the pietists and other religious purists of Nietzsche's lifetime.[83]) The despisers of the body are also the idealist philosophers who profess that ultimate reality is spirit, consciousness, or ideas, while the material world is declared non-existant, illusory or a confused idea. (Such notions are found, according to Nietzsche, in Hegel, Leibniz, Berkeley and other philosophers.) The idealist posits a God, spirit (Hegel's *Geist*, Fichte's *Ich*, Kant's *transzendentales Ich*)—some variety of universal consciousness—as the highest good and standard of reality. Thus both types of spiritualist degrades matter as the antithesis of the good—as unholy, absurd, polluted—and seeks the "better" world, the "true" world and the "after" world.[84]

The basic dichotomy between body and spirit arises with the naive (=childlike) dualist notion of personal identity. The despisers of the body reduce the dualism to a spiritualism in which the highest good and underlying standard of reality is spirit. Zarathustra, on the contrary, reduces the dualism to a physicalism. He finds the underlying principle of all reality to be the body. Like the dualist, he is aware of the presence of spirit in the world, but he is awakened to the dependence of spirit on the physical. "Body am I entirely and nothing else; and soul is only a word for something about the body."[85] In an inversion of the spiritualist principle, Zarathustra proclaims that body is the independent being, whereas the spirit is dependent: there can be a physical universe without spirit, but there can be no spirit without an encompassing body, as the spiritualists imagine. Zarathustra, then, is rejecting the notion of a disembodied spirit.

Zarathustra does not conceive matter (=body) to be stable, indivisible solid atoms, mere chunks of stuff, as did the Greek atomists, nor as mechanically behaving elements moving through space, as did the classical materialists of the seventeenth and eighteenth-centuries. Rather, for Nietzsche, matter is a creative force that is purposive and intelligent in the strongest sense of the word. "There is more reason your body than in your best wisdom." The bodily organism is a vast multiplicity in collaboration toward an inner purpose (=a plurality with one sense) and a vast opposition of members within a commonwealth (=a war and a peace), that organizes contrary drives and sublates conflict in pursuit of a collective goal.[86] Thus it shows greater purposive action (=is the Great Reason) than does the subordinate and superficial processes of consciousness (=the little reason).

As part of its purposive activity, the body has created the spirit. According to Zarathustra, the spirit is an instrument (*Werkzeug*)[87] for the body, a tool created that it might fulfill the aims of the body. "The creative body created the spirit as a hand for its will." While our conscious life (=thoughts and feelings) appears to us to be the guiding force of our actions, the body is the genuine origin of the laws and reasons for human actions (=mighty ruler, unknown sage). The idealist takes the ultimate self to be the ego (*das Ich*), but Zarathustra declares that the body is the underlying manipulator of the self (=leading string of the ego) and the determinant of the self's thought processess (=prompter of concepts). While the spirit is the self's consciousness of itself (=says "I"), it is but one small and late development of the organism: the body proves itself to be the fundamental principle of the self (=*does*"I").

The spirit is spoken of as the eyes of the self, as the hand for its will and its toy and tool. But what *is* the goal of the body, that it would create the spirit? What the body wants to do above all else, it most fervent wish, is "to create beyond itself." That is, the body strives to enhance the power of its life.[88] It is not content to remain with the vegetative, reproductive, motive processes: the nature of the organism is to organize present processes for the creation of higher processes.[89] Spirit is added onto the prior organic processes and is itself an organic process (=something about the body). It is the latest and smallest development of the organism, but not necessarily the last or the best. The fundamental error of the spiritualist is that he misinterprets this process to be fundamentally different from the others, i.e., non-organic, non-material, and to be of greater value than the "lower" processes and to be the standard of reality. That is, spirit is taken to be real and independent reality.[90] According to Zarathustra, however, the superaddition of spirit is one more level, or stage, in the progressive creativity of life. The organism seeks to create beyond itself; that is, it seeks to enhance its power in life. And indeed even the inorganic will later be held to strive for such extension of power. All bodily nature is a force attempting to enhance its power: this is later identified as "the will to power."[91]

The error of spiritualism is, however, not one of reasoning. Misinterpretation of the spirit, according to Zarathustra, is itself an action of the body: when the body loses the will and strength to create beyond itself, it turns against life and desires its own destruction. Contempt for the body is envy of the healthy body and a disguised drive for self-destruction. Thus the spiritualists at every turn confirm the primacy and worth of the body. Longing for the spirit is fundamentally longing for the disembodiment of the self. But since the self rests only on the firm foundation of the body, disembodiment is another word for death. Thus the spiritualist longs for the conditions that would spell his demise. And so it was with the afterworldly: they sought a spiritual world, a disembodied world, a spectre which in reality means the negation of life. And indeed the teachers of virtue want sleep without dreams, i.e., eternal sleep throughout the night of death. These three types are, then, in stark contrast to the life-enthused spirit of the three metamorphoses. Zarathustra speaks as a teacher only to those who are inspired with earthly, bodily life. To all others he wishes destruction: the teachers of virtue are blessed, for they shall soon drop off (=perish); the afterworldly are admonished to recover, but Zarathustra speaks to them as one recovered among the deadly ill; and he would not change the despisers of the body, but have them "say farewell to their bodies—and thus became silent."

The *body*, with its stages of self-overcoming, is the principle for understanding life, and its highest creation is the basis for the highest values of man.[92] The highest creation of the human organism, though, is the individual in which every level, every process, of the organism is in its healthiest state--and that individual is the *overman*.

5. On Enjoying and Suffering the Passions

The overman is once again the concern of this section, although the notion is not mentioned by name, in keeping with the admonition, "Inexpressible and nameless is that which gives my soul agony and sweetness and is even the hunger of my entrails." Zarathustra's notion of the overman is the agony which hungers his soul, and his virtue of self-overcoming is the passion he suffers. "Man is something that shall be overcome"—this leading idea of the Prologue is the equivalent of "the overman shall live." But for the overman to exist, mankind must go beyond itself by setting great ideals and overcoming great obstacles, which is to say that great virtues must be willed, for great virtues are the means to greatness. But by undergoing such great efforts, man must commit his entire being to the service of his ideal, and so when he perishes, he perishes of his ideals.

It is the hard doctrine of Zarathustra here that man must again suffer great passion, succumb to a ruling, driving, *overwhelming* force which will spell his demise (=perishing). It is easier for him who has one commanding passion.

> My brother, if you are fortunate you have only one virtue and no more; then
> you will pass over the bridge more easily.

This is a restatement of the doctrine in Prologue, section 4:

> I love him who does not want to have too many virtues. One virtue is more
> virtue than two, because it is more of a noose on which his catastrophe may
> hang.

The surpassing of modern man (=passing over the bridge) by perishing of one's own virtues (=going under) is *great* virtue: modern man has only *small* virtues, and so must suffer the passions (=grow an evil) out of conflict of his discordant virtues (=war and battle). Domesticated man still has much of the beast of passion in him, and to rejuvenate this nature, it is necessary that the passions must be suffered once again.[93]

To suffer a passion, one need not will it as a universal moral imperative (=human statute), ground it rationally (=the reason of all men), consider it revelation (=divine law), nor consider it assurance of an eternal reward (=overearths and paradises). The passions will by nature be irrational and will arrive (=build its nest), develop (=dwell) and create the future (=sit on its eggs) with the unreason of natural drive (=bird). The highest goal (the overman) need have no general meaning (=name) nor community (=in common with the people).[94] It is an autonomously chosen, if irrational, moral law *for the individual* and will bear the mark of the individual passion. If one must speak of the personal, inner, overwhelming power, it is best to stammer.

6. On the Pale Criminal

In a note to this section Nietzsche writes, "the pale criminal imprisoned and Prometheus in contrast! Degeneration!"[95] Both the Pale Criminal and Prometheus dare to break the commands of god ("Thou Shalt" and Zeus), but the Pale Criminal shows remorse for his affront with a self-disgusted ego: Prometheus shows defiance from a self-strong ego.[96] Prometheus is the lion who would then turn into the child and create a new order of values for man. The

Pale Criminal is the lion whose single virtue has spelled his undoing. The sublimity of the criminal rests in his ego, in his self-estima-
tion—but the lion without will is despicable and ought to be put out
of his mercy (=a quick death). As anticipated in the last section,
not all who go into the desert battleground of virtues are strong
enough. And as was said in the Prologue, section 7, he who is
possessed by one great passion creates "more of a noose on which
his catastrophe hangs."

Like Dostoyevski's character Raskolnikov,[97] the Pale Criminal
raises himself above the law and commits a crime, only to suffer
from guilt thereafter. Both were equal to the deed, but the memory
(=image) of the deed that remained proved to be a hypnotic barrier they were unable to overcome. "The criminal is treated by the
moral man as the accessory of one particular act—and they treat
them so, the more this one act was the exception of their essence:
so it works like the chalk scratch with the hen.—There is much
hypnotism in the moral world."[98] The greater the crime, the more
of an exception to the law it constitutes and so the more reason is
revolted by it. Reason follows the rule. The reason of the Pale
Criminal freezes before an image of the deed (=chalk streak stops
a hen). This is the lion, the rule-breaker, the nihilist, in crisis. After
destroying "Thou Shalt," the lion has returned to become the beast
of burden, and discovers the horror of its act. This is his "madness
after the deed," which proves to be a noose of his own making.

Those who would judge the Pale Criminal kill as well: their
"goodness" and "justice," they believe, allow them to kill and sacrifice in a different sense—punishment *for* murder, not a *second*
murder. But punishment for its own sake is meaningless revenge.
The Pale Criminal has accomplished the overcoming of man in his
own ego—and for this he must go under (=perish). But the judge
kills someone without overcoming himself or another. Thus the
judge himself is on trial here: why does he kill? An undergoing with
an overcoming is justified: it is a means to the goal of overman.[99]
But the execution of the meta-moral man without thereby improv-
ing man is bilious revenge. The criminal has acted out the crime of
his inner life; this crime is commited by the judge as well, but due

to his prudence, in imagination alone. By means of his own passions, the criminal has been brought to his demise: the judge kills out of "goodness" and "justice," not passion. The criminal has justified his own death: but the judge has yet to justify his own continued existence.

Superficially judged, the motive of murder in the cases of the Pale Criminal and Raskolnikov is theft. Nietzsche's depth psychology, however, considers the criminal who breaks the moral proscription "Thou shalt not kill." To portray the action as robbery or revenge is "madness *before* the crime." The deep reason for the crime is degenerative passion, an expression of his disturbed body. Were the deed to be viewed as one out of passion, the burden would "roll off," but the image of the deed has left him *pale—* passionless. He wanted to have *reasons* for his crime, but without irrational passion, he feels guilt as if it were a lead weight.

Nietzsche considers all spiritual illness to be a symptom of physical distress.[100] The criminal type is a strong type of man who exists under unfavorable conditions which turn his strong drives into degenerative forms, such as depressive affects, suspicion, fear, dishonesty.[101] The physical disturbance (=diseases, ball of snakes) expresses itself as a lashing out at the world (=catch prey in the world). The weak or weary in will want to hurt that which they cannot overcome, which means to adopt the form of hurt and suffering considered evil at that age—at one time doubt, heresy or witchcraft, in this age *theft*—violation of private property. But the deep motive is *blood*: the criminal wants passionately to achieve satisfaction by murder, but his reason revolts and substitutes the more "reasonable" motive of robbery. This is a purely naturalist, materialist, anthropological interpretation of "evil," and so it affronts those who would believe in witches and devils.[102]

Zarathustra is by no means endorsing all forms of criminality in this section. Its real purpose is to serve as a case of depth psychology reminiscent of previous sections. In other writings, Nietzsche gives a physiological investigation of criminality to the conclusion that it is a form of physiological degeneration. Thus the criminal is not at all the overman. However, the criminal's animal nature is still evident and he strives with one great passion to overcome man, and so he finds limited favor with Zarathustra.[103]

More important than praise of the criminal is indictment of the judge. The red judge is the kantian moralist and any other type who values *retribution*. Although the red judge neither understands nor shares the leonine nature of the criminal, he judges the latter by the camel-like standards of "thou shalt" and "thou shalt not." Justice as retribution demands *punishment* in proportion to the crime. And so the red judge gives the death penalty to a murderer who may actually be a higher man. The judge is a passionless herd animal who seeks to judge the one who struggles to overcome man. He is one of the "good and just" in the Market Place who indirectly cause the downfall of the higher man. But the judge's virtue, justice as retaliation, like the virtues of all last men, is a means to mere longjevity and contentment. The red judge[104] is a sign that the last man holds the power in human society today; the Pale Criminal is a sign that the overman is slowly on his way.

7. On Reading and Writing

This is the only speech of the entire book without a designated audience;[105] Nietzsche, through the voice of Zarathustra, directly addresses the reader concerning the relation of reader to writer. Literacy was once taken to be a sign of divine abilities, later of great learning, but has finally become a possession of even the most common man. But reading Nietzsche is not the passive entertainment of the mass consumer of words who reads any newspaper.[106] Writing in Nietzsche's vein is writing with one's innermost being (=blood);[107] he wants to be learned by heart--thought through from within, committed to memory, felt with passion, reworked as if one's own creation.

To understand Nietzsche from the *inside* is to understand his philosophy of life. Life is not something which must be borne out of mere inertia, but is rather the object of greatest value. "We love life, not because we are used to living, but because we are used to loving." This dramatic and beautiful statement is meant not only as a contrast to christianity, but also to Schopenhauer, who professed that the world is sorrowful and meaningless. Whether to love life or not is itself not a matter of rational choice, but when one finds a purpose in existence, i.e., the overman, even the "madness" of great striving attains a reason. (The discovery of reason even in madness is an inversion of Hamlet's tragic worldview.) True, life has its many burdens, but to fold under its weight is for the weakling (=rosebud), not the strong type. (Nietzsche's anti-christian image here should be compared to the "lillies of the field" parable at Matthew 6:28 and Marx's parody thereof.) Zarathustra's greatest danger (=devil) is the spirit of gravity, that is, the weakness of spirit that would succumb to the grave concerns of life, making him solemn, serious, thorough and "profound." The average man lives in the blackness of depressed spirit through which "all things fall." Zarathustra's real spirit is to fight gravity and rise upward. He is "well disposed toward life" and finds empathy with affirmative beings (=soap bubbles, butterflies), even if they are derided as "light foolish delicate mobile little souls." Relief from gravity allows Zarathustra to assume an extraordinary position over man (=elevation) from which man's engulfing tragedies and seriousness become plays, as human affairs were for the Greek olympian gods.[108]

The question of values now becomes a light-hearted affair: while his readers still take truth/falsity, good/evil, life/death seriously, looking outward and upward for solutions to be *given*, Nietzsche looks down—like the sun over earth, Zarathustra from his cave, the animals flying over man—out of a gayness born beyond these false dichotomies. Nietzsche's thoughts are audacious and require like-minded courage, *active* thought, and lightness. To destroy belief in the gods creates dangerous, devilish thoughts in their stead (=goblins), but Zarathustra prefers these dangers to the seriousness of the restrained, burdened spirit. This requires that the good reader be able to go from peak formulation (=aphorism) to peak, comprehending the entire mountain range of his thought without getting lost in the vastness of his writings.

The weakling creates gods in his own image, but Zarathustra can no longer take such gods seriously. Rather, he would only believe in the dancing god Dionysus, who "dances through me."

Dionysus is never mentioned by name in *Zarathustra*, yet he is as central to the work as the idea of the overman. In *Die Geburt der Tragoedie* Dionysus is an "artistic power . . . which breaks forth out of nature herself, *without the mediation of the human artist* . . . . " More specifically, the dionysian is the natural drive to the non-imagistic arts (whereas "Apollo" is the natural drive to the imagistic arts), which expresses itself at a variety of levels of life, but which is most analogous to the compulsion to intoxication. That is, Dionysus embodies the drive to enhanced feelings of power seeking release in gesture, passion, song and dance and Apollo personifies the drive to power released in vision, dream and poetry.

Nietzsche revised the notion of the dionysian by the time of *Zarathustra*, as Silk and Stern have recognized in *Nietzsche and Tragedy*: 1) the purely dionysian is later seen as impossible: there is always the apollonian in art, 2) Dionysus is later contrasted to Christ, not Apollo: Dionysus and Apollo are conflated as an anti-christian ideal, and 3) Dionysus is later a life force rather than an artistic drive.

In his autobiography, Nietzsche clearly states the relation between Dionysus, Zarathustra and the "overman."[109] Zarathustra is the *advocate of the overman*, which is none other than *Dionysus himself*. The notion of the dionysian is the very notion of the overman. This notion of a highest type begins as an ideal over Zarathustra, but is eventually actualized by him: Zarathustra is said to be the overman actualized to the highest degree of reality. (Nietzsche's chapter on *Zarathustra* in *Ecce Homo* is critical for understanding this crucial point.)

So it is that Zarathustra believes in himself: he finds his god in himself, dancing through this *earthly body*, in an experience of self-diremption which Nietzsche elsewhere associates with poetic inspiration and creation of the gods.[110] Zarathustra is the advocate of this god Dionysus and his mystery teachings.[111] Now he can only parody the christian god in the image of an ass,[112] a mere beast of burden, who bears life as a burden. In his own image, Zarathustra creates a god who is the ultimate Yes-sayer, who affirms even the most tragic parts of life, and who dances through all nature as the vital driving force overcoming life and bringing it back into existence in an eternal cycle.

8. On the Tree on the Mountainside[113]

Nietzsche returns in this section to the themes set out in the Prologue and "On the Three Metamorphoses." The youth is one who has successfully metamorphosed through the camel and lion stages, but like the Pale Criminal, he is not yet able to assume the right to posit new values: he is not yet the child, but rather "the lion in crisis."

Like the Tightrope Walker, he wills to "cross over," but the youth also undergoes all the dangers of the tightrope. He fears that he has metamorphosed too fast and will suffer the hesitation which would spell his downfall. He is spellbound by those who pass him by with leaps and bounds. He comes to be contemptuous of his crossing over, or of the loneliness of the wire. And he looks back at his past steps and stumblings. But above all, he is spellbound by the evil he is involved in. By parable, Zarathustra captures the essence of the youth's horrors: "The more he aspires to the height and light, the more strongly do his roots strive earthward, downward, into the dark, the deep—into evil." The youth is hypnotized by the depth of his evil, and is in danger of undergoing the Pale Criminal's "madness after the deed."

The youth's danger is not that he would become one of the "good"—a sleeper, an afterworldly despiser of the body—but that he would remain in the lion stage as complete nihilist. The youth is a "sufferer of the passions," and would let his passions free (=dogs out of cellar). Hesitation would allow the passions, however, to turn into small virtues. Those who would give up their hopes and strivings out of prudence devolve into hedonists with their little pleasures. But the spirit that would metamorphose must become a child, the creator of new values, who assumes the right to his highest hope, to become the hero in his own soul.

Zarathustra knows well the dangers facing the youth; to "discover" his soul, Zarathustra had to "invent" it. That is, to understand the youth, Zarathustra had to have gone through the same crisis.[114] The youth is an image of a former self, and Zarathustra is clearly moved by him. Zarathustra offers three parables using the image of a tree. Like the tree, the youth is threatened more by an invisible force (=inner tension) than tangible force.[115] As with the tree, this inner tension is necessary if one is to "cross over," for what would grow upward must send roots downward. And like the tree, the youth must wait for its lightning (=overman). But parable alone cannot resolve the youth's anxiety, and so the section concludes on a note of hope in crisis.

9. On the Preachers of Death

After the personally moving experience with the youth of the last section, Zarathustra returns to the multitudinous preachers of death—the gravediggers,[116] sleepers, afterworldy, body despisers, the virtuous, and others—with particular vehemence, repeating the message of Prologue 8, that such men must be passed by and left to their innermost death wishes: "And let this be the doctrine of your virtue: "Thou shalt kill thyself! Thou shalt steal away!" "

10. On War and Warriors[117]

This apparently straightforward paen on war cannot be taken at face value. Nietzsche here endorses war in a figurative sense, whose principles are taken from war in the literal sense. Zarathustra recognizes a former self in the warrior (*Kriegsmann*), who is sharply contrasted to the soldier (*Soldat*): the former is the wager of spiritual struggle and overcoming, while the latter is the undifferentiated (=uniform) herd animal of the state.[118] War and the soldier are the essence of the political state,[119] which comes under vehement attack in the next section. Far from an endorser of patriotism,[120] Nietzsche was an ardent supporter of individualism, and a detractor of all things collective. No friend of might and bloodshed for its own sake, Nietzsche, who served in the Franco-Prussian

War, repeatedly warned Germany that its military prowess was no evidence of cultural superiority.[121]

In military hierarchy Nietzsche finds a particularly clear expression of the nature of life: all members are ranked in a pyramidal fashion with command coming from above and obedience practiced below. War in the literal sense is a measure of discipline within a people. In the paradigmatic political state, the warrior is a mere means toward the production of the military genius—in themselves, soldiers have no value and are sacrificed to service of something higher in power, i.e., the state and its commander.[122]

War in a figurative sense is the center of Nietzsche's concern here, but the speech reflects the lessons learned in life's school of war in the literal sense.[123] War in his sense is an inner[124] struggle of values (=your war shall you wage—for your thoughts). This struggle reflects the nature of existence, for life is itself war in a way which bridges the literal and figurative senses of the trope.[125] Zarathustra teaches a doctrine of the radical inequality of man and divides him, between those strong enough to command and those who would obey: thus Zarathustra does not "spare" those who would overcome themselves (e.g., the youth of I.8). As in the war between states, sacrifice must be for something higher: Zarathustra's war is for the progress of man toward the highest type. The warrior is the highly disciplined individual—while not yet the lion, he is the camel (="thou shalt" sounds more agreeable than "I will"). His self-sacrifice is not the recalcitrance of the slave, nor the loss of self-love (as with the Pale Criminal), but is the warlike virtues of bravery, self-control and sense of duty of the hero, i.e., the distinguished individual. Cultivation of these virtues is, for the warrior, an end-in-itself (=it is the good war that hallows any cause), though his obedience is only a means toward an end (=the overcoming of man). In the cultivation of virtues required for this task, "war and courage have accomplished more great things than love of the neighbor."

This section is above all an inversion of the evangelical sentiment of "peace on earth, good will toward man."[126] The christian wants peace of soul, and is one sort of the "peaceful" or "unarmed" psychological type.[127] The weak type wishes only to have non-strenuous work as a means to contentment and long life. This feminine type values what is harmless (=pretty and touching). Thus the warrior appears "ugly" and "heartless"; but to Zarathustra, the beautiful does not have absolute value in comparison to the sublime. In the evangelical commendation to peace, the weakling rejects struggle in both the figurative and literal sense, and so seeks the opposite of the very essence of life itself, and so reveals an underlying afterworldly, morbid wish to escape from life. In contrast, Zarathustra endorses the warrior, or "armed," psychological type, who foregoes contentment, longjevity and pleasure. In praising the warrior type, Zarathustra praises life itself, which is a sublime war of all against all. Zarathustra's highest affirmation of life, the yet-to-appear doctrine of the eternal return, is elsewhere[128] associated with Heraclitus, who taught that "war is the father of all things." Here the "highest thought" for which Zarathustra wages "my war" is the overman, i.e., the complete man who affirms life and reflects it in all its sublimity.

11. On the New Idol

The vitality and health of the human spirit, which has been the central concern of the book implicitly or explicitly from its opening, becomes the yardstick of value against which the modern political state is measured. (The standard of life as the ultimate measure of value is a notion reworked from Goethe. For discussion of Goethe in this context, see *Schopenhauer als Erzieher.*) While the state claims to *be* the people, the sum of all human efforts, it is rather the very *death* of human spirit. The great individuals who formed the early communities[169] of man out of formless herds used an ideal to inspire and unite man: the state later used compulsion (=sword) and reward (=a hundred appetites) to harness the already formed peoples for its purposes. But this *political* structure is essentially foreign to the *spiritual* life of a people. A genuine people is unified by an ideal and a system of *customs and rights*. The modern state mixes all groups together, and it bears a sure sign of this mixing in its babble-like confusion of values. A people unified and pure is evidenced by a single set of *customs and rights*; the state is a hodge-podge of *laws* imposed on a motley patchwork of ethnicities. This melting pot produces the undifferentiated man of the masses (=the all-too-many) and therefore spells the disappearance (=death) of ethnic uniqueness, multiplicity and all forms of individuality.

In this section Nietzsche uses the word *Volk*, which Kaufmann translates as "people." It implies blood relation but should extend to include such groupings as clans, tribes, nations, et alia. Unlike Wagner and his friends Artur Gobineau and Stewart Chamberlain, Nietzsche did not think of people along strictly racial lines. *This section, along with the preceding and following sections, is in direct opposition to national socialism, militarism and all types of Vaterlaenderei.* To appreciate the subtlety of Nietzsche's thought, it is important to divest it of any connotations of "race theory." (Of great interest here is chapter eight of *Jenseits von Gut und Boese*.)

The political state appears to be the work of divine, superhuman design in human affairs (=ordering finger of god), an appearance which fools not only the foolish and dull, but great spirits as well. Nietzsche is thinking here of Hegel,[129] but also of Plato and others who speak in such spiritualizing and deifying terms. Zarathustra fears that the higher man, after his victory over christianity, will involve himself in the intrigues and adventures of the state. But the task of the higher man is to set up a new value over man and thereby unify a new people, one alien to any political structure. The state offers fame and riches to the higher man, as Satan (the false idol) tempted Jesus (the higher man).[130] But the state seeks the endorsement of the higher man only to attract the many.[131] Like the old idol (christianity), "the new idol" takes on a "finery of divine honors." But the state is really a machine of death (=hellish artifice) which, like Goya's depiction of Gargantua, feeds on human sacrifice. Not only the wicked criminal drinks the poison of the state, but also the law-abiding man, such as Socrates.[132] The figurative death of peoples in ethnic mixture is matched by literal death in war, which he calls the "slow suicide" of a people.[133]

In the political state, the lower man, symbolized by the monkey, holds power. The will to political power aims at a form of wealth that is mud and excrement relative to the goals Zarathustra envisions for the higher man. Rather than any form of involvement in, or reform of, the intrigues of the state, Zarathustra advises total non-participation and moreover expatriation from the all-too-many. The call to leave fatherlands for fresh air anticipates the later section, "On the Blessed Isles." On one of the nearby isles, "Fire Isle," the monster of the state is revisited in Hades in section II.18, with equally shrill condemnation. Zarathustra's goal is absolutely and unalterably non-political and anti-political:

> Where the state *ends*—look there, my brothers! Do you not see it, the rainbow and the bridges to the overman?

It is hard to imagine that any philosopher who has written these words is nonetheless linked in many people's minds with German fascism. But we must wait until III.7 to find that Nietzsche anticipated, and reviled, future propoganda campaigns to link his name with "something terrible." In the meantime it is important to remember that Nietzsche took his own advice to heart, forfeiting his German citizenship and spending his days at his beloved refuges in Northern Italy and Switzerland.

12. On the Flies of the Market Place

Zarathustra delivers to his companions the lessons learned in the Market Place. The Market Place is the realm of public life inhabited by the crowds (=flies), i.e., the "all-too-many," "superfluous," and "rabble" of previous sections, and by the man of the people (=the great man), who is the Jester of the Prologue. This "great man" is only the "actor of great things"—the politician or leader of mass movements whose greatness resides only in their ability to make great publicity (=noise) concerning events which affect the masses. He takes credit for the events which attract the most attention (wars and other world historical events), and is lauded by the masses as a "great man." But the truly great men are creators of value, whom the masses do not comprehend. In comparison to the inventors of new values, the great men of the masses—the Hitlers, Lenins and Churchills of history—are merely "showmen," a theme of the last section. The "great man" understands only violence, propaganda and popular movements. And when he creates a god in his own image, "he believes only in gods who make a big noise in the world," and this god is the "new idol," the state. But the truly great events of world history are the creation of new values, done away from the crowd (=invisibly) without fanfare and applause (=silently) by the solitary man.

The "great man of the masses" arrives in an hour of crisis in stern seriousness (=solemnity), whipping the rabble into a fury and demanding a rash, partisan, extreme, political/military action, and so he delivers only superficial solutions to the superfluous. But against these idolators of the state, Zarathustra commends neither support nor reaction, but non-participation and abandonment. The masses only injure (=sting) the truly great man with their endless superficial moralisms, demands and flatteries, draining his spirit (=blood), making him bitter and bilious (=poisoned). (This aspect of Zarathustra's teaching brings to mind Shakespeare's *Timon of Athens*.) All small people secretly resent greatness although they may laud it in public out of prudence: greatness is a reminder of what they are not (=their bad conscience). The great see through the superficial, who do not comprehend greatness, but who only follow those who seek the favor of the rabble and demean themselves as "men of the people." The Market Place, the arena of mass movements, nation states and war, is not the natural place for a creator: he must seek solitude and quiet, that his thoughts may ripen in fresh air and bloom into truly great fruits for mankind.

13. On Chastity

Zarathustra has advocated, and practiced, the search for solitude. But unlike the ascetics (e.g., the afterworldly, preachers of death, teachers of virtue), Zarathustra does not deny the sexual and social nature of man. To dispel any possible misunderstanding,

Zarathustra delivers two consecutive speeches on the social/sexual nature of man.

Zarathustra is disgusted by the two extremes of human sexuality, hedonism and abstinence. The hedonist is the "enjoyer of the passions,"[134] whose indulgence comes from lust (=mud and heat), not from natural drive (=animal innocence). But Zarathustra does not teach abstinence (=slaying of the senses) either, for when the passions are repressed, they find *indirect* expression in consciousness (=mud has spirit). The repressed man's spirit is tortured by the drive for satisfaction, resulting in the creation of *ressentiment*, bad conscience and other negative reactive affects. Thus many who would slay their senses develop far worse maladies than hedonism.[135] The sado-masochistic image of eternal punishment is built from the material of this repression (=mud and heat). Especially important here is the image of the gravediggers in Prologue 8 and their morbid fascination with eternal punishment. Such depth psychology deals with the base in man but does not make the moral judgment of considering all sexuality as "dirty," and in any case it refuses to become superficial (=shallow water) by avoiding the matter.

Zarathustra recommends solitude but not chastity. He advises a healthy harmony with the sexual drive (=innocence of senses) without bad conscience, which does not mean the *denial*, but rather the *refinement*, of the drive.[136] Zarathustra's own chastity is a result of his natural instinct for solitude, and is neither a universal imperative[180] nor an apriori law for himself, but is a convivial harmony of drive, conscience and consciousness. This is in contrast to Jesus' commendation at I Corinthians 7:2,7, who would universalize his own chastity. Zarathustra also suggests that his teaching would change as the instinct for isolation leaves him. In any case, he is not a "despiser of the body."

14. On the Friend

This section is intended to temper the previous sections' endorsement of solitude, and is important for understanding the nature of Zarathustra's companions (=friends, brothers), and indeed is important for understanding the mysterious "overman." The hermit's meditation is an inner dialogue between I and Thou. But for hermits, contemplation is always serious self-criticism (=too many depths): the friend is a self outside oneself, like the hermit's "Thou," but is positive and elevating (=has height). Affirmative belief (=faith) in the friend is a projection of self-love outside of the self. Desire for a friend betrays loss of self-love and often is envy of what the self feels itself to lack. The nature of the individual is cast outside himself in his relation to Others. The Other is thus another self: it is a projected self-report, as god was taken to be the projection of the religious self outside itself. The friend is the other self in which one's highest expectations are projected.

The best friend is one who embodies something one is not, but would willingly strive to become. In the friend one has that which is beyond oneself and that which one seeks to overcome (i.e., to excell). Thus the friend is not the mere mirror image of oneself, but is the ideal self, and thereby a sort of "enemy." Like the gods, our created ideals of the inner life, the friend is someone outside oneself to be emulated, surpassed, and so dethroned. Likewise, if one is to be a good friend in return, one must present something worthy of surpassing. Thus, if one shows oneself to the friend in all one's imperfections (=nakedness), the friend recoils. Were man ideal (=gods), then he would have cause for shame in hiding any feature (=ashamed of clothes). Thus in oneself one must raise one's natural attributes to their greatest attainable degree, to present the most ideal expression of all one can become. *But this is to overcome oneself: this is to move toward the overman.* "You cannot groom yourself too beautifully for your friend: for you shall be to him an arrow and a longing for the overman." This is not to cosmeticize: rather, it is to improve in a genuine fashion.

The good friend is one who reflects what we are and what we are not, what we can become and what we cannot. He is "a rough and imperfect mirror." When we see the friend *in stasis*, not overcoming himself (=asleep), we recoil at this death-like non-vitality, as he recoils at our imperfection: thus he brings one in touch with one's own "overman." The good friend does not violate one's individuality: he guesses at the innermost secrets of the Other, but does not spoil them by bringing them into the light too quickly, and so knows when to keep still. And just as one's own true essence is divined by the intuition of the friend, so the overcomings of the friend (=what he does while awake) is seen only in the innermost subjective recesses of oneself. The innermost recesses are symbolized by the dream: "Your dream should betray to you what your friend does while awake." (This image comes to the fore in II.1). The secret of the Other's objectivity is found in the self's greatest subjectivity. Thus knowledge of the friend's needs and wants are intuitively grasped (=guessed) and yet his privacy is respected by avoiding public display of emotion. The friend may need and want compassion, but his nature demands it to be expressed without public tears (=unbroken eye), and instead with a sign of quietude and strength (=the glance of eternity). Among the solitary type, compassion must resemble a nut: feeling (=delicacy and sweetness) nurtured within an outer expression of inspiring firmness and strength (=hard shell).

Friendship is a type of independence: the master/slave relation typical of all-too-human love is stifling and stunting for both: friends grow and ripen and heal one another on equal terms. The love between the sexes involves an injustice, a No-saying (=blindness, night, lightning, assault) with what is found to displease. Women are antagonists with one another (=cats and birds), envious, sneaking, conniving and are seldom real friends. Or "at best" they put all difference aside and ruminate with one another (=cows).[137] Indeed, the vast majority of men are herd animals as well (=comrades),[138] without individual difference, rather than true friends. The very exceptional solitary human is the only one capable of real friendship. Zarathustra's companions are such friends, and despite his solitary nature, Zarathustra makes no secret of his longing for them: "let there be friendship!"

15. On the Thousand and One Goals

In what is perhaps the highpoint of Part I, Nietzsche's central notion of ethics is brought to the fore. The central teaching of the

historical Zoroaster is the notion that the universe revolves around
the struggle between good and evil. Nietzsche's Zarathustra brings
this cosmic projection of ethical struggle back to earth, but reaffirms the all-powerfulness of valuation in human affairs. In doing
so, Zarathustra abandons any particular partisan role in the struggle, in contrast to Zoroaster (who took the side of good). Instead
Zarathustra assumes *an anthroplogical perspective,* and invalidates
questions of good and evil by abandoning the moral perspective altogether and adopting an extra-moral perspective. Zoroaster ini-
tiated the great struggle between good and evil: Nietzsche's
Zarathustra returns to overcome it.

Valuation is the essence, the first principle, the *arche* of human
spirit; without the uplifting, vitalizing, sustaining and motivating
power of value (=esteem), man could not meet the cruel power of
nature. A genuine people (*Volk*) is preserved by the valuations of
good/evil it places over itself: to lose that valuation, or to adopt another, is to lose the very self-differentiating principle of its identity.
To preserve itself as a self-same unity, a people must preserve its
sense of good/evil. From an extra-moral perspective, the multiplicity of valuations evidences an ethical relativism: there are many
senses of good/evil (the number 1000 is meant to highlight this),
but *the one true sense of good/evil does not exist.* There is no
good/evil in itself but only (many) goods and evils *according to a
people.* From the perspective of one standard, all other standards
are mistaken (=delusion and wickedness): thus between ethical
standards there is only incommensurability. From an extra-moral
standpoint, however, the issue of *the* right standard is sublated,
overcome, gone beyond.

The content of a people's valuations is formulated in a definite
set of prescriptions and proscriptions (=a tablet of the good) which
they place *over* themselves, meaning that the "tablet" is an absolute
standard from which no one is exempt and which is taken to be a
self-sufficient external standard of greater worth than the people
itself. But from Zarathustra's extra-moral perspective, each tablet
of values is an expression of a people's progress over the obstacles
they must surmount (=their overcomings). The proscriptions and

prescriptions of every people is "the voice of their will to power":[139] valuations express the history of a people's spirit, its driving force of life, as it overcomes its hindrances. In the language of a previous section, the tablet of good expresses "the metamorphoses of the spirit" of a people.

The particular content of a standard is *conditioned negatively*[140] by what a people has found most difficult to overcome, what has cost them the greatest amount of willpower. What is easy to do is not praiseworthy: a people values what they have done in the hour of their greatest exertion. The good is that which for a people seemed impossible, but what was achieved at great cost. The good is also *conditioned positively*: it is whatever is the highest essence of a people: that is, the unique feature which each member has, but which is rare outside of the people. That feature which has raised them above the others (=makes them rule and triumph and shine) and which gives them a shared resource and wealth (=awe and envy of neighbors) is that which is esteemed as good by a people. This essential feature of a people is esteemed as *the greatest good* (=the highest), is taken to be the standard by which all members and outsiders alike are evaluated (=the measure), and is taken to be the ultimate value which makes sense of their struggle in life (=the meaning of all things). This good as negatively and positively defined is the highest good, the *summum bonum*, which they call holy.

In the image of his god, one recognizes the man. In the innermost spiritual need of a people, one sees the wealth and poverty of a people: in their worldview (=land), depiction of afterlife (=sky) and social morality (=neighbor) one sees what is hardest for a people, what has cost them the greatest willpower and what it is that they take to be their own highest essence.[141] In the highest goods of the Greeks, Persians, Jews and Germans, one sees what each people has found the hardest and what each held as most essential. This is to discover the very essence of the man in that which he places above himself (i.e., his "overman").

Seen extra-morally, good and evil are nothing other than human invention. Good and evil have an entirely human meaning: there is nothing superhuman in their origin, essence or meaning. Zarathustra's extra-moral perspectivism is a type of anthropological reductionism.[142] Man alone is the measure of good/evil--there is nothing whatsoever non-human involved. Values express the very essence of man: man by nature values and all valuation is human by nature. The secret of good and evil is the essence of man. Man alone, of all animals, creates religion: the essence of religion is nothing other than the essence of man. Man is the esteeming animal.[143]

Esteeming, valuing, is the creation of a tablet of good and evil: the tablet "in itself," to be discovered or revealed, does not exist. This creation of value is, from the extra-moral viewpoint, the one and only source of value (=through esteeming alone there is value). Without placing a value above oneself, creating *something above man over man*, life itself could have no meaning or purpose (=the nut of existence would be hollow). This is the task of the child in the metamorphosis of spirit—to create meaning in life and to esteem what is found to be hardest and rarest. To create value is to presuppose having rejected all previous values (=a creator always annihilates): thus the lion comes before the child. But before the No-sayer comes the "Thou Shalt" of a genuine people: the individual is only "the most recent invention." Man's history begins with groups, with "peoples," and their collective values. To bear such values is the task of the camel of the spirit.

The value which man would place above himself, over man, is an expression of his deepest love. (The "love" of which Zarathustra speaks is neither the standard romantic notion nor the platonic love of knowledge, but rather enthusiasm and optimism in an ideal over the individual, as Schopenhauer had functioned for Nietzsche at the time of *Schopenhauer als Erzieher*.)[144] But love that would create tablets of the highest good must be able to *command and obey*. Love must be strong enough to command the creation of values: it must also allow itself to be commanded, i.e., obey, in the surrender of itself to the service of something "higher." The creator and ethical lawgiver is nothing without those who would take up the standard. The egoism of the lion means the death (=going under) of a people. The original peoples of the earth have all perished from the egoism of the modern state, hedonism and the individualism of modern man. Thus the patriarchal peoples are not revivable. *New peoples must be created*. But this requires *new esteemers*, new creators of values, and not idolators of the state, nor jesters nor preachers of death. But for a truly great people to arise, love must once again be rekindled: love is the fire in the children's new sun—the new value over man on this earth. Zarathustra is he who sees the need for an overman and sees the means to this end. But the necessary conditions are still lacking: modern man still rules and the last man still threatens to become the destiny of mankind. Violent gyrations of a jester, to use a now familiar image, could still destroy man before a higher type is taught.

Until man discovers, *invents*, what he truly *can be*, he remains the *not yet truly human*. The inspiration that would ignite all peoples (=thousand necks) to strive beyond themselves is still lacking. Zarathustra's overman is the expression of what would be required for all people to overcome themselves and rescue mankind from "the last man." The overman is "the work of lovers" that would unite mankind in a great project. But the overman is a value created by man for himself, against himself, over and beyond himself. Zarathustra, while able to see the necessity of the overman, is as yet unable himself to *become* the overman. And so he asks the question which will be answered for him only much later: "tell me brothers, who will conquer it? Who will throw a yoke over the thousand necks of the beast?"

16. On Love of the Neighbor

This section incorporates the observations of the last two sections. According to Zarathustra, the friend is the self-aware individual (=I, *das Ich*), whose example leads another to their own self-awareness. A neighbor (*der Naechste*: lit. "the nearest") is an average man of the crowd without distinction (*Du*), who can give only a superfluous or falsified self-awareness to another. The undifferentiated man ("thou," or "you": in Zarathustra's biblical German, the same) must be avoided if the "I," or "ego," is to develop: the opposite of the friend is not the enemy, but the all-too-similar.

The oblique sentence, "even if five of you are together, there is always a sixth who must die" has as one of its meanings, that in a collective (=five) the individual (=the sixth) is unable to develop (=must die). Zarathustra recommends instead an ideal self (=the farthest). One's ideal self begins abstract (=ghost) and must be slowly actualized (=given flesh and blood). A friend is a sort of higher self who hovers over man, inspiring self-overcoming: the best friend teaches how to love, for if his love is not to be overwhelming, one must learn to absorb love (=sponge) and so will eventually saturate and overspill oneself. This learning to love prepares the way for the self-love of the overman.

Man's highest love, *esteeming as holy*, proceeds from the Thou to the collective ego (the "herd," or "the people") and then to the autonomous individual (=the "I" or "ego"). First, God is deified; second, Spirit is deified; finally, the individual is recognized as divine. Disintegration of herd consciousness (=world rolling apart) becomes integration of the individual (=rolls together). The apparent "evil" involved in setting oneself above the crowd results in the *good* of the individual. Many apparently meaningless events surrounding oneself (=accidents) along one's path of development (=circles) find meaning only as the self slowly develops. Love of the individual, rather than of the neighbor, is a new sort of tablet raised above the old type ("Thou shalt"). Self-love is not the hedonism of the "enjoyer of the passions," nor the egoism of the great man.[145] Self-love is rather the heresy of the individual's defiant "I will," which threatens all peoples hitherto and the very conditions of human life as it has been known. As human history continues to develop, then, Nietzsche sees an ever greater role played by *individuals*, even if they must still struggles against gargantuan governments and rigid social institutions. In this struggle, Nietzsche is one of world history's greatest champions of individualism and free thinking.

17. On the Way of the Creator

"On the Way of the Creator" is an extremely rich, if overlooked, section that illuminates the themes of the nearly oblique speech

"On the Three Metamorphoses." Its other companion section is the upcoming "On Child and Marriage."

Zarathustra begins with a question for a friend, "Is it your wish to go into solitude?" This is indeed the question facing the "camel of the spirit" in I.1 and it is with an affirmative answer that the first metamorphosis (from spirit to camel) takes place. After a further loss of commonly accepted values (=conscience), the second metamorphosis occurs and camel becomes lion. In turn, the lion, the reactive nihilist, comes to an end when it is asked, "Do you want to go . . . the way to yourself?" For this way is the third metamorphosis from lion to child. Thus "the way of the creator" is "the metamorphosis of the spirit" culminating in the child, or creator. This child/creator is " . . . a new strength . . . a new right . . . a first movement . . . a self-propelled wheel . . . . "[146]

He who attempts to cross over the last metamorphosis—the higher man—must not become the Jester of Prologue 6 with his "convulsions of the ambitious." The great attempter must have an *idea, a great thought*. Of course, many so-called great thinkers are mere hot airbags: Zarathustra demands that one's "dominant thought" be *autonomous, genuine, positive* and sufficiently far "over and above" oneself to present an *ideal*.[147] But when one climbs up the ladder of self-overcoming, the very isolation and elevation give rise to feelings of desperation, nihilism, melancholy and the like. The lion must "murder" such feelings if his "dominant thought" is to be an affirmation.[148]

The "brother" of this section is yet another figure for the "higher man" of the Prologue, for "you pass over and beyond them . . . . " And so it is that all higher men will be envied and hated and finally crucified by "the good and just."[149] Whether it be Christ, Napoleon or Zarathustra, *the higher man is brought to his downfall by the man of reaction and negative will*. Against the reactionary, Zarathustra counsels "passing by," for any *direct action* could only become a *re-action*, thus multiplying the problem.

But the man who withdraws from activity suffers from the seven devils of loneliness. He must therefore convert his great misfortunes to advantages: his burdensome loneliness must give him new strength. The solitary man is moved by a love that includes a great contempt. "The lover would create because he despises." Great love and contempt for mankind together drive the solitary man into isolation. Thus his relation to mankind is painful: the object of his love and contempt has trapped him in a dilemma of love and rage. Nonetheless Zarathustra bids the solitary man on his journey, for his purposes will be someday achieved, even if "justice" must "limp" behind.

The lion cannot halt with his object of love/contempt: he must want to "create over and beyond" himself. Zarathustra is the higher man who would create the active, affirmative man, or "child." But since the child can only be created in oneself, any metamorphosis into child entails the *destruction of the present self.* In self-overcoming, the higher man builds something "over and beyond himself"—the overman. Thus Zarathustra repeats "with my tears" the passage from Prologue 4 that "I love him who creates over and beyond himself and thus perishes."

18. On Little Old and Young Women[150]

For Nietzsche, woman is intricately bound to the question of truth and knowledge.[151] Woman is the enigmatic (=riddle) and opaque (=stormy film) being, whose truth is hidden like a child concealed in a coat. But for all her deception, woman, truth, has no substance: the solution to her riddle is a vacuity, her waters shallow, the veil (=coat) the entire truth (=child). Woman is the passive principle of life, who obeys, who recedes when approached, who is attracted when pulled away from, who *loves*—she is surface water. Man is the active principle of life: he commands, wills, seeks adventure—his rivers run deep. Together the sexes form the procreative principle of life—command and obedience,[152] whose goal is the generation of something over and beyond itself—the *child.* Zarathustra calls for the complementary raising of each principle to its highest degree: man should pursue dangerous play, while woman should develop her capacities of love and hate.

But the radical duality of the sexes generates a cleft of knowledge: to man, woman is a riddle. But woman knows man better than he knows himself. Zarathustra, however, bridges the cleft to woman: he knows her, as does the little old woman. In an exchange of roles, he receives something from woman, and so becomes pregnant with a truth. (The child under Zarathustra's coat prompts his companion to remark, "is it . . . a child born unto you?" There is another, subtler change of roles: in language alluding to Luke 1:37, the little old woman quips that all things are possible with women. The male christian god—who is deep, eternal truth—is replaced by a human female figure, whose truth is changing and superficial.) The secret of woman is that her appearance is her truth: she has no inner essence and there is no real cleft between the sexes; there is only life, which is command and obedience (=don't forget the whip). Rather than addressing woman separately from man, Zarathustra is more interested in exposing the *vacuity of truth*: truth (=little old woman) confirms this assessment about herself (=young woman) and delivers a truth which is itself a vacuity thinly covered.

19. On the Bite of the Adder[153]

Like Jesus, Zarathustra delivers a parable on love of the enemy, retaliation and judgment.[154] Just as he inverted Christ's doctrine of neighborly love, so Zarathustra here inverts Christ's admonition to love of the enemy. Unlike the "good and just man," Zarathustra would requite evil, not with good, which shames the offender and thereby causes *ressentiment*, but with another evil, mitigating the guilt of the offender, or with a sign that the evil has done no harm or some good. Christian love of the enemy, like that of the neighbor, leaves all involved with an impoverished spirit: in this case, the offender is shamed and the offended left stifled in his outrage at the offense.

Zarathustra, like Jesus, also raises love above the will for punishment. As in I.6, the "just" man and his "justice" is exposed as lust for the knife, and is held below the original offense. Retribution of kind for kind is impossible. Zarathustra's principle is "I give each my own," meaning that he prefers to be the strong individual who can absorb many wrongs without abandoning himself to the self-destructive passion of revenge.[155] But for this one must be able to allow harm from others.

Best of all is not to judge in terms of "evil," "guilt" or "revenge." If evil is returned with a little evil the spirit is purged and calmed. This psychological treatment finds moral categories to be of no use: it is concerned purely with the deep psychology of crime and punishment. Thus the moralist considers the doctrine "immoral."

20. On Child and Marriage

This section is the third panel of a triptych that includes "On the Three Metamorphoses" and "On the Way of the Creator." As in "On the Way of the Creator," one of Zarathustra's friends has expressed the will to "cross over"—this time in the metaphoric guise of a will to marriage and paternity. Zarathustra warns that not everyone has the *right* to desire a child (=creation) and marriage (=affirmation). Only the lion--"the victorious one, the self-conqueror, the commander of your senses, the master of your virtues"—has the right to attempt the metamorphosis to child. The autonomy and innocence of the lion must be used to create *a higher self, something "over and beyond" oneself.* Only the *fundamentally healthy type,* "perpendicular in body and soul," can hope to achieve a higher self. Zarathustra is thinking here of a self which fulfills the greatest potential of "becoming what one is" (=production) rather than standard repetition of normalities (=reproduction).

In the creation of a higher self, *affirmation* plays the crucial role. And where there is a *double affirmation*—as in the double "I do" of marriage—there is a creation "over and beyond" the two individual affirmations, i.e., a child is born. The identification of the marriage trope with double affirmation is natural and straightforward, but *who is it* that enters into such a wedlock? As can be shown only much later, it is the pair Dionysus-Ariadne who are meant here.[156] Dionysus represents here *command and restraint* in opposition to his role in *Die Geburt der Tragoedie.* The "caves and woods" imagery surrounding him suggests the wanderer's loneliest moments, or "stillest hours." Ariadne represents active force as such, *anima* pure and simple. When control desires active force and active force desires restraint, the two elements of life—command and obedience—give birth to the autonomous, self-created and self-guided creator, or "child." The marriage of command and obedience takes as its seal the "nupital ring" of eternal return. Only when both dominant and dominated say "Yes!" to the eternal return of the same will there be such a "child."

The "child" of this section is the same as that of I.1, I.17 and II.1: it is a metaphoric image standing for *the higher self*. And this "one that is more than those who created it" is the overman. Nietzsche is therefore in no way speaking *literally* of children and marriage: that would be an interpretation appropriate for the genetics-minded "Ape." Nietzsche's message "On Child and Marriage" delivers no advice on *human reproduction*. As in Prologue 4, his message is an *existential imperative*: "over and beyond yourselves you shall love one day." Zarathustra's type of marriage, like his love, involves contempt: before the higher man is driven to the overman, a great contempt must threaten to consume his entire being. When marriage is construed as an intersubjective affirmation after a period of nihilism, Zarathustra pronounces it "holy" relative to the base and capricious values of the all-too-many.

21. On Free Death

Like Schopenhauer,[157] Nietzsche endorses the practice of suicide as found in antiquity. Unlike Christianity, the ancients held life to be worthwhile only within qualitative limits: the ignoble christian on the contrary regards life to be prolonged unconditionally. (This does not mean, of course, that the christian preserves his own life at the cost of others. But life is taken by the christian to be a gift from God which ought not be ended by any person other than God himself: he is, then, necessarily against abortion, euthanasia and suicide.) Thus the christian is a slave to death, while the noble man is his own master, even over death. The superfluous mass of humanity lives without purpose or direction and yet fears death and avoids it at all cost. Such meaninglessness is worse than never being born at all. (Silenus, the dionysian forest god of Greek mythology,

taught "To die is second best for man: best is never to be born at
all." Zarathustra holds this wisdom as truth only in the case of the
superfluous.) Zarathustra teaches that death is not merely the cessation of life, but its consummation, completion, perfection and
crowning moment. Even in death, the example of the higher man is
an inspiration: his death is a hope and promise to the living that life
can be perfected and mastered. For the goalless man, death is best.
For the higher man, dying under his own command is best, after a
life full of struggle and personal overcoming in which a goal is created and a heir to that goal secured. Man is a fruit on the tree of
life: some die too early, some too late. Inertia and fear cause man
to die after his time: disgust with the earthly and melancholy cause
others, like Christ, to die before their time. The right time to die is
when maturity of spirit and heart have been achieved, while they
are still ripe and "taste best." What constitutes maturity of the spirit
is an evolving notion in *Zarathustra*. The primary focus here is on
lightness and optimism versus gravity and melancholy. Christ would
not, or could not, laugh (Luke 6:25) and, according to Nietzsche,
suffered from a longing for death. Dionysus, the laughing and
dancing god, longs for recurring life, and serves as an antithesis to
Christ.[158]

The preachers of *thanatos* preach a doctrine of servitude to
(=patience with) the earthly. Zarathustra longs for the force which
would jolt the weak while preserving the strong. The "preachers of
quick death" are those who would deliver a doctrine so terrifying to
the *weak* that they would be overcome: yet the doctrine must also
inspire the *strong* to great strivings in which their spirit is sacrificed
for the advance of higher man (=to die fighting and squander a
great soul). This is the as-yet-to-appear doctrine of the eternal return. The higher man will also die quickly: he is *not* to be *spared*.[159]
But his life and *death* result in a creation of a goal outside himself:
he creates an ideal (=throws the golden ball), a sun (=overman),
which lights his life and gives direction. When man's ability to reach
for his ideal declines (=sunset), the ideal and the actual spirit are
one (=a glow around the earth), and the time for dying (=going
under, sunset: *Untergang*) is soon at hand. To remain past one's

own meaning and direction is to become feeble and incapable, "a toothless mouth."

Zarathustra has created his sun, his golden ball, his overman, and has achieved his great victories and found his truths: he is becoming all he can and should be. But part of his self-legislated commandment is to not *outlive* his purpose and meaning. Thus he has already begun his Going Under, though he is not yet at sunset: he now affirms his return to the *earth*, which is his origin, destiny, essence and love. He now lingers only to see his friends cast their star skyward, and to discover a final doctrine which fulfills his destiny and shakes the tree of life.

22. On the Gift-Giving Virtue

The speeches of Part I have taken place in "the Motley Cow"; Zarathustra now prepares to return to isolation. Thus will end the first cycle of the movement which structures the entire book--that of descending from, and ascending to, the isolation of his cave.[160]

Section 1. The disciples' gift is emblematic of the overman. Its golden substance is an image of the highest value because, like gold, the overman is exceptional (=uncommon), intrinsically valuable (=useless), exemplary (=gleams) and inspiring (=gentle splendor). The sun radiates its golden essence as an overflowing burst of innermost power from itself. To give away an overrichness of oneself is the most intimate gift-giving. Innermost self is the substance of valuation and estimation whose essence is *love*.[161] Zarathustra's highest value is a self-love which overflows to others and causes the receiver (=moon) in turn to shine. Not love of the species, but rather of what is highest, rarest, most refined and strongest is the love Zarathustra exhorts. This love is a sort of fire ignited and fueled by *hope for man* and kindled by hope for the self.[162]

He who gives himself wants to find and accumulate the goods of the earth, that he might take them, create something beyond them, and give them to man. His promethean humanism is the polar opposite of the poor in spirit, who cannot love and so steals values from the creator. (The opposition of Prometheus and a criminal appears in I.6. Prometheus steals the gift of fire from Zeus that he might give it to man, whom he loves. The criminal, poor in spirit, takes for himself what is not his in an effort to comfort himself and satisfy his hunger.) Spiritual poverty is a condition caused by bodily degeneration.[163] Humanity is a vast spectrum of well-being between mean conditions of survival (=genus) and supervitality (=overgenus): a degeneration of vitality is expressed in an incapacity to esteem and love beyond the self, while the overabundant in vital force overflows with affirmation and esteeming. Weariness of life results in an impulse to *thanatos* (i.e., to the preachers of death).[164] Repeating the materialist-naturalist principles of previous sections, Zarathustra identifies the primal ground of moral concepts and judgments as the body. When the body is healthy, the senses are elevated and the spirit is in turn elevated, which is expressed as an *esteeming*; a degeneration of the body impoverishes and atrophies the senses, causing the spirit to turn against itself and life, or to take the values others create. Mankind's greatly divergent circumstances and resources result in a great many divergent states ranging from degeneration to supervitality, and so a multiplicity of expressions of the relation between will and the world.[165] Gift-giving evidences an overabundant will which wants to create and give: the emblem of the staff is an image of a will powerful enough to shine like the sun and gleam like gold, guided and directed by a dominant thought and purpose.[166] Giving and receiving will be the major theme of Part II.

Section 2. The basis of Nietzsche's optimism about man is the great range of possibilities still open to humanity. Man's essence is open-ended and the possibilities to create with the earth's treasures "unexhausted and undiscovered." Man is an on-going experiment without bounds and capable of pursuing a multitude of directions simultaneously. With ever greater knowledge of the body, by experimentation and investigation, the primacy of the body as the basis of human nature will appear, and with it greater cultivation of the senses.[167] As a consequence there will be greater elevations of the soul and greater capacity to esteem. Along future paths the body will achieve the conditions of supervitality so that an all-affirmative esteeming of earth, of body, of *life*, will be possible for an entire people. When the goods of the earth are so harnessed, a new people will arise to praise the conditions of their affirmation. At that time, earth will be a site of *the physiological recovery of man*; this, though, will per force ignite a spiritual recovery of man in which weaknesses of human will and their symptoms will be overcome, overthrowing the will to *thanatos* and creating a new tablet of good.

One should note at this point that the physiological conditions of modern man are a record of mankind's history, according to Nietsche, i.e., a record of interaction with nature and its elements. "Alas, much ignorance and error have become body within us." This once again evidences Nietzsche's lamarckianism: "acquired characteristics" are inherited into a personal genetic legacy. Thus the individual can hope to participate in a revitalization of mankind, even if one does not see its ultimate consequences.

Zarathustra's optimism about the possibility of a new beginning for mankind is, however, not unlimited. There are still many dangers inherent in the overcoming of man. Part I has been one long near-monologue concerning the dangers of "crossing over." The imagery of Prologue 6 is once again recapitulated here: "It is dangerous to be an heir. Still we fight step by step with the giant, accident: and over the whole of humanity there has ruled so far only nonsense—no sense." The Tightrope Walker is he who would cross over "step by step": the Jester is the leader of mass movements arising in sudden events out of great accident in public arenas. Over humanity is still the Jester's circus—like nonsense: Zarathustra wills that man put meaning (sense) into existence by commanding accident. The meaning of existence over man is overman.

Section 3. With his disciples at the crossroads, Zarathustra's spirit metamorphoses[168] as the desire for isolation overwhelms him. Since the early experiences of the Market Place, Zarathustra has learned that he must spread his doctrines to other leaders, not followers. Only by becoming leaders, masters of their own fate, will his companions truly follow his doctrine. Zarathustra wants his pupils to become other leaders. He would rather have them attack him (=pluck at his wreath) than remain *believers*. Making an idol of Zarathustra would cause a nihilism once this external source of value tumbles. (The ancient image of the worshipper slain by his own idol is reported by Aristotle at *Poetics* 1452a 7-10.) Thus the paradox evolves that Zarathustra will find his friends again only after they have denied him.[169] The third time together will Zarathustra and his companions celebrate "the Great Noon." (The third time he is with his friends must be Part IV, sections 11 to 20. Thus it is likely that the "higher men" of Part IV are these very disciples, once they have found, and followed, their own way.) Those who would "cross over" will celebrate themselves as higher men, and their knowledge of themselves as the truly divine will stand over them as the sun at noon. To embrace a promethean love of man is to replace god with highest man as the highest value. Thus the advent of man's great self-love is the death of all gods as the center of the universe of values.

Notes

1. The entire first section of the Prologue may be found as *Froehliche Wissenschaft* section 342 (*KSA* Band III page 571) under the title "Incipit Tragoedie," with minor variation. The final published version of the Prologue bore no title, but Nietzsche had planned at one time to entitle it "On the Overman and the Last Man." I retain this title as a mnemonic device.

2. For further information concerning the relation of the historical Zoroaster and Nietzsche's Zarathustra, see: Emil Abegg's "Nietzsches Zarathustra und der Prophet des alten Iran" in *Conferences prononcees a Geneve sous les auspices da la Fondation M. Gretler*, (1945), pages 64-82. See also Peter Puetz' notes on page 291 of the Goldmann Klassiker edition of *Also sprach Zarathustra*. For information about Emerson and Nietzsche's Zarathustra, see *KSA* Band XIV pages 279 ff. For a comparison of Zarathustra as portrayed here and Nietzsche himself, see *Nietzsche kontrovers II* edited by Rudolf Berlinger and Wiebke Schrader (Wuerzburg: Koenighausen u. Neumann, 1982), page 110. And for the major secondary source on ancient Persian zoroastrianism, see *Zarathustra* Wege der Forschuung Band CLXIX. Bernfried Schlerath (ed.). For English-only readers, see Mircea Eliade, *A History of Religious Ideas*, Volume I, translated by Willard R. Trask (Chicago: University of Chicago Press, 1978), pp. 302-333.

3. This is borne out in notes from the *Nachlass* (see in particular *KSA* Band X 524). An explicit analysis of *ueber*-concepts by Feuerbach is of great interest in comparison with Nietzsche (see: *Ludwig Feuerbachs Saemtliche Werke* edited by Wilhelm Bolin (Stuttgart: Fromann's Verlag, 1905), Band VII, under the title, "Der Gottesbegriff als das Gattungswesen des Menschen"). Nietzsche's use of *ueber*-concepts is largely *in pace* Feuerbach's analysis, though there are wide divergences in their programmatic usages of such concepts.

4. For a superb article concerning the vertical dimension, see F.D. Luke's "Nietzsche's Imagery of Height" in *Nietzsche: Imagery and Thought*, edited by Malcolm Pasley (Berkeley: University of California press, 1978), pp. 104-122.

5. See I.3, I.17 and II.19.

6. There is at least one other very noteworthy example of the misanthropic hermit in world literature; namely, Shakespeare's *Timon of Athens*. It is certain that Nietzsche was familiar with this tragedy, and it is not surprising that there are many similarities between them in imagery and thought. The two characters also have many dissimilarities, and their two types of misanthropy should be contrasted.

7. This is borne out by comparison with I.3.

8. This comment is supported by II.3 and II.4. The comment is important to include here for a complete understanding of the difference in spirit between the Hermit and Zarathustra. Concerning the Hermit, see IV.6.

9. See commentary to Prologue 1.

10. See *Basic Writings*, p. 717 (*KSA* Band VI page 300): "Other scholarly oxen have suspected me of darwinism on that account . . . " where the subject under discussion is *der Uebermensch*. In the immediately preceding passage, Nietzsche explicitly supports my account: "The word "overman" as the designation of a type of supreme achievement, as opposed to "modern man," to "good man," to christians and other nihilists . . . . " A passage of extreme interest here is I.22: "Upward goes our way, from genus to overgenus." This language is called a "parable" in the immediately following sentences of I.22. It is beyond doubt that Nietzsche looks at man from an anthropological standpoint, i.e., as one animal among many. And since Nietzsche is a lamarckian to the extent that he believed the inheritance of acquired characteristics to be true, it is at least arguable that the *Uebermensch* could well become an *Ueber-Art* from a biological viewpoint in Nietzsche's thoughts. Yet it is Zarathustra's message in the Prologue and throughout that *man has not yet become all he can become within his present biological constitution*. Nor would there be any guarantee that physiological evolution would mean spiritual evolution (—indeed, this is the very problem with man). Thus evolution is neither a necessary nor a sufficient condition for the *Uebermensch*. Modern man must will the overman in *this* body and on *this* earth: there is still much to be done with man outsdie of genetic considerations.

    Yet this is not to say that Nietzsche sees the species as static according to an aristotelean model. Life itself is that which overcomes itself and produces something higher. And since man is subject to the same sort of environmental and natural changes that brought to an end the reign of the dinosaurs, it is likewise possible that man as a species will vanish. This viewpoint is part of Nietzsche's denial of the christian concept of *man as an eternal creature of god*. But Zarathustra is not suggesting here that man pursue some sort of speculative eugenic engineering.

11. Man is in fact the *Ueber-Affe*, a qualitative leap above the ape, and yet still all-too-simian. See *KSA* Band X, 160.

12. See for example *Ecce Homo* III.1 and IV.5, along with the later sections of *Zarathustra*: II.12, II.21 and IV.13. The mixing of identities between Zarathustra, the overman and the devil is a major theme in the book.

13. See II.21.

14. "Transcendent" here means belonging to a supernatural realm at a total remove from nature. The overman, while a concept implying qualitative superiority, does not reside in the otherworldly realms of metaphysics or religion.

15. Here one finds dramatic evidence of the deep, though unacknowledged, debt in Nietzsche's philosophy to the German philosopher Ludwig Feuerbach. In a fragment from 1867-68, i.e., Nietzsche's period at Bonn University, Nietzsche quotes Feuerbach's dictum, "Content yourself with the given world." Nietzsche's remark thereto is that this phrase "is the ethical canon which materialism has given rise to." (My translation of both Feuerbach and Nietzsche: the fragment "Zu Democrit" is found at *Historische-Kritische Gesammtausgabe* Vol.3 page 335, while the Feuerbach quotation comes from *Grundsaetze der Philosophie der Zukunft*). This ethical canon becomes "Remain true to the earth" in *Zarathustra*. Another famous nietzschean dictum "body am I entirely and nothing else" is in fact a reworking of a feuerbachian phrase. The new zarathustran goal for man of "body and earth" finds its direct predecessor in the feuerbachian legacy. Karl Marx was another philosopher of the nineteenth-century who adopted Feuerbach's call for a non-supernaturalist ethics. The young Wagner moreover was a feuerbachian during a major phase of his creativity. Wagner's later turn away from Feuerbach to Schopenhauer was the fatal turn separating Nietzsche from Wagner. When Wagner turned away from feuerbachian "body and earth," he found his own truly schopenhauerian self: when Nietzsche turned away from Wagner, he found his own feuerbachian self.

16. This passage parodies Genesis 4:10.

17. One may well think of St. Augustine's *Confessions* in which the saint, as an example of evil, adduces stealing an apple from an orchard, wherein the theft is committed for its own sake.

18. By "teleology" I mean here an ethic which gives ultimate ethical priority to a final end, or purpose, over a means. "Deontology" refers to an ethic which sets morally sanctified limits on the use of a means for a final end. The common phrase, "the end justifies the means" is an expression of teleology. The notion of unalienable human rights is a deontological concept. Kantianism and christianity are the best-known deontological ethics: eudaimonism and utilitarianism are well-known teleological ethics. The final end, purpose, highest good of the nietzschean ethic is the overman.

19. See commentary to Prologue 1.

20. An unusual note from the *Zarathustra* notebooks (*KSA* X 134) states, "The overman has by his overflowing of life all the appearances of the opium smoker and of the frenzy and dance of Dionysus: he does not suffer from the after-effects." (My translation.) The analogy between use of narcotics and creativity is a leitmotif in *Die Geburt der Tragoedie* and the *Nachlass*.

21. See here *Morgenroete* 50 (*KSA* Band III 54-55).

22. The sentence "Ich liebe den, der freien Geistes und freien Herzens ist: so ist sein Kopf nur das Eingeweide seines Herzens, sein Herz aber treibt ihn zum Untergang" alludes to a quote by Napoleon: "Das Herz gehoert zu den Eingeweiden." (See *KSA* Band I, p.69). The theme is taken up again on pages 205-206 of Band X: "Ich liebe die freien Geister wenn sie auch freie Herzen sind. Mir ist der Kopf wie der magen des Herzens—aber man soll einen guten Magen haben. Was das Herz annimmt, das muss der Kopf verdauen." See also *Zarathustra* III.12 sub-section 17: " . . . the spirit *is* a stomach!" Compare with Ludwig Feuerbach's gloss on the German saying "man ist, was man isst"—"One is what one eats." See *Saemtliche Werke* Band X pp.65-68.

23. See *KSA* Band XIV, pp.283-4.

24. See *KSA* Band XIV, p.284. All allusions claimed by Montinari have been checked against the Luther Bible in German.

25. The sentence "I am not the mouth for these ears" is an allusion to Matthew 13:13.

26. In a note from the *Nachlass* out of the *Zarathustra* period, Nietzsche writes, "The opposite of the overman is the last man: I created him at the same time as the former" (*KSA* Band X, p.162; my translation).

27. See *KSA* Band X, p.160.

28. The flea-beetle (*Erdfloh*) is a beetle that leaps like a flea.

29. See commentary to Prologue 3.

30. The image of ice and fire alludes to the ash image of Prologue 2.

31. See comments to Prologue 4.

32. This becomes clear in Prologue 7.

33. August Messer, in his *Erklaerung zu Nietzsches Zarathustra*, (Stuttgart: Strecker u. Schroeder, 1922), argues that "excited and radical agitators" are meant by the image. "Damit sind eben jene aufgehetzenden und radikalen Agitatoren gemeint, denen kein Fortschritt schnell genug geht, die sich und anderen einreden, das Vollkommene koenne mit einem Schlag, am einfachsten durch Gewalt erreicht werden" (page 15). The Jester does indeed suggest that the progress of the Ropewalker is not fast enough and, as we have argued, the Jester is one who believes progress is possible through a single blow. However, as develops in the next section, the "purpose" of the Jester was merely to protect the mean and strike at the enemy of the people, *not* to secure *real* progress. Further, if the Jester is indeed the representative of the mean, agitation is not to be associated with him. It is better to broaden the possible meaning of the Jester symbol here, to include all those who, for whatever reason, wish to skip steps in the metamorphosis of the spirit.

34. See Matthew 4:19. The metaphor of the fisher of men is extended in "The Honey Sacrifice."

35. For confirmation of this interpretation, see Prologue 9.

36. Messer's *Erlaeuterung* is confused on the numbering of the sub-sections at this point. The entirety of the commentary to what he calls sub-section 7 is in fact the beginning of sub-section 8. The actual sub-section 7 receives no treatment from him whatsoever.

37. Messer's generally fine commentary is confused by the figure of the Jester. In particular, the relation of Jester to Zarathustra is confused. Messer gives a contradictory account, and comments that Nietzsche uses his associations loosely (see page 15 of *Erlaueterung*). Rather than associating the Jester with the man of the people, he begins by associating him with radicalism and then attempts to argue that Zarathustra is the true leader of the people (*echter Volksfuehrer*) without discerning the mass-movement character of the Jester and without explaining what he means by *Volksfuehrer* (see page 15 of the *Erlaueterung*). Our associations clear up these confusions by bringing into harmony the various levels of meaning to the Jester. The identity confusion between the Jester, the devil and Zarathustra must be presented as such, rather than becoming a victim of the confusion.

38. That is, in contrast to Marx, the progression of human spirit is not a political struggle, much less a struggle of economic classes. For elaboration of the nietzschean "political" philosophy, see Tracey Strong's *Nietzsche and the Politics of Transfiguration* and Karl Loewith's *From Hegel to Nietzsche*. Strong is too literal in his interpretation, but makes many fine points and is a "must" for those interested in Nietzsche's politics. Loewith's account, on the other hand, is not to be underestimated. Unfortunately, Nietzsche's politics has attracted more poor scholarship than any other aspect. For my inter-

pretation, see comments to II.18 and I.10 inter alia. An excellent source for clearing up previous confusions is Massino Montinari's "Nietzsche zwischen Alfred Baeumler und Georg Lukacs" in *Nietzsche Lesen*.

39. Messer's account of the gravediggers' scene is very good. Though arrived at independently, my comments follow closely Messer's *Erlaeuterung* pp. 16-17.

40. And for the association of the scholar and the average man, see section 206 of *Jenseits von Gut und Boese* (*KSA* Band V pages 134-44).

41. See here especially *KSA* Band VI page 293; "Der Gelehrter—ein decadent."

42. See Prologue 4.

43. This is a variation on Psalms 146:5,7.

44. Messer twists in the wind for an interpretation of this scene, and leaves his comments at the level of conjecture. He sees the Hermit as a symbol of philosophy, resting this association on the possession of light in darkness and on the Hermit's isolation. Isolation, while a virtue generally in nietzschean ethics, does not make the isolated a symbol of philosophy (e.g., the Hermit of Prologue 2). The light is explained in the next section: when Zarathustra awakes, he claims repeatedly that *ein Licht ging mir auf*, and indeed it is the realization that other companions are needed, a lesson which the Hermit has not learned. So while he is only halfway from the crowd, contact with the Hermit has *enlightened* him as to what is needed: the Hermit is however unaware of both his need and the nature of the problem: that is, while he *has* the light, he is unaware of its *meaning*.

    While Messer recognizes the confusion between spiritual/bodily food, he suggests that this symbolizes the desire of the philosopher to apply his own system, regardless of subject matter. Further, he does not connect this confusion with the "bad sleep" of the Hermit, but suggests that restless sleep is a symbol for not wanting to be troubled with matters of difference, and that the Hermit for that reason is a dullard. Finally, he suggests that Zarathustra leaves the Hermit because the latter is no genuine human spiritual leader and that this is the reason Zarathustra declines to stay and eat, rather than the notion that the Hermit has nothing spiritual to offer. Thus Messer himself falls victim to the confusion about sustenance.

45. This observation was made to me by Prof. Douglas Browning at the University of Texas at Austin.

46. By "moral autonomy" I mean the capability of forming one's own moral standards rather than to accept pre-formed, pre-existing standards of behavior. Kant brought the importance of moral autonomy forth, and the various issues surrounding it occupied the German idealists and romantics after him.

47. For an excellent discussion of Nietzsche's animal imagery, see T.J. Reed's "Nietzsche's Animals: Idea, Image and Influence" in *Nietzsche: Imagery and Thought*, edited by M. Pasley. Reed is very critical of Nietzsche. For an interesting piece on the image of eagle and serpent in *Also sprach Zarathustra*, see "Eagle and Serpent in *Zarathustra*" in *Nietzsche-Studien*, (Berlin: DeGruyter Verlag, 1977), no.6, pp.240-260.

48. See commentary to III.12.

49. See end of Prologue 9.

50. This superficially contradicts the negative evaluations of the Jester elsewhere (see commentary to Prologue 9). Messer becomes confused and writes this off as an example of Nietzsche's use of conflicting imagery. But the contradiction is superficial. So far as the Jester's "springing over" entails a "going under" for the Ropewalker, Zarathustra endorses the image: the fundamentally different, appended, meaning of the image—that man might be sprung over without many accumulated tribulations—is not contained in what Zarathustra teaches here. The motley symbolic meanings patching together the image of the Jester reflect his motley nature. His very motleyness confuses Messer here.

51. See II.12. Hegel makes an interesting contrast and comparison here. See also II.12.

52. See Prologue 10, II.6, I.8, IV.13 and III.11.

53. See David S. Thatcher's "Eagle and Serpent in *Zarathustra*" in *Nietzsche-Studien* Band VI (1977). Thatcher assembles a number of interesting sources that Nietzsche *may* have known of. Most of the material in the article is only loosely tied to the actual symbolism of eagle and serpent: there is a shortage of analysis of the text itself.

54. See commentary to Prologue 1.

55. *Geist* is a technical term in German Idealism, beginning with Hegel. For Hegel's sense, see Robert Solomon's "Hegel's Concept of *Geist*" in *Hegel: Collection of Critical Essays* A. MacIntyre (ed.), 1972.

56. See Matthew 4:1-11; Mark 1:12-13 and Luke 4:1-13.

57. Sections II.8 and III.11 contain explications of the lion image.

58. This is the method of Hegel as he describes the stages of spirit (*Geist*). This section could be viewed as a parody of Hegel's *Phaenomenologie des Geistes*, but as Hollinrake points out in *Nietzsche, Wagner and the Philosophy of Pessimism*, it is much more likely that Lessing and Goethe are alluded to. See Hollinrake, page 7.

59. See Prologue 2. "Verwandelt ist Zarathustra, zum Kind ward Zarathustra . . . ."

60. The end of the metamorphoses as described by Zarathustra is the child. But the child is the spirit which assumes the right to posit new values: the new value of the child is the overman. Note well that the metamorphosis of spirit need not end with even the overman: development of the spirit is open-ended. Zarathustra sees spirit only so far as the overman.

61. There is not a single argument as such in *Zarathustra*: its substance is constructed from *imagery*, not from argumentation, though this is not to say that there are not a great many principles behind the images. *Zarathustra* resolves all questions to a matter of aesthetics, with the meaning of existence as the subject matter of the main question. Only as an *aesthetic phenomenon* can the world be justified. The imagery built around his principle is meant to reach the passion of man rather than his reason: the overall aesthetic quality of the book is intended to communicate the passionate affirmation of life which constitutes the ultimate "argument" for his worldview.

62. See *KSA* Band XIV page 286 for this note. Unfortunately, the citation given (N V8, 104) is incorrect. The quotation is given in full, however, at *KSA* Band XIV page 286.

63. The sage's admonition to adopt virtues is an allusion to Exodus 20:16, 14 and 17. The admonition to "chew the cud" alludes to the herdlike nature of the Last Man, as in Prologue 4. The image of green pastures alludes to Psalms 23:1,2 and John 10:11. "Green pastures" also poses an opposite image to the lion's desert.

64. See Prologue 2.

65. See Prologue 8.

66. It was Ludwig Feuerbach who introduced the comparison in *Das Wesen des Christentums*. Marx made Feuerbach's comparison famous in his dictum, "Religion is the opium of the people."

67. Feuerbach's *Das Wesen des Christentums* (1841) created a tremendous sensation in philosophical and popular circles. It greatly influenced the Young Hegelians (Stirner, Bauer, Strauss), Karl Marx, Kierkegaard, Nietzsche, Scheler, Freud, Heidegger, Sartre, Martin Buber and Karl Barth.

68. This is the fundamental notion of *Das Wesen des Christentums*. "The divine being is nothing other than the human being, or rather, the human nature purified, freed from the limits of the individual man, made objective—i.e., contemplated and reversed as another, distinct being." See *Essence of Christianity*, translated by George Eliot, (New York: Harper Row, 1957), page 14.

69. Feuerbach says, "The future life is the present in the mirror of the imagination: the enrapturing image is in the sense of religion the true earthly life—real life only a glimmmer of that ideal, imaginary life. The future life is the present embellished, contemplated through the imagination, purified of all gross matter; or, positively expressed, it is the beauteous present intensified." (Eliot trans. page 182).

70. Zarathustra says that the body wants to "crash through these ultimate walls with its head, and not only with its head." Concerning the projection of the non-rational in human nature into the supernatural, Feuerbach writes, "The homeric gods eat and drink,—that implies eating and drinking is a divine pleasure. Physical strength is an attribute of the homeric gods: Zeus is the strongest of the homeric gods. Why? Because physical strength, in and by itself, was regarded as something glorious, divine." (Eliot trans. page 21.)

71. While Nietzsche and Feuerbach share materialist and naturalist orientations, the similarities and differences of their systems are too complex to discuss here.

72. Zarathustra says, "But "that world" is well concealed from humans—that dehumanized inhuman world . . . is a heavenly nothing." Feuerbach writes "All existence, i.e., all existence which is truly such, is qualitative, determinative existence . . . . An existence in general, an existence without qualities, is an insipidity, an absurdity." (*EC* page 15.)

73. Zarathustra says, "the belly of being does not speak to humans at all, except as a human." The self-positing of all measure by man himself is an important principle behind Nietzsche's and Feuerbach's (divergent) perspectivisms. Zarathustra says, "this creating, willing, valuing ego . . . is the measure and

value of things." Feuerbach writes, "Man, especially the religious man, is to himself the measure of all things, of all reality." (*EC* page 22).

74. The word Nietzsche chooses, *das Ich*, is the technical term of German idealism (esp. Fichte and Feuerbach) expressing the subjective locus of consciousness. It is also the word Freud uses, and which is translated into English as *ego*. The certainty of the body and its senses was a major principle of Feuerbach's empiricism. After Hegel's *Phaenomenologie des Geistes*, such certainty had become a sophisticated matter. See Marx Wartofsky's *Feuerbach*, (Cambridge: Cambridge Press, 1977).

75. Feuerbach uses *ueber*-concepts in a technical sense, including *uebermenschlich* and cognates. The so-called "C" edition of *Das Wesen des Christentums* contains many uses of *ueber*-concepts, which are translated by George Eliot as *super*-. But of particular interest is "Der Gottesbegriff als das Gattungswesen des Menschen" in *Saemtliche Werke* Band VII. Knowledge of Feuerbach's analysis is an extremely helpful tool for understanding Nietzsche's use of *ueber*-words, a tool employed throughout this commentary.

76. Nietzsche sees the creation of previous superhumans as signs of weakness. His own superhuman, however, is created out of strength. For Feuerbach, the creation of any and all superhumans is a natural tendency of man to objectify himself. Feuerbach remains within the German metaphysical tradition when describing the creation of gods: Nietzsche goes to French moral psychology for such an account.

77. Zarathustra says, "Alas, my brothers, this god whom I created was man-made and man-madness, like all gods! Man he was, and only a poor specimen of man and ego . . . . " Feuerbach writes, "Man—this is the secret of religion—projects his being into objectivity, and then again makes himself an object to this projected image of himself thus converted into a subject . . . . " (*EC* pages 29-30).

78. *Die Geburt der Tragodie* was written during Nietzsche's schopenhauerian period. *Zarathustra* was written in the optimistic recovery thereafter. Nietzsche's concept of Dionysus undergoes a major change precisely for this reason. See Silk and Stern's *Nietzsche on Tragedy*, (Cambridge: Cambridge University Press, 1983), page 246 and footnote 37 on page 419 for a brief but accurate description of this change.

79. The tropes of "body" and "earth" are major programmatic notions for Feuerbach as well.

80. Feuerbach writes, "The supernatural body is a body constructed by the imagination, for which very reason it is adequate to the feelings of man." (*EC* Eliot trans. pp. 783-4.)

81. In *Preliminary Theses on the Reform of Philosophy* Feuerbach writes, "Theology is *belief in ghosts.*" See *The Fiery Brook: Selected Writings of Ludwig Feuerbach* edited and translated by Zawar Hanfi, (New York: Doubleday, 1972), page 157. Nietzsche was familiar with the *Preliminary Theses*.

82. Zarathustra parodies Peter I 1:19 and Matthew 26:27. Cf. Feuerbach's analysis in *EC* chapters 6, 16, 19, 21 et al..

83. For a description of pietism, see *Encyclopedia of Religion and Ethics*, edited by James Hastings, (NY: T&T Clark Publishers, 1956) and *Encyclopedia of Philosophy*, edited by Paul Edwards, (NY: Macmillan Publishers, 1967), Vol. VI and A. Ritschl's *Geschichte des Pietismus*, three volumes, (Bonn: 1880-86).

84. For a note on these forms of world-defamation, see *KSA* XIII pp.34-35.

85. This is possibly a reworking of Feuerbach's dictum: "The body belongs to my being; indeed, the body in its totality is my ego, my being itself." (My translation of *Grundsaetze der Philosophie der Zukunft* section 37.) Nietzsche was familiar with Feuerbach's materialism.

86. See Kaufmann's *Will to Power*, pp.375-76, note 707.

87. Here *Werkzeug und Spielzeug* (tool and plaything) highlight the origin of spirit in *utility for life.*

88. See *Will to Power* 707: "becoming conscious is obviously only one more means toward the unfolding and the power of life." Or *Will to Power* note 688: "My theory would be: that the will to power is the primitive form of affect, that all other affects are only developments of it." Or note 644:""Spirit" is only a means and tool in the service of higher life, of the enhancement of life." All of Book Three Section II (in Kaufmann's organization) is important to this point.

89. See the remarkable note 676 in *Will to Power*.

90. See note 707 in *Will to Power*.

91. See II.12. All of Book Three Section II of *Will to Power* is relevant here. See esp. note 688: "that all driving force is will to power, that there is no other physical, dynamic or psychic force except this."

92. See here note 676 in *Will to Power*.

93. See *Will to Power*, note 684: "*Third proposition*: the domestication (the "culture") of man does not go deep—Where it does go deep it at once becomes degeneration (type:christian). The "savage" (or, in moral terms, the evil man) is a return to nature—and in certain senses his recovery, his *cure* from "culture"—."

94. The notions contained in this paragraph are found in a note from 1887-88 (*Will to Power* 317).

95. See *KSA* Band X page 134. (My translation.)

96. For an excellent translation of the Prometheus myth, see David Green's *Greek Tragedies* (University of Chicago Press, 1960), Vol. I.

97. Raskolinikov appears in *Crime and Punishment*. Though Nietzsche did not know of Dostoyevski at the time of this writing, Nietzsche's understanding of the criminal type bears an uncanny resemblance to Dostoyevski's. Further, in published works after *Zarathustra*, and in his notebooks, Nietzsche brings his agreement with Dostoyevski to the fore, and under discussion of the very themes of this section. In particular, see *KSA* Band VI pp. 146-48, 201-03 and *Will to Power* 233, 434 (esp)740 and 788.

98. See *KSA* Band X page 64.

99. "Your killing, O judges, shall be pity and not revenge. And as you kill, be sure that you yourselves justify life! It is not enough to make your peace with the man you kill. Your sadness shall be love of the overman: thus you shall justify your living on."

100. See *KSA* Band III page 176-78 for example.

101. See *KSA* Band VI pages 146-48.

102. See in this context the criminal as debtor (*KSA* V pp.307-08), decadent (*KSA* VI pages 68-69); the naturalization of crime finds particular expression in *Will to Power* 233 and 740.

103. There are a number of aphorisms in which Nietzsche speaks positively of the criminal: see *KSA* III page 160 (law-breaker as future law-giver), *Will to Power* 233 (Dostoyevski's criminal worth more than one hundred "broken christians") and *Will to Power* 740 (the rebel not contemptible in himself and possessing good instincts). Above all, *the criminal should not be judged by an isolated act*: see *KSA* V pages 308-09 and *Will to Power* 740.

104. The color red, as Messer (page 35) points out, probably refers to the judicial robe of Nietzsche's time. As well, it fits the image of the judge as animal sacrificer. The animal, in this case, is of greater value than its sacrificer—this is Nietzsche's radical point. Red also serves as a contrast to the *pale* criminal.

105. All other speeches are directed toward a specific group (e.g., "the afterworldly"), or "my brothers," meaning the group of companions Zarathustra has assembled. Such features are never accidental: like all masterpieces of art, every aspect of *Zarathustra* is intentional at some level or another.

106. The text parallels a note from the *Zarathustra* period: "Another century of newspapers—and all words will stink." (*KSA* X page 73: my translation).

107. Another meaning to the expression "blood is spirit" is the physicalism we have previously noted. Words were once thought of as pure spirit (=god), then spirit was found to be blood (=body).

108. See *KSA* pages 302-305.

109. See *KSA* VI pages 343-349. See credits in footnote 78 above for summary of alterations in the concept "Dionysus."

110. See in particular *KSA* I pages 47-48. A number of diremptions occur in *Zarathustra* at critical junctures, in which he views himself from outside himself. The experience of Zarathustra in IV.10 is none other than an idealized account of inspiration experience. Zarathustra is the visionary of Dionysus. Nietzsche, in *Ecce Homo*, claims the same sort of experience for himself during the creation of *Zarathustra* (see *KSA* VI pages 335-342).

111. "Mystery teachings," that is, the overman, will to power and eternal return. These are all posed originally as riddles to be solved.

112. The wording of the ass image alludes to and parodies Matthew 21:5 and Zachariah 9:9.

113. The biblical text to be compared with this section is Matthew 19:16-26, Luke 18:18-30, Luke 10:25 and Mark 10:17-27.

114. Messer (page 39) writes, "The youth's soul is shamefully closed, but the soulknower knows nevertheless to make an image of him (he "invents" it so to speak, in order to "discover it")"—my translation. The image (*Bild*) Messer refers to is the tree metaphor. But this analysis is superficial. In the previous section, the impenetrability of spirit was taught: only one of one's own type (=blood) understands one's problems. In I.9, Zarathustra will address another former self—the warrior. There are many former selves presented to

Zarathustra (see esp., II.19). When the youth is surprised at Zarathustra's insight, the latter smiles because of the intimacy of their relation and the ease of task. Zarathustra could never have seen through the soul of the youth, unless he had previously undergone (=invented) the same experience. The youth is a former self of Zarathustra.

115. The image of the wind is an allusion to John 3:8.

116. The gravediggers are seen here as those "for whom life is furious work and unrest." This corroborates further the previous identification of the gravedigger with the scholar and his death wish. (See especially II.14 and III.9.)

117. Of extreme interest in connection with this is *Der griechische Staat* (*KSA* I page 764 ff.) and the eighth chapter of *Menschliches, Allzumenschlisches* (*KSA* II page 285 ff.).

118. For another occurrence of the wordplay on "uniform," see *KSA* I page 775.

119. See *KSA* I page 775.

120. See e.g., *KSA* III page 16. Examples are legion.

121. A good (short) biography is Ivo Frenzl's *Friedrich Nietzsche: An Illustrated Biography*, (New York: Pegasus, 1967), translated by Joachim Neugroschel: see pages 36-38 on military service. Also see Curt Paul Janz' *Nietzsche* Vol.I pages 364-82 for a more in-depth account. See also *KSA* I page 159.

122. See *KSA* I page 775 ff.

123. See Schlechta's edition, Vol.III page 432 and 921.

124. See Schlechta's edition, Vol.III page 911 for explication of inner/external war distinction.

125. See *KSA* VI pages 84-85.

126. See *KSA* VI page 170.

127. For contrast between armed/unarmed, warlike/peacelike psychological types, see Schlechta's edition Vol. II page 795.

128. See *KSA* VI pages 312-313.

129. See *KSA* I page 708. Hegel et al. are probably meant by those whose thoughts are stolen by the State and called "education." See *KSA* I 710-11 and 742.

130. The phrase "It will give you everything if you will adore it, this new idol" alludes to Matthew 4:9.

131. Probably alluding to Hegel (see here: *KSA* I pages 302-311).

132. Incredibly, neither Naumann nor Messer notice the allusion to the death of Socrates by poison at the hand of the state. That Nietzsche intended the poison as a symbol of the afterworldly, as Naumann contends, rather than the very appropriate mention of Socrates, is highly unlikely. Messer takes the poison to allude to the philosopher's self-compromise in giving his best to the state. But Nietzsche here is speaking of literal death, at least in part, as evidenced by the passages before and after.

133. For the comparison of war to suicide, see also *KSA* III, pages 565-568.

134. See comments to I.5.

135. The inversion of the biblical parable of devil and swine alludes to Matthew 8:28-32.

136. See I.20.

137. Messer argues that the bird-and-cats image symbolizes women as irrational and moody, the cow image symbolizing women as good-natured, caring mothers. But neither reduction is plausible, since one must above all else explain the relationship of women *to each other*, i.e., as *friends*, not as mothers. Naumann arrives at a more plausible reduction of the images. He writes, "Women are still cats, who know to hide malice under velvet paws, or birds, fond of sweets, flighty; or at best (worst?) cows, patient, ruminating." (My translation.) The image of ruminating cows is almost certainly correct: they "chew the cud" together, as one says, recalling the stereotype of the gossiper. Unlike friends, cows have put all difference aside and are herd animals. But Naumann still does not capture the essential relation *between* cats and birds: sneaking, pursuit, ambush, antagonism. Rather than "hiding malice under velvet paws," women are antagonists with one another, but not for the purpose of self-overcoming.

138. See *KSA* X page 91 3[1] and I Corinthians 13:13.

139. This is the first appearance of "will to power" in the works published in Nietzsche's lifetime. We defer discussion of it until commentary to II.12. An interesting discussion occurs in Walter Kaufmann's "Nietzsche's Discovery of the

Will to Power," in his *Nietzsche* (Princeton: Princeton Press, 1974), 4th edition and W. Mueller-Lauter's "Nietzsches Lehre vom Willen zur Macht" in Band III of *Nietzsche-Studien*, pages 1-61.

140. Here I adopt Feuerbach's terminology in "Der Gottesbegriff als das Gattungswesen des Menschen," in Band VII of *Saemtliche Werke*. See comments to Prologue 4.

141. This is the central notion of Feuerbach's philosophy.

142. By "anthropological reductionism" I mean the method of resolving all religious dogma, imagery and objects into the human, all-too-human factors which are their origins. Nietzsche's anthropology is laid out in M. Meckel's "Der Weg Zarathustras als der Weg des Menschen. Zur Anthropologie Nietzsches im Kontext der Rede vom Gott im *Zarathustra*" in *Nietzsche-Studien* Band IX.

143. This observation begins the "Einleitung" to Feuerbach's *Das Wesen des Christentums*.

144. For a striking anticipation of the overman as a principle of love, see *Schopenhauer als Erzieher* (*KSA* Band I pages 340-41).

145. The festivals derided in this section, which one might imagine along the lines of German military parardes of the 19th-century, are directly related to the "great man," "Jester" and "Market Place." The "actors" of these festivals are the "great actors" of I.12. In a note to this section Nietzsche writes, "In patriotic festivals the audience still belongs to the actors" (my translation of *KSA* XIV page 291). Montinari suggests comparison of this passage and Amos 5:21.

146. See comments to I.1. Sections I.1, I.17 and I.20 are so closely related as to be three panels of a single triptych.

147. Of special interest is I.13, I.18 and, for contrast, Matthew 19 and I Corinthians 7.

148. See I.18.

149. The image of "the god who limps" and "these animals entangled in the heavenly net" is a strong reference to the myth of Ares, Aphrodite and Hephaestus. The formulation of "blessing what god has not joined" refers to, and inverts, Matthew 19:6.

150. This section should be contrasted to I.13, I.14 and I.20.

151. For a highly provocative investigation of this theme, see Jacques Derrida's *Spurs*. The interpretations of this section, II.10 and II.15 given in this commentary are influenced by Derrida.

152. See II.12.

153. Compare primarily with I.6.

154. For love of enemy, see Matthew 5:43-48. For retaliation, see Matthew 5:38-42. For judgment, see Matthew 7:1-6.

155. See I.12.

156. *Summary of allusions to previous sections*: Moral conscience is the echo of "Thou Shalt' in the ear of the lion. Zarathustra puts the question to the lion, Do you have the right and strength to become a child? The ambitious rabble (=great men, monkeys, jesters et al.) lust after power but have no genuine ideas (=they bellow). The child would will negative and positive freedom, and would create its own tablet. Unlike the Pale Criminal it would judge and avenge itself. The child would *create* an overman (=throw a star out into the void) as Zarathustra already has at the book's outset: Zarathustra has "compelled the very stars to revolve around himself," and so becomes the center of his ethical universe. (See comments on this copernican revolution in Prologue 1.) To nurture the overman one must suffer the burdens of overcoming, oppose the "last man" and, above all, avoid mass political movements. (See comments to I.10, 11, 12, 13 and 16.)

157. See the essay "Vom Selbstmord" in *Parerga und Paralipomena*.

158. See commentary and footnotes to I.8.

159. See I.10.

160. See Appendix 2 for the structural interpretation which supports this contention.

161. "When you are above praise and blame, and your will wants to command all things, like a lover's will: there is the origin of your virtue." In section 2: "Let your gift-giving love and your knowledge serve the meaning of the earth." "You force all things to and into yourself that they may flow back out of your well as the gifts of your love."

162. For the equivalent image of Zarathustra carrying fire to the valley and ashes to the mountains, see commentary to Prologue 2 and footnotes thereto.

163. See commentary and notes to I.6.

164. See commentaries to I.2, 3, 4 and 9. The duality of *thanatos* (death) and *eros* (love, life) is used in this connection to indicate connections between Nietzsche and Freud in terms of basic themes.

165. As previously indicated (see comments to I.4), there is no real distinction between world and will: reality *is* will. But Nietzsche identifies the body as the form of this will. Thus when he uses "body" he is referring to a more fundamental *will*, which is an extended notion of physicality.

166. For future sections corroborating the above interpretation, see II.19, III.4, III.12.30 and IV.13.15.

167. "With knowledge, the body purifies itself; making experiments with knowledge, it elevates itself; in the lover of knowledge all instincts become holy; in the elevated, the soul becomes gay."

168. "and the tone of his voice had changed" (*seine Stimme hatte sich verwandelt*). His spirit metamorphoses (*verwandelt sich*) as well between sub-sections 1 and 2. Thus in full circle back to I.1, the spirit is seen in metamorphosis from the camel (=among fellow man) to the lion (=isolated) to the child (=future man creating overman).

169. This is an inversion of Matthew 10:33.

Prefatory Remarks to Part II

After Nietzsche finished Part I in February, 1883, he convalesced in Genoa's Piazza Barberini.

> It was on a *loggia* high above that Piazza, from which one has a fine view of Rome and hears the *fontana* splashing far below, that the loneliest song was written that has ever been written, the "Night Song." Around that period an indescribable melancholy was always about me, and I found its refrain in the words, "dead from immortality."[1]

This "Night Song" is one of Nietzsche's finest lyrical compositions. It would later become the ninth section of Part II. One might say, only half metaphorically, that the Piazza of Part II is built around the *fontana*-like "Night Song." Fountain imagery indeed underlies most of Part II. Nietzsche gave his own commentary to the "Night Song" in two sections of *Ecce Homo*, a sign of its great importance to Nietzsche.[2]

In the summer of 1883, Nietzsche returned to Sils-Maria, Switzerland, "the holy spot where the first lightning of the *Zarathustra* idea had flashed for me."[3] There he wrote Part II in a ten-day spurt of activity. The central theme of Part II, giving and receiving, was anticipated and preformed in the Prologue and Part I. This theme presupposes a distinction between *the one who gives* and *those who receive.* The one who bestows his love and wisdom gives his gift to those who are barren, passive, unproductive or otherwise empty. In Nietzsche's usage, the giver gives the gift of *values for life.* Givers are value creators, or "esteemers," such as Mohammad or the historical Zoroaster. The vast majority of mankind must receive value in life from him who *gives value to life.* Between the man overrich in spirit and those poor in spirit lies the slope of human equality. Looking down on the barren masses, the value-creator feels a *pathos of distance*, or feeling of superiority, much as the almsgiver feels over beggars. The tension between the desire to *release* overrichness and the desire to *maintain one's distance* thus becomes an important leitmotif. Correlative to this theme, of course, is the initial motif of friendship in tension with solitude found in Prologue 1.

Philosophically speaking, giving and receiving are notions that are signs for more fundamental principles, i.e., active and reactive force. Zarathustra the giver represents active force whereas his audience, friends and critics represent reactive force. Zarathustra's dilemma is simple: if he activates himself he must come into contact with reactive force, which is offensive and dangerous. But if he does not activate, he is reduced to an unacceptable, and ultimately impossible, passivity.

The first section of each Part introduces the major imagery to follow. Thus section II.1 presents the imagery of Part II in a small set of elegant metaphors. The basic image of Part II is *downward flow* (:remember the Piazza *fontana*). Throughout Part II there is a downward flow of Zarathustra's love for man (=mountain streams) and his wisdom (=rain). At the zenith of the vertical dimension is *the one who gives*, or Zarathustra. This apex is his mountaintop of solitude. His love of man and his wisdom pour down from his solitude like a raging storm of water. Below him, at the nadir, are *those who receive.*

In a strong sense, Part II, like Part I, depends on the Prologue and its critical distinction between the overman and the last man. For *the one who gives value to life* is none other than the overman and *those who receive* are none other than last men. It is their permanence, and possible victory, that disgusts Zarathustra to the point of endangering the fulfillment of his destiny. Overcoming this disgust is the primary task of Part III.

Notes

1. *Basic Writings* p.758: *KSA* VI 298.

2. *Ecce Homo* "Warum ich solche gute Buecher schreibe" sections 7 and 8.

3. *Basic Writings* p.758: *KSA* VI 341.

Commentary to Part II

... and only when you have denied
me will I return to you. Verily,
my brothers, with different eyes
shall I then seek my lost ones;
with a different love shall I then
love you.

(Part I sec.22(3))

Part II

1. The Child with the Mirror

This section, originally entitled "The Second Dawn,"[1] invites comparison to the Prologue, section 1, which was the first dawn. Once again, Zarathustra speaks to himself in the solitude of his cave, beginning the second cycle of the plot line.[2]

Zarathustra is awakened from the first of several dreams in the book[3] to the realization that his teachings are in danger: among his friends (=seeds), whom he has bid to follow their own paths (=scattered), are those moralists (=weeds) who would only pose as higher men (=wheat), and who now misinterpret (=distort) Zarathustra in terms of the christian notions of good and evil. (That this event would occur was foretold in I.22. The passage foretelling this event was Nietzsche's own choice for introductory quotation to Part II.) As in Prologue 1, Zarathustra undergoes a metamorphosis, and rises like the sun, ready once again to pour out his golden essence downward to man. Four parallel metaphors arise to symbolize Zarathustra's condition; weather, water, emotion and speech. At the zenith of the vertical dimension is the storm, the lake, his overladen soul and his teachings. An overabundance of each results in a downward overflow of rain, river, flowing love and speech, paralleling the going under of Zarathustra among men and the solar phases of the overman (=sun). At the nadir of the vertical dimension stands mankind, both the few friends (=islands) and the many foes. Those who are below are frightened at the great effulgence overtaking them from above, and misinterpret it as the raging of an evil god. (The misinterpretation of a higher being by a lower being is a persistent theme in Part II.) The storm over man is however the superhuman wisdom of Zarathustra, which, like a lioness, has undergone a gestation and birth process, and now seeks to roam wild once more, displaying both its strength and gentleness.

To those friends who have proved themselves to be beyond good and evil, Zarathustra now prepares his new psychological insights as if they were spears, and summons his greatest energy (=wildest horse) to begin anew a battle of values. The lioness who would "roar gently" is an emblem of the simultaneous coupling of the sublated concepts "good" and "evil" found in the overman. (This lion reappears at the beginning of the Great Noon in IV.20, and has already occurred at I.1 and I.17. The conflation of lion and child images in this section is different from that expressed in I.1. The image of the camel, which rushes into the desert in I.1, is here conflated with the image of the lion. Though this section bears strong resemblance to Prologue 1 and I.1, the symbols are in constant transition, with each and every element being raised to a new level of meaning.) The ambiguity within all of Zarathustra's imagery between metaphorical and literal conflict is fully intentional and never resolved.

2. On the Blessed Isles

Just as Part I had raised the notions of the Prologue to a clearer, more conceptual, less imagistic, level of comprehension, so Part II raises the concepts of Part I to a more concise, if still abstract, formulation, building in particular upon sections I.3 and Prologue 3. In his first speech to his reassembled friends, Zarathustra compares the overman not to the last man, as previously, but to the gods of world religion. The general conceptual movement of this section strongly reflects the programmatic direction of German idealism; namely, returning to man that which he has previously placed outside himself.[4]

In a copernican revolution, after the fashion of Kant,[5] Zarathustra finds the measure of truth, reality and good not in the external object, nor in a Divine Subject, but in man himself. That which is true, real and valuable is a creation of human reason, imagination, will and love. Thus they are reflections of the human faculties. (Nietzsche of course often criticizes the very notion of faculties, as well as other concepts of German idealism. I in no way claim that Nietzsche himself was an idealist, much less a kantian. I claim here that the central conceptual movement of Zarathustra's ideas reflects the revolutionary twist of perspective underlying German idealism and romanticism.) To know ultimate truth, reality and good is to know man as the measure of all things; the world itself becomes a blessedness to him who finds himself at its center (=lovers of knowledge). The incomprehensible and irrational is that which is outside the bounds of human faculties—the unthinkable, unwillable, unsensible. Gods of world religions are based upon mysteries which pose a paradox to human understanding. The gods are merely conjectural beings outside the possibility of thought and sensibility, and by nature not objects of the will. Hitherto man has placed his superhuman phantasies in supernatural realms (=upon distant seas). Zarathustra wills that the external—superhuman, supernatural, objective—be returned to earth and embodied man. Like Kant, Zarathustra sets a limit on human speculation by restricting the measure of the real, ideal and true to the limits of the human.[6]

God is a conjecture which falsifies human experience, turning time and change into illusion, presenting paradoxes which swoon the understanding and make the body turn from itself; thus such conjecture is called "the turning disease." Theological visions of god as the One, the Plenum, the Unmoved, the Sated and the Permanent are only derivative images (=parables) of the earthly and bodily.[7] To the extent that the gods falsify man's experience and turn him against himself, they are conjectures that are misanthropic.

To imagine the gods as the Permanent is to expose the nature of the creator as he who wants-no-more, esteems-no-more, creates-no-more: Zarathustra does not want man to undergo this great weariness.[8] Robbing man of conjecture is to rob the creator of faith, the eagle of its height. But the lies of the poets, their flights of fancy to otherworlds, should be replaced by creative flights of the spirit which celebrate and advocate and justify the human experience of impermanence, sorrow, transformation and struggle. Creativity is the redemption of the overcomings man undergoes: it re-juvenates life and removes its gravity. Creation is itself a process of great struggle and pain, in close analogy to the birth process. (The birth process of the lioness in the immediately preceeding section anticipates this analogy. And the metamorphosis of spirit in I.1 is prototypical creation, resulting in the birth of a child.) Any creator must accept the inevitable painful process to achieve the result of creating something higher than himself. The creator's will must will the fate of him who would cross over, and will the self-overcomings required: he must go through a series of selves to find his most complete and perfected self. Rather than a single identity, the creator has a series of former selves (=hundred souls) on the way to his eventual all-encompassing identity.[9]

Willing liberates: creative will has the freedom *to* create something beyond itself. All of Zarathustra's senses suffer to release their power, to break out of the prison of their limitations: creation is the great liberty, the great knowledge, the great begetting, in which man strives beyond himself in his new found innocence. Creative will overtakes the creator and compels him toward the raw material of creation. Zarathustra's creative will compels him toward *man*; man is the material, the means, by which something higher is formed. Present man, like the restraints of the individual, is a prison from which the creative will liberates itself. Zarathustra does not will that man create another illusory superhuman of the imagination: this is not his *liberating* will. Real creation requires sustained overexertion of the will toward a goal. A god is not a possible creation of human will, but the complete and extra-ordinary individual *is* attainable for man. According to Zara-thustra's expectations, the overman will eclipse even the greatest men hitherto, and will require the harnessing of a great collective will ranging over generations (=fathers and forefathers) in a colossal human project in the likeness of, for example, the great architechural wonders. But the product is man himself, a miraculously higher man who exceeds all previous standards of man. In present man lies the outline of what man can be, what man should be, i.e., the overman. But "modern man" is a resistant and still imperfect substance (=hardest, ugliest stone): to create the overman means therefore that the hammer of the will must spell the undergoing of the imperfect.

This seemingly facist doctrine must not be taken at face value. There is a persistent ambiguity in Zarathustra's doctrine of the overman between overcoming *one's own self* and overcoming *others* by external force, which is critical to maintain. There is a further ambiguity between *Untergang* as total destruction and *Untergang* as the "surpassing" of the lower by the higher. Nietzsche's doctrine of self-overcoming is the surpassing of a former self by creation of a higher self: his imagery accomodates the case in which the literal destruction of the individual is included, as well. Zarathustra does not stipulate the necessary destruction of mankind in a literal sense: his overcoming of man, however, is not constrained, as he says repeatedly, by *preservation* of the species. This is certainly one of the most nebulous and dangerous doctrines Nietzsche formulates: extreme caution should be exercised in approaching it.

The overman is for Zarathustra still a shadow, an image of images, the most fragile, lightest, stillest thing on earth. But once inspired by the magnificence of the promise of man, the gods of the imagination no longer matter. Man is now the center of the ethical universe: he is the measure of all things. With promethean *hybris* Zarathustra dismisses the gods as the highest values: "the beauty of the overman came to me as a shadow. Oh my brothers! What are the gods to me now?" The gods are now dethroned as the creators of the universe: man creates truth, the very world, and the highest good out of himself: the gods themselves are made by man in his image, the inverted image of man the creator. "Away from God and gods this will has lured me; what could one create if gods existed?" Zarathustra's superhumanism reaches its highest formulation in this section in a paralogism: "*if* there were gods, how could I endure not to be a god! Hence *there are no gods*." This is a syllogism of the will, not of reason: the gods remain a conjecture unrefuted. But Zarathustra's will to endure and create beyond himself leaves no room for Divine Beings: the complete and extraordinary man is now the highest goal—the man who creates the world in his own image, and is the measure of all things, whose faculties of will, love, reason and creativity are developed together, integrated and unified, each to their greatest degree, in the overman. To enrich man, Zarathustra impoverishes the gods. This enrichment occurs in Part IV.

3. On the Pitying

Man is the ashamed animal. Man does not merely *resemble* the animals, he *is* an animal, but an animal whose shame in particular, and moral sentiments generally, differentiate him from other species. Nietzsche's depth psychology in this section evaluates the extra-moral value of moral sentiments—shame, pity, conscience— from a naturalist perspective.[10]

The pitier, contra Matthew 5:7, is not the blessed man. In his feeling of blessedness and charity he raises himself above the pitied by an act of humiliation. Pity (*Mitleid*) is suffering with (*mit leiden*) another person. Those who are in need are the poor in spirit or body who must receive from others without being able to give in return. He who suffers is ashamed of his need, and whereas there has been such great suffering in man's existence, the history of man is shame.

When charity is offered and accepted, the pitied is put into psychological debt: he feels deeply that he owes something to the pitier, though help was not asked for. The moral notion of guilt derives from the psychological feeling of debt.[11] Debt is a power relation between the more powerful creditor and the powerless debtor. The debtor comes to think of himself in terms of dependence and powerlessness, rationalizing his position in moral terms: "I am indebted (*schuldig*)" becomes "I am guilty (also *schuldig*)." Moral conscience does not arise from an inner voice judging what is right and wrong, nor is it a faculty of judgment placed in us by some god: it is a *moral* interpretation of *power* relationships. Far from being a positive moral force, it is an expression of self-denigration which only duplicates the sorrow of the sufferer in the pitier.

The debtor suppresses his self-reproach out of an instinct for ego-preservation, turning his scorn from himself to his pitier, in a more or less disguised *ressentiment*. A great evil deed out of *ressentiment* is preferable to many small repressions, for the former is a *catharsis* (=opened boil) while the latter is a degenerate self-consuming syndrome (=creeping fungi).[12] Feelings of sinfulness and bad conscience, originating in psychological indebtedness, are sources of *ressentiment* which corrupt the entire *psyche* like a disease or, which result in disguised "criminal" deeds.[13] Thus Zarathustra completely rejects the value of pity and similar moral sentiments from an extra-moral (that is, psychological) perspective.

If one must pity others (suffer with them), it is best done without the awareness of the pitied (=from a distance). But best is not to pity at all, for pity is basically a multiplication of *sorrow*, which is not a positive force in itself. Pity, bad conscience, charity, shame, indebtedness, *ressentiment*, need and sorrow are things which must be overcome, if man is to become psychologically healthy. What man should learn is a feeling of joy about himself. Joy expresses man's innocence and teaches him to feel good about himself and others. This affirmation of human existence is not joy *in* another's suffering, but joy *despite* sorrow. (Still less does joy mean the herd-like contentment of the last man, hedonism or the sleep of the virtuous. Joy is felt about the highest elements of mankind—higher man—and the greatest joy is felt by the overman. Man must strive to overcome himself for real joy to be sustained. Joy is the experience of creating a higher self in one's own person.)

Moral sentiment never solves a problem, but is itself a problem. Man cannot afford a religion which represents the world as sorrow and redemption as afterworldly. The sufferer overcomes himself and his need when he relies on his own efforts: this brings life-affirming joy (=the great love). Thus the life-affirmer sacrifices himself and his neighbor alike to the trials of life, that the human condition might overcome. Along life's course the great comfort is to have a friend; yet the friend is not the pitier, but another self in which the sorrows of life are temporarily laid to rest in shared joy (=bed), i.e. another self who makes prolonged rest *uncomfortable* (=field cot), thus stimulating the friend to renewed overcoming.[14] Far from incurring a debt, one is thereby inspired to the great love of life, which overcomes the existing need and creates something beyond itself (=creates the beloved). Christian "virtue," as will be seen more deeply in the next section, judges the world to be sorrow and creates a false beyond, a soft bed, for sorrows.

4. On the Priests

This section builds primarily upon II.3, I.9 and Prologue 2. Nietzsche's anti-clericalism, a legacy principally from Voltaire, grew increasingly hostile throughout his career.[15]

As in Prologue 2, Zarathustra here passes by the religious man without violence (=sleeping sword),[26] for, like the Hermit, the priest is sometimes a higher individual (=hero), and many of them suffer greatly. And in any case, when one struggles against them (=attacks), one risks contagion with their spiritual diseases (=easily soiled). (In contrast, see commentary to I.17. Zarathustra's pity in this section presents a difficulty of interpretation: how far are we to accept his thoughts about priests in this section, when they occur in a state of uncharacteristic emotion?) Zarathustra declares that "my blood is related to theirs," expressing the message that the clergy, like Zarathustra, suffers spiritually.[16]

It is clear that Zarathustra's conciliatory speech here is born of pity and compassion: despite his last speech, Zarathustra pities (=suffers with, *mitleiden*) them for their false values and delusive words. Since priests are the most vengeful of all groups,[17] he advises all to pass them by.

Priests seek an afterworldly solace from the sorrows of life. But as in the medieval fisherman's fable,[18] his solace (=island) is a false value and delusive words (=monster), which festers psychological illness (=sleeping calamity), like the fungi of II.3, eventually overtaking them (=eating, devouring). As in Matthew,[19] the priest builds huts on his solace: these *churches* are the spirit-stifling (=musty) abodes of those repentants who humiliate themselves (=crawl upstairs on knees)[20] rather than striving upward (=soaring). As in II.3, the damage of shame is brought to the fore: the death-oriented priest[21] shames himself before the challenges of life (=pure sky) and hides in the tomb-like sanctuary of the afterworld. What gives the priest his greatest pain, and yet is his greatest love, is *man himself*: thus he pictures God as his greatest love—*man*—but as man only insofar as the priest knows him, i.e., as man the sufferer. Thus the priestly type imagines a *suffering god*. The christian god, as explicitly stated in II.3, has died out of love for man, because this god's creator, the christian, like the Hermit of Prologue 2, is unable to bear his love for man, and thus perishes by it.[22] Christ is the suffering god who dies on the cross of his unbearable love for man.

Death images are the expressions of the *thanatos* in the priestly soul; their apparel, speech, songs, and buildings evidence their melancholy souls (=ominous frogs). The spirit of the priest is made of needs (=gaps) which are filled by their god (=stopgap). Like their god, priests' souls perish (=drown) in their pity for man. The monster upon which they crawl to safety (recalling the fable image again) is only *more pity*, objectified, personified and set into the beyond as the pitying, suffering man/god.

And like the shepherd Jesus,[23] priests drive their herd "one way." The immortal souls claimed by the priests for man cannot disguise the petty, herdlike diminutive spirits of the herd and shepherd. Both the herd and their shepherd are all-too-human. As a testimony to the truth of their faith, some priests become religious fanatics and attempt to validate their cause in martyrdom (=signs of blood), after the fashion of Christ himself. But fanaticism proves only the hatred at the core of all true believers—a *ressentiment* born out of life's disappointments—and not the truth of the belief.[24] Where vengeful emotion (=sultry heart) couples with unemployed reason (=cold head), the psychological type "Redeemer" arises. There have been many higher types other than the Redeemer, and there will be many other higher types for Zarathustra's friends to overcome. (Zarathustra himself is a higher type his companions will have to overcome, "lest a statue slay them," as in I.22.)

Despite the rise of higher types among man, he is still too average, conforming and underdeveloped, or in short, "all-too-human." Zarathustra's depth psychology has allowed him to see the various types of man at their foundations (=nakedness). The *healthy, vital,* no-longer-human type has yet to appear: this type marking a break from the ageless illnesses of mankind is the *overman.*

5. On the Virtuous

Zarathustra has given a general critique of christian psychology in the opening sections of Part II; now he escalates his attack against the "good and just" by considering a spectrum of notions of virtue.

In this speech Zarathustra does not address the christian, whose contentment (=slack and sleeping senses) must be shattered by fire and brimstone preaching (=thunder and heavenly fireworks). It is an *aesthetic sense* (=voice of beauty) which he wishes to employ in persuading his friends (=the truly virtuous).

The common feature of the spectrum of virtues under consideration is that they all suppose a reward for virtue. Even the higher man still bases his notions on belief in a moral world order (=reward and punishment). Their virtues in the Here and Now (=on earth, today) are still not motivating enough: the virtuous still want the reward of heaven and eternity. But Zarathustra's most basic teaching is the absence of moral order (=reward and paymaster). Further, he does not accept any sort of teleological concept of virtue: virtue is not even a self-satisfied feeling (=own reward), but is more purposeless sacrifice than a means to an end. (The notion here is one of self-propulsion and self-creation along the lines of later existentialism, rather than that of pre-formed purpose and pre-existent essence.)[25] The deep psychological mechanism (=foundation of the soul) of the christian still drives the higher man: Zarathustra's ideas (=boar's snout, plowshare) will upearth the soiled psychology of the past to make way for new motives and truths.

The psychological motives of the good and just—revenge, etc., —express the will to punish and mortify: true virtue is, on the contrary, the will to love and create. Virtue is not a reaction against what others do: it is an instinct, a drive, of the innermost sort, as is the mothering instinct, which wishes to create something beyond itself.

The phrase "thirst of the ring" alludes to the as-yet-unformulated doctrine of the eternal return. Thirst is a need, an instinct, for something external (i.e., water). The "ring" is a metaphor introduced in I.1, symbolizing the creation of a higher self, as a point which moves only to return to its origin.[26] Creativity in Zarathustra's sense is creation of a higher self by *becoming what one is*, i.e., by actualizing the potential residing in oneself. Every ring is a point which moves away to return to itself: the virtuous man is driven by an internal compulsion (=striving) to complete and actualize the higher self which lies within himself, but whose nature he does not yet know. The drive of the virtuous man is a creative, mothering instinct desiring a child.[27] It therefore bursts of wave-like energy, developing what is internal and potential, as a child bursts forth. The development of the innermost self outlives the energy source: the "meaning" of one's essence may take many years after the life of the individual to reveal itself: the ultimate nature of the individual's virtue (=sunray) lasts well beyond one's lifespan (=dying star). Virtue is therefore not a deed of short duration, nor something external to the self: virtue is none other than the explosive energy source of life itself, which strives to overpower all barriers and expands its boundaries to encompass its universe, but returning ever again to its origin. (The notion of life and spirit as self-movement runs through German idealism and originates in Aristotle.) This power source is the self: therefore, "your virtue is your self."[28]

Zarathustra parodies a variety of common so-called virtues, exposing their inner essence, as if running amok through a congregation of the "good and just."[29] There are those whose virtue is merely surrender to external force (=spasm under the whip).[30] Others call the repression of vice to be virtue, and when their vice finally emerges it is christened "justice." There are those who sink into their passions (=drawn by devils), but simultaneously call their own counter-image "virtue."[31] There are those who also allow their passions to go out of control (=carry stones downhill), but who are incontinent (=creak) and call their self-contradiction (=brakes against wheels) "virtue."[32] Others follow standards of behavior automatically (=clocks),[33] identifying virtue with regularity of norms. There are those who have only minute virtues (=handful of justice), but who seek to tyrannize others by imposition of their impoverished souls. For them, to be just (*gerecht*) is to be revenged (*geraecht*). (In German, *Ich bin gerecht*—Iam just—and *Ich bin geraecht*—I am revenged—have only the most minimal phonetic difference. Considering that Zarathustra's teachings are *speeches*, the tool of homonyms is a powerful linguistic means of persuasion.) Like the true believer who envisions the eternal punishment of the damned as entertainment for the blessed, he wants to mortify the flesh (=scratch eyes) for the sake of his own sick spirit.[34] And there are those whose virtue is merely prudence in dangerous situations (=sitting still in a swamp), accepting authority rather than making waves amid hostile creatures (=those who bite).[35] Others have showpiece virtue, the churchgoers who gesticulate and go through motions without religious emotion (=heart). Still others see virtue as necessary for life and property: the real name of their virtue is the "police." And there are those small people who find fault in others, and believe themselves faultless in their criticism (=the evil eye). Some want to be aesthetes of the spirit (=edified and elevated) without having real spirit, while others want involuntary bliss (=to be bowled over).[36]

Everyone thinks that he knows what is good and evil, and most believe that they themselves are good. Zarathustra has looked at the expression of the innermost essence of the "good and just" as it is developed in their self-expression, and finds that they are reward-oriented. But Zarathustra does not have "the evil eye": his task is not to find fault and convert the congregation, but to instruct his friends of the pitfalls therein. All christian "virtues" are reactions which build heavenly and hellish visions around self-judgment and self-reward, judgment and damnation of others. They are all psychological illnesses which identify the aim of virtue as reward and selflessness. Thus they avoid the responsibilities to themselves while securing an immortality of the soul. But Zarathustra teaches virtue as *self-development*.[37] Inner essence develops through a chain of selves as over generations through mother and child.[38] Virtues are the stages of self-expression which the person goes through on the path to self-revelation. Since the self is not a pre-formed, pre-existing essence, but is rather radically *created*, the process of self-formation is true creativity, not mere mechanism.[39]

The "good and just" have lost their illusions of virtue (=toys, words) in the wave of Zarathustra's teachings. But like the waves of the ocean, the new tide will bring a flood of brilliant new virtues and characters. The overman is himself the ocean whose relentless waves bring forth great individuals (=colorful shells) whose wonderfulness will prove a consolation and inspiration to others. The old notions of virtue will be swallowed by a tide of higher values and exemplars. The rising tide is a sign for the advent of a great teacher whose flood will drown the old and wash ashore the new. The advent of a new age of great individuals and virtues will be reminiscent of the creation of great epochs of man (e.g., the Renaissance): the highest expression of the new spirit will be the overman (—here without historical precedent, but analogous to Michelangelo).[40]

6. On the Rabble

Zarathustra now turns his attention to the *lowest man*, the *basest, most common*, spiritually *most impoverished* man. The rabble are by no means identifiable as a socio-economic class: it is rather a *psychological* type. The *power-rabble* are the true believers of mass movements of all types[41]—socialists or facists, democrats or tyrants—whose claim to right rests only in might and a disgenuine claim to equality. They are the spiritually poor—revenge-seekers, power-hungry, greedy—who would topple all those placing themselves above the crowd: their hero can only be "a man of the people." The *writing-rabble*—the popular press and the "famous wisemen"—use the word in its lowest form to entertain the masses, overthrow the worthy, or rationalize the superstitions of the masses.[42] The *pleasure-rabble*—hedonists, utilitarians, eudaimonists—seek pleasure of the lowest form, soiling the highest goods of the earth and body, and soiling the highest ideas (=dreams).[43] The rabble in general are the parasites within the human species.[44]

The rabble point to a fundamental inequality of man. In comparison to human spirit at its highest, they lead a life more animalic than human.[45] Yet at the same time it is undeniable that the lowest man still has spirit. This means that the rabble is an ineradicable element of the human species: it is an inevitable, if the lowest, expression of *espirit*. Even if it were to be momentariliy abolished, it would regenerate. Thus the most base nature of man is still included in the totality of the species along with the highest exemplars.[46]

This is the realization that Zarathustra finds hardest to swallow: his nausea with the lowest man nearly extinguishes his love and expectation for man.[47] Though the necessity of the lowest man is explicitly stated here, it is the challenge of the rest of Part II, and all of Part III, to transform the notion into the doctrine of the eternal return.[48] The saving factor in Zarathustra's struggle is his discovery of "the highest spheres"—solitude—which is pictured in terms of his hermit cave, with the imagery of the Sils-Maria area. (Sils-Maria in the Ober Engadine, Switzerland, was Nietzsche's summer resort and location for the creation of much of *Zarathustra*. That Swiss images are reflected in the book is confirmed by a number of later letters.)

7. On the Tarantulas

In this section, one of the most important in Part II, a number of notions central to Part I and the Prologue are raised to more concise formulations and interrelated. In addition, this is a major statement of Nietzsche's ideas on *revenge*, a central concern of his philosophy. (In a note to this section, Nietzsche writes, "Purification from revenge—is my morality.")[49] The major purpose of this section is to answer a question facing Nietzsche's psychological theories: if all values are expressions of the esteemer's will to *over*power,[50] how are we to account for the will to *equal* power in egalitarianism? Bristling with suggestive imagery, this speech also raises questions about Nietzsche's "aristocratic radicalism" which were only anticipated in the previous section.

The tarantula of Zarathustra's parable is the *rabble-rouser*: he is the *preacher of equality* who stirs up democratic-socialist feelings within the masses. *Revenge* is the poison of this spider, a toxin of the *psyche* which puts the spirit in a swirling storm, upsetting its perpendicularity and creating an all-consuming bile which must be released through a variety of subtle means.

Unlike "the virtuous" in II.5, Zarathustra does not "sit still in the swamp . . . avoiding those who want to bite": he disturbs and provokes the rabble-rouser, that the latter be forced to reveal his inner essence.

Zarathustra employs his depth psychology to penetrate the secrets of the egalitarian, showing his true colors. The soul of the tarantula is *black*: this bilious soul harbors the darkest motives of the human spirit. The inner essence of the tarantula, which it calls its virtue, is the *will to equal power*: this is the drive of all relatively inferior individuals, expressing itself in the will for equal socio-economic or psychological power. Underlying this will however is the will to *overpower*: the drive for superior power is disguised and repressed within the weak as will to equal power: once this will is realized, the will to *over*power becomes operative. Within the oppressed, the will to overpower is a *will to tyranny*—what Zarathustra calls "tyrannomania of impotence." Aggrieved conceit and repressed envy, once unleashed, become a fanatical drive for revenge against the previous master. Thus the socio-economically or politically oppressed become tyrants who form democratic-socialist dictatorships in the image of the previous masters, while the spiritually impoverished and repressed form dictatorships of theocracy, burning heretics and wreaking revenge on the worldly. The "good and just" man—christian, socialist, democrat—lacks only the power to become the evil and unjust man: when this power is finally achieved, the egalitarian will transform into his opposite.

The will to over power, to revenge and regress, is the psychological motive behind the will to judge and the will to punish. Like the red judge of I.6, the preacher of equality practices a "justice" which is the expression of his own mania of impotence, and which aims at punishment, bloodletting and death. Whether it be the Inquisition, socialist dictatorship of the proletariat, the bourgeois justice system of private property or otherwise, the will to punishment is a violent motive of revenge rather than an objective, absolute standard of right. The preachers of equality, as judges and punishers, are none other than the preachers of death in I.9.

Naumann[51] is almost certainly correct to identify the tarantula of the parable first and foremost (though of course not exclusively) with the socialist Eugene Duehring. Nietzsche consistently identifies him with the swamp of revenge,[52] and as the proto-socialist who seeks to overthrow and punish all those who set themselves over the people. He is the "tarantula on the path of thinkers." And when Zarathustra says, "some preach my doctrine of life and are at the same time preachers of equality . . . " it reflects a similar formulation elsewhere aimed at Duehring.[53] Like the alpine climber who goes too far into the cold, only to be overcome, the socialist Duehring is totally consumed by his own bilious envy.

Underlying this speech against egalitarianism are issues involving human nature and reality. Zarathustra's notion of the overman presupposes a real inequality among men, and one that is endorsed to widen ever greater. Without the greater worth of a relatively *higher* type, the doctrine is of no consequence. But this does not mean that Zarathustra's notion is a totalitarian will to uniformity. Far from suggesting that all men should agree in striving after a single shared ideal, the doctrine of the overman presupposes that a great many directions in overcoming man will be attempted. His "great love" of the overman presupposes that there are "a thousand bridges and paths" beyond man, some leading higher than others, many conflicting with one another. Only the tyrant drives his flock One Way. In the universal strife upward, over and beyond man, relative differences among men (inequality) will only increase. That some paths will require a war of values is also expected and affirmed as part of his "great love." The various peoples of mankind will create conflicting tables of values, conflicting gods (=images and ghosts) in a great war of values (=the highest fight). Such was it in the great age of the tragic Greeks. Zarathustra is suggesting that man overcomes himself when a multiplicity among the gods, among overmen, occurs.[54] Since the creation of values and overmen is the highest expression of the self, and since many higher selves are required in the overcoming of man, the love of the overman is the exact opposite of a will to *one* "good and just" way, to *one* "law and order."

Life itself is a struggle among its elements.[55] The clash of values among mankind is a symptomatic expression that man and his esteeming powers are alive. The christian's "good and evil," the socialist's "rich and poor" and Zarathustra's own "high and low" are only a few among the multitudes of tables of value produced as man lives and struggles. All life is struggle, and all struggle results in *power relations*, which are expressed in human consciousness as *moral values*. Life is a natural struggle in which individuals are eventually extinguished (=overcome). In the effort to overpower another, a lifeform strives for greater power: the will to equal power is only an intermediate step for the weak.

Nature establishes an ever-altering hierarchy among its species and members in a complex and subtle system of commanding and obeying. Zarathustra recognizes the inequality inherent in nature and man. For him, the ancient temple is an architechtural symbol of the pyramidal, stepwise inequality among all things. Rather than turn from life, Zarathustra affirms the struggle and inequality (=war) inherent in life and values (=the beautiful). All elements of life are things that attempt to "cross over" to something beyond themselves (=values and arches), requiring an overcoming and a "going under" for another (=a breaking through, contradiction among steps and climbers), as with the Jester/Ropewalker image of the Prologue. Zarathustra affirms the struggling, vital individual as divinity, and exhorts men to struggle with one another, like the gods of mythology.

Just as Zarathustra underwent an attack of pity directly after his speech against it, so he here succumbs to the poison of the tarantula, *revenge*. Before his swoon, he asks to be tied to the column of the temple, as Odyssesus was tied to the mast to resist the fatal call of the Sirens. Even in revenge, Zarathustra affirms the inequality and power hierarchy of nature by remaining perpendicular to the earth. And like the stylite,[56] he would rather be judged than become the red judge of punishment. Above all, the *perpendicularity* of healthy body and psyche, of a will pointed *to the heights*, is to be maintained against the *centripetal*, all-consuming, disorienting will to revenge   (=cyclone, whirlwind, tarantella). The key to the health of man is a rainbow over the storm, a bridge over whirlpools; that is, *delivery from revenge*.

8. On the Famous Wisemen

The "famous wise men" are the famous philosophers and theologians who seek to provide a rational foundation to the common sense of a people concerning morality, reality and knowledge. Set in direct contrast is the "free spirit" (German: *der freie Geist*), i.e., the thinker who is considered to be the enemy of the people and an affront to the superstitions, mores and all manner of uncritically accepted traditional beliefs. At the foundation of this distinction lies the question of truth. These famous wise men call their attempt to "prove" the popular wisdom and dogmas of the people a "will to truth." The free thinker claims no such will to truth, but is nevertheless in possession of truth borne away from the crowd and without regard to traditional beliefs or "common sense."

This distinction as well underlies the contrast of the camel and lion in I.1. The famous wise men are here the beasts of burden who, as advocates of the people, are dogmatic (=stiff-necked) and sophistical (=clever) like asses—which here fulfills the theoretical role of the camel trope. The ass kneels down to carry the dogma of the people. As anticipated in I.1, the powerful forces of the state seek to lend credence to their claims of legitimacy by gaining the allegiance of a "wise man," an ass harnessed in front of their warhorses. Such wise men, occupying academic chairs and other positions of power, dwell among the people (=cities), share the superstitious religions (=idols) of the tribe, commit themselves to rationalizing these superstitions (=pull the cart of the people), and are well rewarded for their service (=well-fed), but who ultimately remain the bearer of a pre-existing Thou Shalt (=remain beasts of burden).

The free-spirited thinker is the lion of I.1, who flees from his fellow man into the desert. He breaks the reverence of the camel and worships no idol of the oasis. He is no man's slave and always remains the master of his own isolation. Therefore he is forever discontent and critical (=hungry, violent). He is the individual who avoids the rabble, the rabble-rousers, priests, flies of the Market Place, idols of the state, the poisoned wells of the rabble and the other dangers to those who would cross over. Though the lion-willed spirit is not yet the creative child, he understands that metamorphoses of spirit demand a life of self-criticism, self-sacrifice and self-overcoming (=life that cuts into itself). Those "thinkers" who impersonate the lion are the asses in lions' clothing who, while appearing to stray from common opinion through philosophical circumlocutions (=detours) and mental gymnastics (=pranks), still return to the tenets of common belief, which, far from rational and presuppositionless ideas, are instead the sophistry of a provincial worldview of a particular people at a particular time. Since they do not know that knowledge itself requires the sacrifice of the all-too-common spirit, that it requires being blinded by the terrible truths of life which the people cannot face, they remain bad poets who are easily wounded and consequently make knowledge a hospital for the weak. In their sophisms they find a contentment (=happiness) which is none other than a mediocrity of the spirit (=lukewarm water).[57]

In contrast, the beast of prey attacks all accepted beliefs with a thorough-going criticism which risks a total nihilism (=abyss) and replaces contentment with a dionysian glimpse into the intrinsic cruelty of life (=terror of the spirit). Free thinking is extreme activity (=hot hands, action) and extreme truthfulness (=coldness of spirit) brought together. Inspiration is not the neither/nor of mediocre enthusiasm (=voice of god from the people),[58] but a combination of voluntary will in the face of an apparently meaningless existence. (The sentence "it means little that spirit moves mountains" parodies I Corrinthians 13:3. The point is that it means

little if inspiration moves the soul; one must use the will to create
something anew from spirit. Throughout *Zarathustra* there is a per-
sistant motif of inspiration and creation.) Like the red-hot iron
thrown into water to cool (=spirit into pit of snow), the free spirit
is an agony of extremes which does not turn away from life.

It is an overpowering *will* that drives the spirit of the lion, like a
wind fills a boat's sails, and so the free spirit departs from the
mainland of mediocrity, leaving the uninspired ass to watch from
the shore.

Having more or less successfully "passed by" a number of dangers
on his way to the "Blessed Isles," Zarathustra pauses for an inter-
lude of three songs before he delivers one of the most difficult
speeches of the entire book.

9. The Night Song

Zarathustra's language is, from beginning to end, dithyrambic
poetry of a highly musical quality. Each section is built upon a set
of sounds, some of which are used as major and minor themes,
while others are used as point and counterpoint decorating the
themes. Each theme goes through a number of variations according to the desired emphasis and mood and tempo. When a
speech is read aloud, it takes on a beautiful melodic character
forming a complete musical unity. By varying the mood and tone of
the melody, Nietzsche achieves a staggering variety of affects, from
the dramatic to the comic, from the fugal to the symphonic. Sounds
which come to the fore as a major theme in one speech are found
as minor themes, or points/counterpoints, or are entirely absent, in
others. Thus the book as an entirety is a tone poem of great com-
plexity, a philosophical artwork which is not only amenable to music, but is *itself music.*[59]

Images and concepts occur following the same musical principles. An image or concept forming a dramatic major theme in one
speech recedes to the background as a farsical point in another
speech. There is virtually no image, tone or concept which does not
play each role at some point or another. Nietzsche's particular genius as a writer rests precisely in this ability to affect a perfect

transformability between image and concept, tone and idea, coloring and mood, such that his language takes on a life of its own, creating a symbolic world in which the elements are not flat, dead signs, but living, transforming, animated, purified, supercharged independent beings. This creativity within the language allows for a multi-dimensional interrelation between images which defies complete analysis. This achievement is the perfection of the romantic theories of poetry and philosophy as found in Friedrich Schlegel and Hoelderlin.[60] As an artist of the German language, Nietzsche has few serious rivals.

This section, the first of seven songs throughout the book, is one of Nietzsche's finest efforts in any work. While all previous and following sections have the character of dithyrambic poetry, this section in particular demands to be *sung*. What is more, this speech is a very important personal document for Nietzsche, highly self-reflective and supersensitive to the foundations of his own *psyche*.

The significance of the imagery in this section cannot be overestimated: Zarathustra here sings of himself with the imagery of the overman. That is, rather than the overman existing as an object external to Zarathustra, as the sun in Prologue 1, Zarathustra now *is* the sun. At this highly introspective moment, Zarathustra portrays himself at three levels: *eros*, pity and the will. Zarathustra's soul has an inner craving, something "unstilled, unstillable," which like a fountain or the sun, spills over. This is the giving of love which is the first level of his self. But like a sun that pulls its own light back to itself, Zarathustra also has the craving to keep what is his, rather than always giving love and never receiving it. The great danger to his solar superabundance is burnout through indiscriminate giving: his love is always endangered by *all-consuming pity*. Total absorption in the woes of the poor would rob him totally, leaving him with malice and revenge-seeking motives. Zarathustra would like for once to receive (=be night).

The third level of his self is *the will*. This is the basic drive in him which defines his being as abundant (=solar) rather than impoverished (=nocturnal) and which drives him to realization of his inner self (=maintains his orbit in space). One's innermost nature is un-

free: the stars do not choose their orbits, nor can a star choose to
become darkness, nor darkness choose to become a star. Zarathustra's inner self is the incomprehensible force of his solar will—thus
his craving for love, and his fight against pity, are driven by his basic
will. One's fate is not, however, a matter of foregone knowledge or
fact: one may die at the wrong time, have the orbit of the will dis-
rupted, or succumb to any number of dangers. Quantity, quality
and direction of the will is something not within the will's own control.

That this speech is autobiographical on Nietzsche's part is indu-
bitable. That this section is central for understanding Zarathustra
as a character is equally certain. But the (non)identity of the overman and Zarathustra remains problematic: Zarathustra's relation
to his ideal self alters subtly throughout the book. Nietzsche's relation to the character as well, is extremely subtle. In any case, the
Night Song is a particualrly firm foundation from which an interpretation of *Zarathustra* Part II may be built.

10. The Dancing Song

After the solemn, introspective and lonely song of II.9,
Zarathustra delivers a song of wit and playfulness, full of allusions
to the gods—a "dancing and mocking song on the spirit of gravity,"
his arch-enemy, who is the suffering and pitying Christ. Before his
devil (Christ),[61] Zarathustra is god's advocate—but his god is the
dancing, life-affirming, celebrating god Dionysus. Here closely associated with Cupid, Dionysus is the principle of life and
love—*eros*—in contrast to the christian, melancholy, morbid and afterworldly principle of *thanatos*.[62]

Within the lyrics of the Dancing Song, Zarathustra raises the
questions, What is life? and What is wisdom? The imagery and
concepts of his answer strongly recall I.18, and strongly anticipate
III.15 ("The Other Dancing Song") and IV.16. This imagery must
be analyzed along the vertical dimension of the metaphoric space-
time. Zarathustra is a fish swimming in the sea of life. Gravity is a
force that causes him to sink into melancholy: it is the tendency to
experience life as something profound, mysterious and serious

(=unfathomable). Wisdom is a woman who raises Zarathustra out of his melancholy with the irresistable lure of higher values (=golden fishing rod). This wisdom is an uplifting light-heartedness and mockery who seduces Zarathustra out of his meloncholia: she mocks his grave sinking into deep waters, reminding him that real wisdom is an ever-changing, playful surface water of appearance—a reflection of the surface of life. The seductiveness of her appearance, her sarcasm (=laugh) and changability from depth to surface, by blinking her eyes, lead Zarathustra to compare wisdom to a woman.

There is a second woman—life itself—who also seduces and lures with beautiful appearances, whose eyes change between deep and engrossing (=open) and superficial (=closed). But the two women do not merely resemble another: Life is the surface reflection of the fisherwoman Wisdom. That is, there is only Wisdom and her reflection—but Wisdom herself is only a changing, playful appearance. When Zarathustra talks with Life and Wisdom, he is always raised to the playful, ever-changing and beautiful "appearance of appearances."[63] And this is precisely to be pulled from the spirit of gravity. But whenever Wisdom/Life opens her eyes, Zarathustra is fooled into seeing a depth to her soul deeper than the surface, and so sinks into a feeling of the unfathomable. What Wisdom/Life can say about herself, Zarathustra is not allowed to tell her: when he does so, he disturbs the surface, i.e, opens her eyes. Once the reflection is rippled and splashed, feelings of depth and shallowness return.

When the dance is over, and the sun— the golden lure that fishes him from the depths—vanishes, Zarathustra's wisdom leaves him, and he sinks again into melancholy. Death-oriented thoughts of gravity from I.21 return to him and he contemplates whether or not the "right time to die" has passed him by. Something unfathomable (=unknown, moist, chilling, thoughtful) floods in around him and washes his wisdom away. But when Zarathustra loses his wisdom, he also loses his pride:[64] and so Zarathustra sadly begs the pardon of his friends that his solar will to give joy has left him now that evening has come.

11. The Tomb Song[65]

Autonomous creation of personal ideals and values is perhaps the centralmost concern of *Zarathustra*. In the Prologue, the basic alternative between creation of a personal ideal (=overman) or contentment in idleness and nihilism (=last man) was powerfully stated. Part I as a whole concerns the dangers of those who would attempt to fulfill their ideals (=those who cross over). Part II considers the dangers of loneliness and the psychological dynamics between those who are spiritually impoverished to the point of always having to *receive* values. Though it manifests itself in a wide variety of forms, one basic dynamic of the giving/receiving relationship is a purposive undermining of the values given, by those who are subordinated to receive. Zarathustra's own depth psychology contained in the songs of Part II reveals that his greatest fear is loss of self-control in revenge and bitterness, should the small man ever suceed in breaking his spirit. The Tomb Song is a reaffirmation of his own will power in the very presence of his previously broken ideals.

Zarathustra's former values are like the highest values of Nietzsche's own youthful idealism and enthusiasm. Now they lie in his irretrievable personal history (=tombs of youth), unrevivable as highest goals. But though his esteeming of them as highest is a lost possession (=once I possessed you), Zarathustra himself currently is, and forever will be, their fruition (=you still possess me). The evolution of the inner self toward an ideal is a chain of selves and ideals to be worked through:[66] though estimation of particulars will change, the esteeming powers of the strong individual survive their passing away.

Since life esteems the highest goods above life itself, the purposive devaluation of another's values is a greater wrong than murder of the esteemer. (This anticipates II.12.) Those petty fault-finders, No-sayers and detractors among the "good and just" murder the spirit and kidnap values in spiritual crimes of greater magnitude than those concerning property.

Zarathustra then goes through a list of such crimes committed against him, which are in fact thinly veiled allegories of disappointments and sorrows suffered by Nietzsche himself. When he raised the personal commandments "All beings shall be divine to me" and "All days shall be holy to me"[67] over himself in the period of *Froehliche Wissenschaft*, the "filthy ghosts" of christianity came forth from the moral indignation of his friends, causing him a "sleepless agony." When he sought to ground a revival of German culture in the aesthetics of Wagner in *Geburt der Tragoedie*, the philological owls, especially Wilamowitz-Moellendorf,[68] blocked his academic career, rather than giving him the hearty welcome he had expected. Further, from his closest friends broke out the *ressentiment* and envy (=putrid boils) of the small man, while his neighbors sought to foul the philosopher's path itself, even after his ideals had vanished.[69] Even once he had overcome all these affronts, and overcome his own nausea and revenge-seeking, his closest friends and family suffered from his "immoralism." Thus his philosophical companions (=bees) and his own works (=honey) were corrupted in his own eyes. Those who came to him as "incurably shameless, impudent beggars" were pitied until their parasitism brought his own abundance into doubt. And when he offered his thoughts to his fellow man (=sacrificed what was holiest), they, like Abel,[70] demonstrated their piety by offering the fatty and smokey gifts of Jesus in contrast. When Nietzsche was first inspired by the dancing god Dionysus, during his wagnerian period, Wagner himself (=my dearest singer) reconverted to a christian aesthetic (=horrible dismal tune) and became a melancholy christian (=gloomy horn). The *Parsifal* opera soured Nietzsche on Wagner just as his inspiration was at its highest. The Dionysian joy in him at that time was to deliver the highest parables of the highest things: due to Wagner's reconversion, this had to wait until *Zarathustra*.

How did Nietzsche endure such wounds?[71] Only through the will to continue, which has been celebrated in the other songs, and which will be explicated in the next section. His will is the unburiable: it bursts the rocks of his tombs, remaining unchangable and invulnerable like a spirit surviving death. Achilles was vulnerable only in his heel: Nietzsche/Zarathustra is invulnerable only in his heel, i.e., in his dancing will. Despite the deaths of his youthful values, Nietzsche/Zarathustra's youthful spirit lives on in the child-like idealism of the creator: the child will redeem the dead. The dead ideals sit in his soul like spirits in tombs, awaiting resurrection. Nietzsche/Zarathustra is his own Redeemer: he justifies his own struggles rather than looking to the Beyond. But only where there are overcomings are there justifications.

12. On Self-Overcoming

This speech, originally entitled "On Good and Evil," is the high-point of Part II and one of the most important sections of the entire book, for Zarathustra's ethical relativism is here grounded directly in his most basic worldview. This section comes at the midpoint of the book, if one counts the ten sections of the Prologue equally with the speeches. As Nietzsche's note indicate,[72] Part III is preformed by this section: Zarathustra overcomes himself in Part III as a parallel to the overcoming of man. Thus the doctrine here is both the generalization and projection of human nature onto reality, and of Zarathustra's nature in particular: there is a perfect parallel in terms of self-overcoming between life in general and Zarathustra in particular. This speech also stands in an important relation to the deep structure of the book: the doctrine of the overman, having appeared in almost every section hitherto, occurs hereafter in only four sections. The doctrine of will to power receives its most fundamental formulation here and will appear only once more by name. And the doctrine of eternal return, only enigmatically anticipated hitherto, comes to the foreground hereafter as the central notion of the entire book. Thus in a real sense this section is a continental divide within the geography of the text. (The most important sections to compare are I.1, I.10, I.15 and II.11.)

In previous sections Zarathustra had exposed the wisemen's will to truth as the will to power, and had admonished his disciples to reject religion and speculative metaphysics by limiting ideas to the thinkable and representable.[73] Under such constraint, thought remains an objectification (=smooth mirror, reflection) of human spirit without religious mystification and distortion, a human product rather than a glimpse into "the belly of being." As with "truth," so-called "good and evil" and valuations of all sorts are products of the human will to power. The value-giver and his dominating will to power seek to guide the course of human history by creating new notions of good and evil, and by then setting the new tablet of values *over a people* and its collective will to power (=river of becoming). Those who receive values act with insignificant resistance (=broken waves) against the direction-giving dominant will of the value-creator (=keel). The people who flow passively through the currents of human history are thus not the real dangers for the value-giver, but rather the danger comes from other value-creators, who also have the will to dominate human spiritual direction.[74]

Zarathustra then grounds this ethical voluntarism (=my word concerning good and evil) in a presentation of his worldview. In keeping with his principles of thinkability and representability, Zarathustra portrays his most fundamental view of reality by analogy to himself. In a note from the *Zarathustra* notebooks, Nietzsche writes, "Nature must be represented according to an analogy with man, as erring, attempting good and evil—as struggling and self-overcoming."[75] Precisely this occurs in the speech: in imagery recalling I.10, Zarathustra looks once again into the eyes of life and wisdom to discover life's secret; namely, that life is "*that which must always overcome itself.*" Here Zarathustra represents reality in man's image, for man is "something that shall be overcome." Man is the being that overcomes itself: he is also the being that sets the standards of reality, truth and value: thus when he interprets nature, i.e. the whole of reality, he represents it as *pure self-overcoming*. This identity between doctrines is clearly stated in another note from the *Zarathustra* years: "Man is something that must be overcome: that is the doctrine of life as the great self-overcoming."[76] This anthropomorphism of the universe is evident even in Prologue 3, when Zarathustra says, "All beings so far have created something beyond themselves." This self-overcoming nature of life is identified with a "will to procreate" and "a drive to an end, to something higher, farther, more manifold": Zarathustra's will to procreate is his striving for the "child," a "children's land," the "future"—in short, *a new man who will in turn create the overman in himself.* Present man must be surpassed and in this self-overcoming a being must be created that is the no-longer-human human.[77] The overman is Zarathustra's value which he attempts to portray as a *thinkable, representable* being.[78]

The dynamics of self-overcoming are codified by Zarathustra into three general principles: first, whatever lives, obeys; second, he who cannot obey himself is commanded; third, commanding is harder than obeying. (Nietzsche had developed a relatively systematized account of will to power, i.e., of obedience and command, as found in art, nature, society/individual and knowledge, in his notebooks as preparations for a *magnum opus*). While Nietzsche had some interest in pursuing the will to power as a general theory of reality, the basic starting point of *human* reality is never far away. The three general principles of power clearly reflect the nature of human society: there always exists a chain of command from which there is no exception—even the most powerful must *command themselves.* Those who cannot command themselves are commanded by others. Command is more difficult than obedience because in the struggle for dominance in the direction of man, life itself is at stake: those who do not struggle take no risk: those who struggle risk life itself. Thus it was that the Tightrope Walker risked everything, failed and paid for the risk with his own life. *The man who attempts to direct humanity places himself in command over the obedient*: when he places himself over man he becomes the meta-legal individual who "must become the judge, avenger and the victim of its own law." (Important in this connection is I.6: the Pale Criminal is the victim of his own extra-moral values, but fails to become his own judge and avenger. The red judge is an avenger and judge of a law not self-legislated.) In the attempt by man to *overcome himself*, man risks perishing, or "going under."

Just as the will to truth was exposed as will to power, so the will to *equal* power is exposed as will to *over*power:[79] those who serve seek to become masters themselves, whether by commanding those still further below themselves, or by stealing power from their masters. Will to power expresses itself in indirect forms (=*crooked* paths), as well as more overt forms. What life creates it will eventually sacrifice for an increase in power: as the tree sheds its leaves, so the creator opposes his own values.[80] Thus Zarathustra scattered the seeds of his teachings only to leave his companions.[81]

Life always seeks an increase in power, rather than mere darwinian will to existence, for Darwin's principle concerns what is already in possession of the living—but for beings to will more of the same is insipid: all life wants not existence, which it already has, but rather an increase in power.[82] And further, life esteems power above itself and therefore declares its end or goal to be power. This doctrine, though appearing in only three sections,[83] is by no means incidental to the deep structure of the book: with it Zarathustra "shall yet solve the riddle of your heart, you who are wisest,"—this riddle of the heart is the mystery of the eternal return. The notion of self-overcoming is in this section identified with the doctrine of the overman: the identity of self-overcoming, overman, will to power and eternal return is the task of Part III.[84]

Zarathustra closes the consideration of good and evil with one of Nietzsche's most important meta-ethical observations; namely, that the highest values devalue themselves. "Driven on by themselves they must overcome themselves again and again." Every value is a violence to what is deemed evil: the willingness to do violence in valuing is a sign of great hope for Zarathustra. The "hidden love and splendour and trembling and overflowing" of the soul in valuation is a sign of the vitality of human spirit despite its degenerative tendencies, and from it the overman will be created, breaking man's previous values like an eggshell. The creative child must first be the leonine annihilator and breaker of values.[85] By raising a new "highest good" over man, the creator will seem evil in the eyes of the believer in the old values. For those who see a new ideal, keeping silent amid the follies and precarious conditions of modern man is worse than destroying old values: it is a disservice to life and the self-overcoming of man to "sit still in a swamp" (—this image comes from II.5). Man's great promise lies in the future—all circumstances of modern man must be tested against Zarathustra's teachings, and if they perish in the test, then that itself achieves his purpose.

13. On the Sublime

A propos the last section, Zarathustra delivers a densely symbolic speech on those who, while having discovered sublime dionysian truths of life, have not overcome themselves through *an aesthetic justification of the world*. (The notion of giving the world an aesthetic justification is one of Nietzsche's most important and original ideas.)[86] The sublime are those warriors of knowledge who have discovered the "ugly truths" of human existence—mortality, need, sorrow—and strike a defiant pose against them (=swelled chest), but who inwardly harbor contempt and nausea at human earthly existence. Tortured by his pointed truths (=thorns), the sublime man suffers silently in the darkness of his own insights without developing at the same time a sense of the beautiful (=rose), and so he is called "the ascetic of the spirit." (This image of course recalls Christ and more generally the "spirit of gravity.") Zarathustra demands sublimity: in sublimity one overcomes the superficiality of the last man, who knows nothing of life's darkside and does not ask. But sublimity must itself be overcome by a sense of the beautiful: sublimity and beauty are opposite natures, the latter serving as a corrective and healing aid for the former.[87] The *merely* sublime man is both hunter and savage beast: he seeks to overcome himself, he remains the lion of the three metamorphoses (=tiger) without the ability to create an aesthetic justification of the world (i.e., become the "child" of I.1).

Though Zarathustra adheres to an ethical relativism, he overcomes the impass of undecidability between standards by an *aesthetic* choice (=taste). Between leonine sublimity and child-like beauty lies the aesthetic judgment. Zarathustra chooses beauty over sublimity as an aesthetic advance which ultimately achieves a moral force in the doctrine of the overman. Such aesthetic-moral choices are basically irrational and voluntaristic, but life itself is the struggle between standards of "taste." And where life resigns such struggle it invariably degenerates and perishes. As stated in I.15, a people who cannot value cannot exist.

The sublime man turns his back on his ideal of beauty (=sun) and shades his eyes with his hand. This shadow in which he lives is the dark, negative worldview born out of the sublime: the sun is the higher, lighter, brilliant essence of human life, when seen with a sense for the beautiful, especially the overman.Sitting in his own shadow, sublime man turns from the world out of contempt and can only strike postures: only when he *turns to face the sun* will he "jump over his own shadow" of leonine sublimity into the solar overman. Zarathustra would have man overcome himself by basking in the beautiful and earthly, like the white bull, symbolizing vitality, beauty and strength.[88]

The sublime man's leonine annihilation of values hangs over him like a shadow and therein he "grows pale": thus his persona, especially his bad conscience, is closely related to the "Pale Criminal," who is also idled in the lion-phase of the spirit. Zarathustra would likewise have the sublime man transform his entire essence from dark nihilism (=monsters and riddles) into creative aesthetic visions (=heavenly children).

The great-souled man has a gracefulness which cannot be created out of a brute act of will. While Zarathustra sees the nature of life as will to *power*, this power can, and should, be directed to *ever higher refinements and syntheses of drives in an elevating beauty embodied in the complete human being*. The sense of beauty born of profound sublime knowledge is not the tasteless contentment and happiness of the superfluous last man. Nietzsche held throughout his writings that artistic impulse is intimately linked to overcoming the horrors of human life: the deeper the horrors experienced, the greater the overcoming and potential for an aesthetic justification of life.

Those who are the most powerful are those who need to develop kindness to the greatest degree. Overcoming sublimity means the creation of beauty, gracefulness, affirmation, love, kindness, i.e., overflow: this self-overcoming creates the overman and an aesthetic justification of life out of a sense of the tragic. Those who are powerless (=have no claws) cannot be great in kindness and are merely "weaklings." Great goodness requires great sublimity: only those who have a great capacity for evil have a great capacity for good.[89] The "column" of the great-souled man, or "overman," rests on sublimity but strives upward into beauty,[90] and as he does so he must overcome his torrential passion, sublimate the will, harness his power into higher directions—in short, become "internally harder and more enduring." (Important here is I.5.) The highest column is the overman who grows out of the deepest sublimity (god's death) to beauty in an aesthetic justification of life in his own persona.

The image of the soul, hero and overhero (*Ueber-Held*) alludes to the myth of Ariadne, Theseus and Dionysus. Only when the hero (Theseus) abandons Ariadne does the overhero (Dionysus) appear to her. [91]

14. On the Land of Education[92]

Already in Prologue 5 Zarathustra had attacked modern man's greatest source of pride—his education—in an attempt to ignite man's will to overcome himself. Prologue 8 contained a highly allegorical parody of modern scholars in the guise of gravediggers. Zarathustra returns now to the theme of modern education and scholarship with the notions of self-overcoming and the overman still in sight.

Zarathustra was overcome by dread at the first sight of the future man, i.e., the overman, and sought instead companionship with the modern educated man. But Zarathustra's contemporaries are *motley*: they have no unity, uniqueness, inner drive, fruitfulness or self-identity, and so they borrow bits and pieces of traditions and beliefs from past cultures which they patch together in a haphazard fashion. The speeches of Parts I and II occur in the "Motley Cow"—that is, in a town symbolizing the spotted and dappled present circumstances and condition of man.[93] Modern man's "leader" is the Jester of the Market Place, described as a "fellow in motley clothes," who is not a genuine spiritual leader but rather a parody of real leadership. The Jester has no ideas of his own, but adopts a clown-like appearance with which he entertains the masses in a haphazard and violent fashion, as a replacement for real leadership.

The modern scholar is a patchwork of knowledge about past cultures which he substitutes for his lack of substance. Rather than a creative, fresh and original source of ideas, the scholar is the characterless gravedigger of stale thoughts and dead beliefs. What the scholar excavates he wraps around himself in an effort to appear substantial, but the gravedigger of the spirit is himself nothing more than a skeleton. Directly alluding to Prologue 8, Zarathustra says of modern man, "You are half-open gates at which gravediggers wait." The scholar is on the edge of human society, waiting for culture to die so that he may dig it up. (In Prologue 8 the gravediggers are met at the edge of the city.) By himself he is not active, but waits like a vulture for something else to perish—thus his *reality* is the *perishing* of something else.[94] Nietzsche had given up philology and scholarship early in his career and had warned against the overuse and abuse of the historical sense in his early writings.[95]

Zarathustra would rather live among the souls of former great men in hell than among the soulless contemporary scholars.[96] Even the most dubious aspects of his vision of the overman (=all that is uncanny in the future and all that has ever made fugitive birds shudder) is preferable to contemporary scholarly education. Though in fact impoverished and starved (=scarecrow, skeleton, thin around the ribs), modern man takes delight in his lack of belief and superstition and sees himself as an advance over all previous men. But his very motleyness ruins the credibility of modern man and his scholarship. Modern scholarship is a laughing-stock in relation to education in previous ages (e.g., Greece, Renaissance), when the *entire* person, *body* and mind, were cultivated to their greatest degrees of health and creativity: modern man is so emaciated and effeminate that Zarathustra can no longer take him seriously. (Zarathustra's imagery of a god making woman from the rib of man parodies Genesis 2:22.) By using so many allusions to Greek, German and christian classics in this section, Nietzsche shows his scholarly abilities while parodying scholarship. Nietzsche himself had been a brilliant star within the stodgy German scholarly tradition, but by coming into contact with classical cultures, he thereby understood intimately the schism between classical and modern education.

Zarathustra's real burden is not the stings of the small scholarly type (=bugs, winged worms), just as Nietzsche was not overcome by the swarming negative reaction against his work. Zarathustra's "heavy burden," rather, is the doctrine of the eternal return (—the major theme of Part III). The ultimate overcoming of modern education and man is progress toward the future and future man, i.e., the overman, who will justify the fragmented, impoverished and previously purposeless history of man. This will be accomplished only when contempoarary education is replaced by *a cultivation of the entire human being, perfecting and synthesizing his powers and drives to their highest extent.*

15. On Immaculate Perception

An important clue as to the targets of Zarathustra's attack in this speech is provided by its original title, "On the Contemplatives." Schopenhauer's ethics evolved around the notion of the intrinsic futility and sorrow of the will, and he taught that the will could be (partially) overcome only through suspension of the will and quietudinous contemplation of the world. Kant's notion of the beautiful centers on the disinterested contemplation of the pleasurable. Wagner's christian conversion was taken by Nietzsche to signal a rejection of healthy sensualism in favor of the contemplative. These three primary aspects of "immaculate perception" are synthesized in the following passage:

> To be happy in looking, with a will that has died and without the grasping and greed of selfishness, the whole body cold and ashen, but with drunken moon eyes.

The moon trope symbolizes contemplation: it sneaks about the windows of earth hoping to peek at beautiful life without touching her or exercising the will; its abstinence from the earthly disguises a deeper lust for life, resulting in a bad conscience and shame at its desires.

The choice of the moon as a trope for the contemplative is a masterstroke. When lying on the horizon, the moon takes on an oval shape which 1)allows for a pregnancy metaphor, and 2) highlights its deceptiveness. Nietzsche changes the German phrase *Mann im Mond* (man in the moon) to *Moench im Mond* (monk in the moon), highlighting 1) its ascetic nature, and 2)its deceptive qualities (i.e., the "face" formed out of mountain ranges). This image of the moon crawling about windows fits perfectly into the metaphor of a voyeur, or "lecher." The bad conscience of the lecher also coincides with the moon's feature of only coming out at night. Further, the moon is essentially a large mirror for the rays of the sun and thus 1) is totally passive, but 2) nevertheless reflects another's rays: thus it is dishonest and has a bad conscience. Having chosen two heavenly bodies, Nietzsche is allowed metaphorical space for expressing the contrasting relations of moon and sun to the "earth," which is a trope for the bodily, natural, material and sensual. At the light of dawn, the moon slowly fades from sight, "caught and pale." The paleness of the moon thus allows the connection of bad conscience between the contemplative, the Pale Criminal and the sublime man at a single stroke. "Daybreak" is further the title of an early book by Nietzsche in which he progressively, if slowly, dispels the influence of Wagner and Schopenhauer. Finally, the gender difference between moon (*der Mond*: masculine) and sun (*die Sonne*: feminine) allows for a linguistic deepening of the overall beauty and economy of this imagery.

Immaculate perception is the voyeurism of schopenhauerian willessness, kantian aesthetics and wagnerian anti-sensualism. As such, it is lecherous toward the earth and deceptive in its abstinence. In contrast, the sun shines openly and innocently on the earth and represents active will, creativity, joy in becoming and in earthly delight.

Underlying the multifarious oppositions of moon and sun is the basic dichotomy posed in Part II; namely, the contrast of giving and receiving.[97] Schopenhauerian resignationism forfeits the active will, which justifies the sublime through the beautiful. (The sublime man is the lion-like spirit who *receives* a sense of the sublime from nature without *giving* an aesthetic justification to the world.) Kantian aesthetics remains "happy" in the *appreciation* of beauty at the expense of active *creation*.[98] Wagner's asceticism rejects the bodily in bad faith and so remains outwardly passive while inwardly lecherous: it "gives" nothing out of principle but wants to "receive" earthly delight in pornographic viewing.[99] And indeed, the light of the moon is received from the sun, which is therefore the principle of giving incarnate.

The final title, "On Immaculate Perception," is a pun on the dogma of virgin birth fitting perfectly with the attack on Wagner's asceticism. Wagner's anti-sensualism was hidden from Nietzsche during the early 1870's like snake coils in a god's mask, deceptive in its playfulness and seeming divinity while fatal in its anti-worldly dispositions. The "curse" on the contemplative can no more create an aesthetic justification of the world than a sterile woman can give birth to a child. Immaculate perception is nothing other than emasculated creativity, just as immaculate conception is nothing other than barren procreativity; i.e., contemplative creation and virgin birth are both fanciful contradictions. Zarathustra's blasphemous imagery is "small, despised and crooked" words,[100] for he speaks of the truths underlying the lechery of "contemplation," but he will not, for that reason alone, avoid exposing the ugly substance of his past mentors and exemplars. In their stead he advocates a solar love of man which pulls even what is lowest in human nature to ever-higher developments and refinements without shame or bad conscience. This solar love is love of the overman. Innocence, beauty and love are themes within the concept of overman, as evidenced in I.16, I.17 and I.20. The purest will that wants to create beyond himself is the will to the overman. The counter-image of virgin birth is marriage aimed at creation of future man.

16. On Scholars

The speeches directly following II.12 hang together as a unity around the contrasts of creation/contemplation, sublimity/beauty,

bad conscience/innocence, receiving/giving, motleyness/unity, arti-
ficiality/reality, asceticism/sensuality and resignationism/affirma-
tion. Though the intended targets of each section may vary
radically, application of the same principles to divergent subject
matters allows Nietzsche to build complex and ambiguous images
in a metaphorical space whose real interconnections lie deep below
the surface of the language.[101] Superadded to his imagery are
personal symbols and rather esoteric allusions to his other works,
contributing thereby still another dimension to his style and
another challenge to the commentator. Zarathustra's speech "On
Scholars" is a relatively transluscent gloss on Nietzsche's own experience with academia, though its conceptual content does not depend on knowledge of this personal background.

As the tragic poet lies in slumber, the sheep-like scholar Wilamowitz-Moellendorf eats the Dionysian wreath of inspiration from
his head, and proudly declares Zarathustra to have been stripped
of his title "scholar."[102] Zarathustra welcomes his expulsion from
academia and is saddened only by his own underdevelopment relative to the man of the future (=child), who lives in a post-christian
era (symbolized by poppies and thistles growing on the remains of
churches).[103] As in Prologue 8, Zarathustra received no spiritual
food from the scholars and gladly left their ranks. (The Hermit of
Prologue 8 in his isolation, "burning the midnight oil," may well be
seen as a symbol of the scholar, in addition to previous identifications.) Like the sublime man, scholars live in their own shadows
removed from life (=dusty rooms): like contemplatives, scholars
lecherously gape at the vital and fertile (=those who have
thoughts).[104] Scholars grind out analyses (=flour) from the real
stuff of thought (=seed-corn), and when challenged (=seized)
they spew forth a cloud of lifeless quotes and syllogisms (=cloud of
dust). Their motleyness (=multiplicity) is totally removed from
Zarathustra's unified persona (=simplicity), just as the grind of
sholarship (=knitting, clockwork, mills, stamps) is alien to vital
thought. Like the flies of the Market Place, tarantulas, adder of
conscience, etc., the small-spirited scholar prepares his vehement
biting criticisms (=poisons) for those who might be vulnerable. In

building philosophical systems based on presumptions (=loaded dice), he shows a disingenuous *a priori* will to tyrannize.

Philologists of Nietzsche's time rejected him and distanced themselves from him by the publication of polemics and reviews (=built false ceilings) created out of revenge and hate (=all human faults and weaknesses), though his creativity exceeded their small virtues such that he towered over their triumphs even in his own errors. Inequality within human spirit, despite the poisonous protests of the small, is apparent in such elevation. As "one who would cross over," Zarathustra is in the position to call for the overman, though such expectations are not warranted to be voiced by those who are not capable of elevation.

17. On Poets

Zarathustra attempts here to deliver a speech on materialist naturalism reminiscent of "On the Blessed Isles," but is interrupted by a disciple who seeks clarification for the phrase "And the poets lie too much," from the earlier speech.[105] The disciple's challenge for justification receives a rhetorical retort aimed at undermining the rationalist presuppositions of his question. As should have been apparent from previous speeches,[106] Zarathustra's doctrines have their "reasons" in experience: his irrationalism embraces the opinions of taste based on grounds long since lost to memory. Further, since Zarathustra plainly involves himself in the "liar's paradox," a search for a rational account is already precluded: thus he asks the disciple in turn *why* he would *believe* in such an irrational wisdom and wise man. The inept disciple then falls into the critique of "faith" already explicated in I.22.3. After the agile thrashing of the disciple, Zarathustra uses the occasion to return to his criticism of the poets, employing throughout allusions to Goethe, Shakespeare, Homer and the Bible.[107] Poets know too little of life, and so fill their gaps with mysticism brewed from the irrational (=poisonous hodgepodge), exploiting the gullibility of the impressionable (=young females) and even taking beliefs from the superstitious (=old females).[108]

Poets further falsify their account of inspiration either in the *vox populi, vox deus* model previously attacked in II.8, or in the romantic notion of passive reception of "secrets and amorous flatteries" from Nature herself.[109] Images of beings hovering between heaven and earth are the dreams of the romantic artist, privileged above all mortals: the misinterpretation of such visions is the origin of poetry, religion and metaphysics. (The role of dreams in the evolution of culture is a persistent and major, if overlooked, theme in Nietzsche's works. See for example his analysis of the apollinian in *Die Geburt der Tragoedie*.)

In an important passage, Zarathustra reduces the creation of the gods to the experience of poetic inspiration: in the inspired *inner vision*, the visionary—be he dreamer, artist, poet, religious seer—*creates the gods in his own image* (=poet's parables, prevarications). In such experiences, the visionary undergoes an elevation of the senses to such an extra-ordinary extent that he interprets the vision as supersensible, or from the "realm of the clouds." That is, the experience is taken to be verific, yet not of *this* world.[110] Within the realm of the supernatural, the visionary places the superhuman being: "upon these we place our motley bastards and call them gods and overmen." The gods and overmen are *Baelge*, a word meaning 1) pelt of an animal, 2) body of a puppet, and 3) brat or "bastard." Nietzsche's selection of this word seeks to play on this multiple ambiguity: as a reflection of human nature, the gods are the form of man removed from his physical essence (as a pelt is removed from an animal) and superimposed on a supersensible realm; as a creation of man, the gods are puppets of man manipulated within the inner vision; as an unconscious falsification, i.e., being of unknown or disguised origin, the gods are "bastards." Only superhumans—images of the human subtracted from his essential body—populate the super-sensible realm of the supernatural. The gods, in short, are images of man subtracted and abstracted from body and earth to be refracted in the Beyond of poetry, religion and metaphysics.[111] That Zarathustra uses the term overman in the plural signifies 1) that it is a broader concept than his own ideal image of man, and one comparable with the idea of god in revealed religion,[112] and 2) that while Zarathustra is willing to parody his own ideal, a sharp distinction between his ideal and others must be drawn. Zarathustra is "weary of poets," because they set their ideals into the supersensible Beyond, whereas his overman is to be realized within the limits of body and earth. Both the religious visionary and Zarathustra project their ideals: the former however projects the gods into the supersensible, while *Zarathustra projects the overman into man's future.*[113] The imperfections of the dreamer, religious seer and poet are projected into fantasy (=become events) out of inner need (=at all costs); Zarathustra meets his creative need by envisioning *the future man, an ideal over man on this earth within this body.*

Zarathustra reduces metaphysical beings, poetic fancies and the gods of religion to creatures of inner vision. But returning to the beginning of this section, it is clear that the inner vision is further reduced to the material/natural: "Since I have come to know the body better, the spirit is to me only quasi-spirit." As one such inner vision, Zarathustra's overman is on par with the other ideations, with the difference that Zarathustra's overman necessitates the creation of a *healthy, sense-oriented* body. This becomes a reciprocal process: as the body becomes healthier and more aware of itself, the ideals of the individual become of greater service to life; and as man's goals become more closey tied to this life, the idea of the overman is thereby approached. Zarathustra parodies his own idea, because as yet it remains all-too-abstract. But the parody is comfortable since Zarathustra knows that *the future is a possible ground for the perfection of man, whereas the Beyond is not.*

Zarathustra's humiliated disciple becomes angry, because, from beginning to end, the master has used the occasion to answer a serious question flippantly. Indifferent to his disciple, *Zarathustra "gazes into vast distances" and becomes the visionary of the overman* in order to contrast his own vision with that of the poets, dreamers and god-creators. Like the others, Zarathustra has a vision. But his ideal is *the man of the future* (=tomorrow). The world of the gods and other inner visions remains mere appearance: these supersensible thoughts cannot *create* a god in *outer life.*[114] But Zarathustra's thought that "touches bottom"—i.e., the eternal return of the same—*can* itself create the overman. The romantics believe in fantastic ghosts and resort to obscurantism and mysticism (=muddy waters) to appear deep. (Nietzsche probably means here belief in the beautiful soul and spirit, as in the *Sturm und Drang* movement, as well as German idealism—Kant, Fichte, Schelling and Hegel. In connection with obscurantism, Hegel, among others, is probably intended.) In them, Zarathustra finds an attempt to reconcile the natural with the divine and uncovers only remnants of christian belief (=the head of some old god). (According to Nietzsche, most western philosophers, especially Kant and Hegel, retained remnants of christianity within their post-christian worldviews, rather than become totally secularized.) Within the shell of beautiful words lies the slimey intent of "the afterworldly" and "the despisers of the body." Fundamentally, the poets are givers who seek receivers and as such are of Zarathustra's type (=poet). But their vanity in appearance without depth of substance turns Zarathustra away from them. When their essence is revealed, they will be found out to be "ascetics of the spirit," the forerunners of the immaculate perceivers. (The image of approaching ascetics of the spirit anticipates the closely related section II.19.) Thus Nietzsche's critique of the romantics beginning with II.13 is brought into sharp focus in this section.

18. On Great Events[115]

This section may be divided into three sections: the narrative of the sailors, the narrative of Zarathustra's conversation with the hound of Hell and the final scene between Zarathustra and his friends. The sailors' narrative is based on a sea captain's journal Nietzsche had become familiar with in Italy.[116]

Zarathustra's conversation with the Hound of Hell is an anti-socialist, anti-democratic diatribe of no great importance to the remainder of the book. Therein, Zarathustra repeats his characterization of socialists and democrats as rabble-rousers and revenge-seekers mouthing false inflammatory doctrines out of an inner turmoil, who are driven by the will to tyrannize, jealous of nobility and religion, overthrowing the *status quo* without a substitute higher value. Zarathustra's preference for inner revolution is neatly expressed in the phrase, "the greatest events—they are not our loudest but our stillest hours." (This anticipates the title of II.22.)

The real interest of this speech lies in the scene in which Zarathustra reacts to the sailors' narrative. At first Zarathustra flippantly reacts by suggesting the sailors had merely seen a ghost, and then merely his shadow. (The humorous interjection, "I suppose you have heard of the Wanderer and his Shadow" refers not only to Nietzsche's earlier work, but also anticipates the titles of III.1 and IV.9.) Here the Shadow signifies the real difference between Zarathustra and his ideal self.[117] Since Zarathustra himself is genuinely mystified by the cry of the flying man, we may assume it was in fact the Shadow speaking rather than Zarathustra. Indeed, the Shadow knows that it is "high time" for Zarathustra to pronounce the doctrine of the eternal return—knowledge still hidden from the wanderer. This is the very first point in the book in which Zarathustra becomes even vaguely aware of a destiny awaiting him. The Prologue and speeches of Parts I and II now yield to the gradually dawning notion of eternal return.

19. The Soothsayer

As in I.2, Zarathustra listens to a "wiseman's" teachings of total nihilism and world-weariness, reflecting both schopenhauerian pessimism (=doctrine)[118] and christianity (=faith), which announces the coming self-devaluation of all highest values (=all rotten fruit), resulting in the resignation of even the most inspired (=the best) such that, even if inspiration (=fire) were to return to man, it would prove too powerful for his weakened constitution (=would turn to ashes).[119] Even man's understanding of the causes of this nihilism would devolve into superstition.[120] Man's values and capacity to create new values have dried up in this schopenhauerian vision, but man is thereby weakened beyond the ability to take his own life in the service of something over man. The question, "Alas, where is there still a sea in which one might drown?" strongly recalls Prologue 3: "Verily, a polluted stream is man. One must be a sea to be able to receive a polluted stream without becoming unclean. Behold I teach you the overman: he is this sea; in him your great contempt can go under." The "shallow swamp" of II.19 is the "polluted stream" of Prologue 3: both represent the stagnant and superficial conditions of current mankind. The "sea in which one may drown" from II.19 is also the "sea in . . . (which) your great contempt can go under": the overman is the goal in which those disgusted with man may sacrifice themselves (=go under= drown). The Soothsayer's question asks, "where is the overman?" Zarathustra's command to prepare a feast shows his confidence in the overman as a goal for which the weak may "go under." But the Soothsayer will spread his doctrine for decades until the end of Part IV. Thus for him, like the Hindu image of the living dead, "we are still waking and living on—in tombs."

Zarathustra is overcome by the prophesy in his waking life to the point of falling into a death-like coma, and when he dreams, Zarathustra symbolizes this defeat to nihilism in a nightmare in which "I had turned my back on all life." His dream is an allegorical vision in which Zarathustra himself is the living dead, "the best who had become weary of their works."

The disciple's interpretation, plausible as it may be in light of Zarathustra's speeches on life-affirmation, is incorrect in every essential. (The disciple's statement, "Your life interprets this dream for us" is, of course, correct, but the disciple's interpretation of Zarathustra's life is incorrect.) The disciple's interpretation ignores Zarathustra's own identification of himself as the night watchman and instead identifies the watchman as Zarathustra's enemies. Far from the "advocate of life," Zarathustra here guards death and weariness and their symbols (=marks of triumph =crosses): the "overcome life" which stares out of coffins is Zarathustra himself. (Here the phrase "Life that had been overcome" highlights the ambiguity between literal and figurative meanings of *ueberwinden* and *untergehen*. Zarathustra's figurative self-overcoming, or its absence, is given a literal symbolism in this dream.) The keys in the dream are not the rattling gloomy doctrines of the world-weary, but the teaching of the eternal return which will bring vitality to the over-man and will bring the last man strength enough to sacrifice himself for something over man. (The key of eternal return cannot be explicitly revealed yet as such: Part III is the struggle to bring this notion to consciousness.) The wind opening the gates of death is not Zarathustra, but rather a force outside of him: his own efforts to use the keys failed. Zarathustra's cry of "Alpa, who is carrying his ashes to the mountain?" is reportedly a scene from one of Niet-zsche's own dreams, which is tied to the terror of Zarathustra's own death and the cremation of his love for man in a great misan-thropy.[121] Nor is the coffin of laughter Zarathustra, but instead it is an advocacy of life which causes him to cry aloud and awake. The dream, in short, shows Zarathustra unable to overcome himself and in fact being overcome by a weariness with man and life. The starlight illuminating the Mountain of the Dead is not the promise of eternal return he *should* give man, but is rather a source external to him. Thus Zarathustra did *not* dream of his enemies (as per the disciple) but rather he dreamed of himself: and he did not awake to his senses and to himself, but rather he awoke in a daze totally out of touch with the dream's meaning.

After the disciple's interpretation, Zarathustra is no more cer-tain of its meaning than before: he remains distant and in the posi-tion of the weary and sick (=in bed). Only when the disciples lift Zarathustra from his bed is he metamorphosed and only then does he understand the dream.[122] As atonement for the nightmare, Zarathustra celebrates with bodily sustenance, which he wants to share with the body-despising Soothsayer. For Zarathustra has dis-covered a goal in whose service the world-weary may find the strength to sacrifice themselves; namely, the overman. The doc-trine of the eternal return is the test in which the overman distin-guishes himself from the last man. Zarathustra himself is not fully conscious of such a test: its vaguest outline has shown itself in a dream. *The dream's ultimate significance is the great distance be-tween Zarathustra and the overman: i.e., the dream is the realization that Zarathustra would fail the test set before him—a test he has yet to discover.* Thus the disciple's laudatory interpretation finds precisely the opposite meaning of the dream. And so Zarathustra shakes his head in denial, though in the long gaze into the disciple's face Zarathustra finds a reflection of his own unripeness and inability to interpret the dream completely.

20. On Redemption

Nietzsche's brilliant narrative style in "The Soothsayer" is followed by a section of equally masterly narration, sparkling stylistics and profound ideas. As does the previous section, "On Redemption" follows a rather involved path of thought and action, only to end by highlighting the discrepancy between Zarathustra's teachings and his own persona.

Like Jesus, Zarathustra is confronted with a group of cripples whose belief depends on the performance of healing miracles.[123] In Zarathustra's sophistical dismissal of the hunchback's plea, it becomes clear that the belief of the ordinary man means nothing to him and that he would leave the spiritually degenerate and mishappen to their malformations rather than go among them, as did Jesus. Recalling his strong attack on pity,[124] Zarathustra suggests that greater harm than good comes from aiding the neighbor. Suffering at least creates overcoming and spirit, whereas comfort is the condition of the last man. Far worse than suffering from loss of a single faculty is the absence of all but one faculty, which has been overly-developed, personified by the "inverse cripple."[125] Past and present man has developed with a single specialization as his goal: thus some have overdeveloped observation (=eye), articulation (=mouth) or consumption (=belly). Those deemed geniuses by the people may simply be overly-developed at reporting and reworking the ideas of others (=big ear).[126] The total absence of a human faculty is said to be preferable to the overdevelopment of all others, or so Zarathustra spoke to the cripples.

Directly after his pitiless polemic against the cripples, however, Zarathustra speaks to the opposite conclusion as he addresses his disciples. Now the great goal of man is his wholeness and the superdevelopment of all human faculties to their greatest extent—suggesting that the return of faculties to the cripples is indeed a goal for man. Once again, the fragmentation of man is lamented: like a battlefield, the history of man presents only partial human beings in haphazard array.[127] Consequently, Zarathustra's goal for man can be found only in the future, and Zarathustra himself can be seen only as a fragmentary and imperfect reflection of what is to come. And as such, Zarathustra can only provide a vision of, direct the will toward, and begin, but not complete, the creation of *a new man*. Zarathustra's many facets (=promiser, fulfiller, etc.,) have not been brought together as a single ideal that could be placed over man. Just as Zarathustra walks among man as among animals,[128] so he walks among them as among "fragments of the future." The future man—the "overman"—is the individual whose *every* faculty is developed to an extent that was achieved previously only through radical specialization and overdevelopment. The great sensibilities, spirit well-being etc., of previous ages of man would presumably be recaptured in a "One" that would thereby represent something clearly over the previous standards of human capacity, i.e., the superhuman, or "overman." (In a note to this section, Nietzsche wrote, "in the *overman* the You of many I's of millenia has become One.")[129] To see this complete human being, recalling the ideals of Renaissance and Greek education,[130] as the goal of the future man, one must be a seer, for only fragmented clues confront the student of man. (Nietzsche's vision of the future man should be contrasted especially to that of Feuerbach, Marx and Freud.)

The gruesome and tragic history of man's maldevelopment and deformation can be redeemed only if this history finds a *purpose*, i.e., the goal of the overman. This is the meaning of the section's title. Redemption for the christian means salvation by the Redeemer and justice (i.e., punishment or reward) in the next world: redemption for the buddhist and schopenhauerian means escape from the cycle of birth/death/rebirth through personal annihilation (Nirvana): redemption for Zarathustra means exertion of the will, thereby giving purpose to the sorrows of the world. The means to this goal can be none other than action of the will, for only by willpower is the ideal made into the real (="will liberates" the ideal).[131] Man's capacity to will is itself a faculty which has been underdeveloped and malformed, particularly through the unalterability of the past (=It Was), which hinders the will (=puts in fetters) by producing a fatalism (=secret melancholy) and frustration (=gnashing of teeth), reducing human drives to passive contemplation (=angry spectator).

The facticity[132] of the past puts an absolute barrier to man's will which makes the will wrathful and vengeful, striking out in desperation at all joyful and lively things. Here Nietzsche squarely addresses the psychology of the fanatic, for he discusses all those who would seek with one violent blow to reverse all time and order.[133] The ill will of the revenge-seeking fanatic is directed against him who does not share in the violent desperation of the frustrated. Thus he wreaks havoc with the progress of man. Within the human spirit fanaticism has taken hold and has spread like a contagion from group to group, generation to generation, corrupting the motives of even the greatest minds, and resulting in a many-headed dragon of "true faiths" whose corpus is the spirit of revenge. The "true believer" of the "true faith" creates a good conscience for himself by inventing a doctrine of "justice" and punishment aimed against enemies of the "good and just."[134]

Since the will is always confronted by the facticity of history, time presents a barrier to action and thus a source of suffering. The greater the will against this facticity, the greater the sorrow: thus the fanatic finds sorrow in everything and comes to consider the will and existence itself as sorrow and punishment. When the will to existence is broken, the result is an indictment of all existence with the judgment that "all things deserve to perish."[135] Schopenhauerian pessimism (the world as sorrow) and christianity (guilt of original sin) are expressions of such world-weariness. As in II.5, the world-weary long for a moral world order of punishments and rewards in the Beyond as redemption for the sorrows of the world. Man's desire to punish those who do not share in sorrow creates an image of eternal damnation: Hell is an image of the real soul of the "good and just."[136]

The facticity of history is irreversible (=no deed annihilated): since the punishment must fit the crime, the punishment for eternally unalterable guilt is none other than an eternal cycle of birth and death: this is the psychological origin of belief in cyclical concepts of time and reincarnation. Existence is itself guilty and its punishment is eternal return. The belief that "existence must eternally become deed and guilt again" is for the worldweary a horrifying image of endless sorrow. Thus their goal becomes a break in the cycle of birth/death/rebirth by cessation of the will, i.e., by becoming nothing, by annihilation of the self.

Though the past is closed to alteration, the future is open-ended and becomes determinate only through exertions of will. The will creates the future in its own image, bringing an *ex post facto* purpose to the accidents of the past, collecting the fragments of man and assembling them in a future individual.[137] But the will to power is a greater exertion than willing a unity and completion for oneself: it must go beyond affirmation of the self to the ultimate step of affirming all past events. This means to "will backwards" all that has happened as a necessary prelude to the present and to accept the vision of eternal return without the horror of the worldweary. Zarathustra's rapturous vision leads him to unguardedly ask, "Who would teach him to will backwards?" Thus Zarathustra is brought to the point of asking for redemption (=eternal return) from an *external* source. At the last word (*Ger.: Zurueck-wollen*), Zarathustra realizes what he has unwittingly asked. He closely surveys the disciples to see if they have consciously or unconsciously noticed the question, whose only answer is "Zarathustra himself." Convinced that they have not noticed his own fright of the notion (=pacified), Zarathustra makes an uneasy joke hypocritically excusing himself, and laughs. "It is difficult to live with people because silence is so difficult, especially for one is garrulous." Zarathustra means here that he has silenced himself concerning the eternal return *for the sake of the disciples*, whereas it is in fact out of dread of the notion that he is silent.

The sharp-witted hunchback[138] has noticed the discrepancy between Zarathustra's speeches to the cripples and those to his disciples, and asks for an explanation. Zarathustra's flippant retort is volleyed by a devastating question, asking for a justification of Zarathustra's hypocrisy, for the hunchback has understood Zarathustra's inability to fulfill his own challenge to "will backwards." Thus the mishappen hunchback has done what the hapless disciples are unable to do, i.e., stump Zarathustra and expose his own handicap.

21. On Human Prudence[139]

Partly personal apologetic, partly philosophical posturing, this section nonetheless underlines the most fundamental structure of the book.

Zarathustra's "double will" is the high tension between the overman (—solitude, loneliness, ideals, strivings, distance) and his fellow man (—crowd, friendship, ordinary life, comfort, overflow). His upward will is the drive to completion and perfection. The "glance which plunges into the height" is the terrifying vision of the overman in his *inhumanity* and *humanity*. Important to note is the contrast Zarathustra draws between the usual vertigo experience of the cliff climber (looking down, reaching up) and *"my* precipice" (looking up, reaching down). This double will is another trope for the high wire of Prologue 6 stretched between man and overman. (The imagery of this section recasts many elements of Prologue 6.) Zarathustra, like the youth of I.6 and the Tightrope Walker of Prologue 6, has become giddy as he looks upon his goal. (The passage, "You highest men whom my eyes have seen, this is my doubt concerning you and my secret laughter: I guess that you would call my overman—devil" is a gloss on the Tightrope Walker's fear of the devil.) His equal and opposite will is to "cling to man"—to find comfort in the familiarity, friendship and comfort afforded by real (=firm) man. Zarathustra's only movements—which structure the book's plot—are between the terrible heights of the cave and the comfortable friendship of the Motley Cow.

The great tension within the overman between seclusion and human community requires rules of prudence, lest the double will be broken permanently and tension relieved. The first rule of prudence is that Zarathustra allow himself faith in man, lest a misanthropic pessimism send him hurling into afterworldly madness.[140] Thus the higher man may occasionally be led into false hopes. His second prudence is to urge only the capable and self-confident higher man to self-overcoming, while not interfering with the "vain man"—the Jester and great man of previous sections.[141] The figures of mass political movements and popular culture provide a comedy useful to life, as a relief from sublimity.[142] When the vain man is threatened, however, comedy turns to tragedy for man. When the Jester is threatened by the competition of the Tightrope Walker, the comic figure takes on a deadly character tragic for the advance of man. His third prudence is to retain hope for man's capacity for *evil*.[143] Just as the childlike spirit requires a leonine phase, so those who would create the future man in themselves must be strong and "evil" enough to destroy old values. Present man's capacity for good/evil is petty and his domestication great. That Zarathustra not lose hope for man, he must be encouraged by signs of latent will to power. Thereby will he be able to fulfill his upward will without losing contact with real man. The final prudence is to misjudge modern man as those *capable* of a future populated by "gods . . . ashamed of all clothes."[144]

In the next section the double will is temporarily broken, as Zarathustra returns to his cave, completing the second cycle of the book.

22. The Stillest Hour

The imagery of this section was preformed in II.18: "the greatest events—they are not our loudest but our stillest hours." This section contains a great event for Zarathustra, because he accepts the awesome mistress' call back to the terrifying loneliness of the cave. Although his teachings have not made a great noise in the world, Zarathustra has planted seeds, and his inexorable will is already in motion toward his destiny, lacking only the mellowness to advance and withstand his most difficult teaching. Zarathustra's teachings are essentially mature and well thought through (=ripe), yet he is unable to withstand the overwhelming responsibility of self-overcoming (=he is not ripe enough for his fruits). In contrast to I.22, "The Stillest Hour" is a departure without victory, for Zarathustra is still unable to give his friends his greatest gift, the doctrine of the eternal return of the same. Sections II.18 to II.20 highlighted this inability, leading up to the disastrous meeting with the hunchback. Growing despondent in II.21, Zarathustra finally succumbs to self-doubts in this section and leaves in full retreat. Amid a wealth of allusions to previous sections and the Bible,[145] Zarathustra relates a dream/parable of impotence, dread, failure of the will and shame. The struggle to deliver the doctrine of the eternal return, more difficult than that of the overman or will to power, is the goal of the entirety of Part III. As preparation for this struggle, Zarathustra sadly returns to the cave and thus ends the second cycle of the book.

Notes

1. See *KSA* XIV page 295.

2. See Appendix 2 for clarification.

3. Other dreams occur at II.19, II.22, III.10, III.13 and IV.10. The image of the child and mirror in connection with dreams is elucidated in I.14. The friend is a rough mirror which reflects the self. The passage in I.14, "Your dream should betray to you what your friend does while awake" is a prophecy fulfilled in this section. Another important dream occurs at II.19.

4. For an overview of the programmatic direction of German idealism referred to here, see *Natural Supernaturalism* by M.H. Abrams, (New York: Norton and Co., 1971), esp. chapter four.

5. Kant gives a formulation of his revolution in the Introduction to *Critique of Pure Reason*. The copernican revolution in values is a recurring, if not central, aspect of the sun in its phases relative to Zarathustra. See commentary to Prologue 1.

6. See in particular *Religion Within the Bounds of Reason Alone* (1801).

7. The passage, "All the permanent—that is only a parable" is an inversion of Goethe's *Faust* II, lines 12104-05. A similar inversion is prominent in "On the Poets." (See also *Froehliche Wissenschaft* 84 and accompanying note.)

8. In a note to this section, Nietzsche writes, "The Empty, the One, the Unmoved, the Plenum, the Replete, the Not-wanting—that would be my evil: in short: sleep without dream." (My translation of *KSA* XIV page 296.)

9. As previously mentioned, many characters in *Zarathustra* are images of Zarathustra's former selves. See commentaries to Prologue 2, I.3, I.8 and I.10. The notion of former selves comes to the foreground in II.11.

10. The depth psychology of this section bears strong resemblance, and should be compared, to I.6 and I.19.

11. The most important discussion of this occurs in the second essay of *Zur Genealogie der Moral* and *Menschliches, Allzu-Menschliches*.

12. For a similar claim, see I.19.

13. See I.6.

14. See commentaries to I.14, I.16, I.22, II.1 and II.2. The image of the field cot is a direct opposite to the image of the sea monster of pity in II.4. Nietzsche's ideas on pity reflect his frustrations with his friends and acquiantances. Those whom he allowed into his confidence came to pity Nietzsche for his loneliness and often miserable personal circumstances. Nietzsche had become a pitiful figure particularly in the eyes of Lou von Salomé and Paul Reé. Their sympathy, however, was never accepted nor solicited. It was perhaps Franz Overbeck alone who approximated the friend idealized in this section.

15. Important later works on the priestly type include the third Essay of *Zur Genealogie der Moral* and the entirety of *Antichrist*; important early pieces include *Menschliches, Allzumenschliches* I Part 3.

16. For an extremely interesting self-report concerning Nietzsche's feelings about his father, see *Ecce Homo* "Warum ich so weise bin" section 3. For a rounded understanding of this section from *Ecce Homo*, it is essential to read M. Montinari's "Ein neuer Abschnitt in Nietzsches *Ecce Homo*" in *Nietzsche-Lesen* (Berlin: de Gruyter 1982), also published in *Nietzsche-Studien* Band I pages 380-419. Sister Elizabeth Foerster-Nietzsche's struggle to suppress this section makes fascinating reading.

    The textual passage probably alludes to Nietzsche's father, a lutheran minister, and to numerous clerical relatives throughout his family tree.

17. See also section 7 of *Zur Genealogie der moral*.

18. Naumann, Messer and Montinari agree that the image alludes to the fable of the fisherman. (See comments to II.3.)

19. The phrase *Huetten bauen* occurs at Matthew 17:4 in the Luther Bible. Jesus Christ is the monster of pity upon which the priest builds his hut (=church).

20. Messer and Montinari cite a letter to Overbeck (May 22, 1883) as the source of this image. The letter was sent from Rome. Nietzsche wrote, " . . . and yesterday I even saw men crawling on their knees up the holy steps!" (My translation.)

21. See I.2, I.3, I.4 and especially I.9 concerning *thanatos*.

22. For comments on man's projection of himself into god, see comments to I.3. Interesting to compare is chapter 6 of Feuerbach's *Das Wesen des Christentums*, "The Suffering God."

23. See Psalms 23:1.

24. Interesting to compare is Feuerbach's *Das Wesen des Christentums* chapter 27, "Faith and Love."

25. See I.10, I.17 and I.20.

26. See comments to I.17 and the passage from the same: "And as the world rolled apart for him, it rolls together again in circles for him, as the becoming of good out of evil, as the becoming of purpose out of accident."

27. See I.1, I.16, I.17, I.18, I.20 and comments thereto.

28. See *Jenseits von Gut und Boese* section 260.

29. See Naumann II page 49.

30. Kaufmann translates *Krampf unter einer Peitsche* as "spasm under a scourge." But *Peitsche* is straightforwardly "whip." The term "scourge" is a figurative, outdated expression for punishment in general. "Whip" is the only reasonable translation. In I.18 Kaufmann translates *Peitsche* as whip: perhaps he wants no confusion between the two. Messer takes the whip to symbolize self-punishment (*Selbstvergewaltigung*) without argument (see p.69). Naumann correctly sees this as a trope for compulsion (*aufgenoethiger Zwang*).

31. This refers to the sentence, " What I am not, that, to me are god and virtue." This is what Feuerbach calls "the negative condition" of the concept of god. (See comments to I.3 and II.2.) The term "counter-image" is appropriated here from from Naumann's phrase *das Gegenbild des Ich*—the counter-image of the ego. (See Naumann II page 47.)

32. Concerning this image Naumann writes, "And there is virtue as prudent, self-seeking, pedagogical wisdom *exercitum*, grave stupidity in duty, stiff, prudish, tirelessly meddling in everything" (see II page 47: my translation). Messer writes (p.69), "Others avoid evil only out of anxiety and call this inner inhibition—virtue." It is clear however that the image revolves around downward motion (seen previously as passion) *opposed by brakes*—inhibition or cognitive dissonance—which are insufficient to halt the motion, and makes only a big noise. The classical term for doing what one knows to be wrong is *incontinence*. Parodied in this passage are the incontinent who voice conscience while following a path against better judgment.

33. Messer (page 69) takes the clock to be the ordinary pedant, while my interpretation is in agreement with Naumann (II pages 47-48). Both Messer and Naumann agree on the regularity of the clock.

34. Nietzsche quotes Thomas Aquinas at length on the enjoyment of the blessed in the sorrows of the damned at *Zur Genealogie der Moral* First Essay, section 15 (*KSA* V pages 283-85). Many other examples may be found in chapter 27 of Feuerbach's *Wesen des Christentums*.

35. Here an interesting conflict arises. Naumann writes (II page 48): "There is virtue as composed waiting in swampy social conditions, as flight before the strong innovator, although oneself is the better. Here coincides obedience of the higher type to the prevailing opinion and slave morality, humiliation and cowardice." (My translation.)   That is, the swamp-sitting virtue is the cowardice of the higher type under the rule of the slave, in situations such as social revolutions.   Indeed, the threat of biting is associated elsewhere (I.12, I.19) with the socialist type, and small man more generally. This may well be another occurrence of what Brandes called Nietzsche's "aristocratic radicalism."

    Messer writes (page 69): "There are also men whose virtue means not to make a sound and give everyone their rights."

    The image of the swamp recurs in II.21, while the leech-bitten man lies in a swamp in IV.4. These sections confirm our interpretation (and Messer's and Naumann's) that prudence is not meant here. Precisely who is meant by "those who bite" is not ascertainable. It may well be that the swamp-sitter is prudent before evil, a theme of Part I. In any case, Naumann's interpretation seems highly plausible.

36. Messer associates this passage with the inspiration experience (page 70). Naumann writes (II page 49), "There is virtue . . . as cruel self-wounding, often only the working of aberrant erotic urges." Under discussion here in fact is what Zarathustra calls "involuntary bliss." This can be proven only later.

37. Self-development (Ger.:*Bildung*) is a major theme in German idealism and romanticism. See Kant, *Was ist Erklaerung?*; Schiller, *Briefwechsel ueber der aesthetischen Erziehung des Menschen*; Fichte, *Die Berufung des Menschen*; Goethe, *Faust* and *Goethe-Schiller Briefwechsel; Schelling, System des transzendentalen Idealismus*; Hegel, *Phaenomenologie des Geistes* et al..

    For an introduction, see Heine's *The Romantic School, A History of Modern Criticism*, Vol.2 and M.H. Abram's *Natural Supernaturalism*.

38. See II.2: "Verily, through a hundred souls I have already passed on my way, and through a hundred cradles and birth pangs."

39. See Karl Jaspers, "Man as Self-Creator" in *Nietzsche: A Collection of Critical Essays*, edited by Robert Solomon, (New York: Doubleday Press, 1973), pp.131-155.

40. Michelangelo is rivaled only by Napoleon in Nietzsche's esteem. The historical analogy is meant only impressionistically.

41. See I.11, I.12, I.19, II.7 and II.18.

42. See Prologue 8, I.7 (esp), II.8, II.14 and II.16.

43. See Prologue 3-5, I.5, I.16 and II.5.

44. See esp. III.12.19.

45. Thus the animal imagery in this and other sections. But see comments to Prologue 5.

46. See comments to Prologue 5.

47. The imagery of choking on nausea, caused by disgust at ordinary reality, strongly anticipates III.2. This imagery first occurs in *Die Geburt der Tragoedie*. See *KSA* I page 57.

48. As previously noted, Zarathustra's notions go through a path of development. The prominent sections of the development of eternal return are II.6, II.22, III.2, III.3, III.13 and III.16.
    The imagery of the eagle bringing nourishment to the hermit anticipates III.13 and alludes to II Kings 17:6 as well as Greek mythology. (See comments and footnotes to Prologue 10 concerning the eagle.)

49. In a note to this section, Nietzsche writes, "Purification from revenge—is my morality." (My translation of *KSA* XIV page 299.)

50. See I.15.

51. See pages 55-61.

52. Concerning swamps, see *Ecce Homo* "Warum ich so weise bin" section 4 (*KSA* VI pages 270). For the topic of revenge, see virtually all other references to Duehring: *KSA* V page 131: V page 310: V page 370: V page 406: *Will to Power* sections 792 and 1066 (as numbered by Kaufmann): letters to Gersdorff (16.2.68) and to Gast (23.7.85).

53. See *Zur Genealogie der Moral* II.11: *KSA* V pages 309-313.

54. See *Froehliche Wissenschaft* aphorism 143: *KSA* III pages 490-91.

55. See II.12 and *Will to Power* 1067, for example.

56. German: *Saeulen-Heiliger*. This denotes a martyrdom in the christian sense, but is also associated with Hercules chained to the pillars. It is important to associate the chaining of Prometheus to the Caucausus, as well. The allusions to the great heroes and demi-gods of Greek mythology at this section's conclusion are intended as contrasts to the Pale Criminal and "good and just man."

57. The sentence, "You are lukewarm to me," parodies Revelations 3:16.

58. *Vox populi, vox deus*. Lt. "Voice of the people, voice of god."

59. Nietzsche's own reflections on the "Night Song" occur at *Ecce Homo* ("Warum ich solche gute Buecher schreibe" section 7, on *Zarathustra*). My later comments on solar imagery are confirmed here as well. (See also Nietzsche's letter to Rohde on 22.2.84.)

60. For an excellent introduction to Schlegel's theory of poetry, see Rene Wellek's *A History of Modern Criticism* (New Haven: Yale Press, 1955), Vol.2. chapter 1. See also E. Behler's "Friedrich Schlegels *Rede ueber die Mythologie* im Hinblick auf Nietzsche" in *Nietzsche-Studien* VIII, pages 182-210 and A. DelCaro's "Anti-romantic Irony in the Poetry of Nietzsche" in *Nietzsche-Studien* XII, pages 372-379.

61. "The master of the world" alludes to John 12:31 and clearly names Christ as the "spirit of gravity."

62. Extremely important are *Ecce Homo* ("Warum ich so gute Buecher schreibe" *Zarathustra* sections 2 and 6, and "Warum ich ein Schicksal bin" section 8) and *Will to Power* 1052.

63. The phrase "appearance of appearances" is taken from *Die Geburt der Tragoedie*. See *KSA* I page 39.

64. See Prologue 10.

65. The original title of this section is *Die Todtenfeier* (Celebration of the Dead).

66. See I.17.

67. As Montinari notes, these two phrases are the mottos of the first edition of *Froehliche Wissenschaft* and originate in Emerson (see *KSA* XIV page 301). This fact escapes both Messer and Naumann.

68. Messer (p.79) makes the direct identification of the monstrous owl with Wilamowitz-Moellendorf without argument: Naumann (II pages 82-82) argues for its identification with philologists in general.

69. Naumann (II page 83) suggests these last two affronts occurred during Nietzsche's stay in Rome.

70. Montinari for once misses a biblical allusion. As Naumann (II page 85) correctly points out, the imagery of fatty sacrifice clearly alludes to Genesis 4:1-7. In christian symbolism, the smoke of a sacrifice represents the ascent of a prayer to heaven. The vegatarian Wagner used the story as an anti-semitic prop in *Religion und Kunst* (see Series Papier edition of *Mein Denken*, pages 388-89). Nietzsche's point is probably an anti-wagnerian parody; the reborn christian Wagner now offers his own fatty sacrifices whose smoke obscures Nietzsche's non-christian "honey sacrifice."

71. The question, "How did I endure it?" is a variation on Wagner's *Tristan und Isolde* (II.2). The parody of Wagner in this section is pervasive and pointed.

72. See *KSA* X page 522.

73. See II.8 (will to truth) and II.2 (thinkability).

74. See IV.13 sub-section 3: "Overcome these masters of today, O my brothers—these small people, *they* are the overman's greatest danger."

75. See *KSA* X page 495. (My translation.)

76. See *KSA* X page 579. (My translation.)

77. See *KSA* X page 202: "Let man be at the beginning of something that is no longer man! Do you want preservation of the species? I say: overcoming of the species!" (My translation.)

78. See *KSA* X page 137: "Create the overman, after which we have *made* all of nature through us thought, thinkable." (My translation.)

79. See II.8 (will to truth) and II.7 (will to equal power).

80. In this connection, see I.10 for sacrifice in "war" and I.21 for the image of fruition and death.

81. See I.22.

82. See comments to Prologue 3 and footnotes. Nietzsche is consistently anti-darwinian.

83. See I.15, II.12 and II.20.

84. See *KSA* X page 522 for identity of overman and self-overcoming.

85. See Feuerbach: "Only he who has the courage to be absolutely negative has also the power to create something new." Zawar Hanfi (ed.), *The Fiery Brook*, page 146.

86. See *KSA* I page 47: the entirety of *Die Geburt der Tragoedie* concerns this notion. The connection between sublimity and tragedy is given at *KSA* I page 57.

87. The dichotomy of the beautiful and the sublime was a commonplace in German romanticism through Immanuel Kant's *Critique of Judgment* and "The Sense of the Beautiful and of the Sublime" (1764), in *Philosophy of Kant* edited by Carl J. Friedrich (New York: Random House, 1949) and Friedrich Schiller's *On the Sublime*, translated by Julius A. Elias (New York: Ungar Publishing, 1966).
    From Kant's "The Sense of the Beautiful and of the Sublime":

    The sublime *moves*; the expression of a person experiencing the full sense of the sublime is serious, at times rigid and amazed. On the other hand, the vivid sense of the beautiful reveals itself in the shining gaiety of the eyes, by smiling and even by noisy excitement. The sublime, in turn, is at times accompanied by some terror or melancholia, in some cases merely by quiet admiration and in still others by the beauty which is spread over a sublime place. The first I want to call the terrible sublime, the second the noble, and the third the magnificent. Deep loneliness is sublime, but in a terrifying way. The sublime must always be large; the beautiful may be small. The sublime must be simple; the beautiful may be decorated and adorned. A very great height is sublime as well as a very great depth; but the latter is accompanied by a sense of terror, the former by admiration. Hence the one may be terrible sublime, the other noble. A long duration is sublime. If it concerns past time it is noble; if anticipated as an indeterminable future, it has something terrifying."

    Translation is from C.J. Friedrich, *The Philosophy of Kant*, page 4.

88. The white bull was considered most beautiful by the ancients (see Naumann II page 99). Peter Puetz (Anmerkungen zu *Zarathustra* page 293) writes, "*white bull*: embodiment of power and beauty. Perhaps also an allusion to the religion of Zoroaster, in which the image of the bull plays a great role." (My translation.)

89. This principle, which is basic to the notion of the overman, may be found also in Plato's *Apology*. See commentary to I.8 and II.21.

90. This is another occurrence of perpendicularity tropes. See commentary to II.7 for a contrast with tropes of centripetality.

91. The earlier image of "arm placed over his head" alludes to a statue of Ariadne Nietzsche had seen in Rome, though the imagery is inverted. The image of being approached in a dream in connection with a mirror may be found in II.1. For a brilliant analysis of the Dionysus image in this section, see Naumann II pages 103-04.

92. Originally entitled "Von den Gegenwaertigen"—"On the Contemporaries."

93. The locations and audiences of all speeches are given in Appendix II.

94. The sentence, "And this is *your* reality: "Everything deserves to perish" parodically inverts Goethe's *Faust* (I lines 13339-1340).

95. See especially "Vom Nutzen und Nachteil der Historie fuer das Leben," (*KSA* I pages 243-324). Another *Unzeitgemaesse Betrachtungen*, "David Friedrich Strauss. Bekenner und der Schriftsteller" (*KSA* I pages 157-243) concerns the "philistines of culture."

96. The sentence, "Rather would I be a day laborer in Hades among the shades of the past!" alludes to *Odyssey* Book XI, lines 489-91.

97. This theme was anticipated in I.22 and is especially accented in II.9. All speeches in Part II evidence the theme of giving/receiving, albeit in varying connections and to various degrees.

98. The kantian notion of sublimity has already been discussed in II.13: here the complementary notion is criticized. The sections II.3 through II.17 hang together in close association, as did sections II.9 through II.11. Thus the centrality of II.12 is once again highlighted.

99. See commentary to I.3, I.4 and I.13 on "despisers of the body." Also, *Richard Wagner in Bayreuth* section 7 (*KSA* I pages 466-472) is important for relating Wagner with the contemplative and anti-sensualist. Nietzsche indicates at

KSA VI pages 313-14 that *Richard Wagner in Bayreuth* is important for the understanding of *Zarathustra*.

100. Concerning the passage, "But this shall be your curse, you who are immaculate, you pure preceivers, that you shall never give birth, even if you lie broad and pregnant on the horizon . . . ," Naumann (II pages 113-4) writes, "The expression here is modelled on that of Mary's immaculate conception, thereby however Nietzsche appears to have shared the usual mistake that he relates this dogma to the failure of the natural reproductive organs, while it does not want to imply that Mary's creation is successful without natural conception, but rather only maintains that through divine grace the *peccatum originale* is wiped away from the developing fetus: Mary gave birth without the stain of original sin, which according to catholic belief is attached to every newborn." (My translation.)

101. Concerning Nietzsche's style and method of construction in *Zarathustra*, see Peter Puetz' "Anmerkungen," pages 280-286 in the Goldmann-Klassiker edition of *Zarathustra*, F. Masini's "Rythmische-metaphorische "Bedeutungsfelder" in *Zarathustra*" in *Nietzsche-Studien* Band II and Anke Bennholdt-Thompsen's *Nietzsches "Zarathustra" als literarisches Phaenomen* (Frankfurt, 1974).

102. The image of the tragic poet lying in slumber on the hillside comes from *Die Geburt der Tragoedie*. This image is picked up in the next section as well, and may also be found in the critical section IV.10. The ivy wreath is a symbol from the dionysian cults. Wilamowitz-Moellendorf attacked *Die Geburt der Tragoedie* in a series of pampletts. (See also comments and notes to II.11 concerning Wilamowitz-Moellendorf.)

103. See III.16: " . . . for I love even churches and tombs of gods, once the sky gazes through their broken roofs with its pure eyes, and like grass and red poppies, I love to sit on broken churches . . . . "

104. As Montinari points out, there is a striking similarity between this section and Schopenhauer's essay on scholars in *Parerga und Paralipomena*.

105. See II.2. See also "Vom Ursprung der Poesie" (*KSA* III pages 439-442) and "Dichter und Luegner" (*KSA* III page 510). Nietzsche attributes this phrase to Homer.

106. See esp. I.15 and II.12. Interesting is "Gegen das Christentum" (*KSA* III page 485).

107. Zarathustra has already made the following allusions. Goethe's *Faust* II 12104: "and all that is "permanent" is mere parable." Homer: "all the poets lie

too much." Bible (Mark 16:16): "Faith does not make blessed" (I Corinthians 13:9): "We also know too little and we are bad learners; so we simply have to lie." Other allusions will be cited as they occur.

108. The phrase "much that is indescribable was accomplished there" alludes to *Faust* II 12108-9: the phrase "that is what we ourselves call the Eternal-Feminine in us" alludes to *Faust* II 12110. The imagery of magical potions alludes to the many elixirs, poisons, etc., that play a major symbolic role in *Faust*. Goethe's tragedy allows a unique mixture of superstition, poetry, christianity and the superhuman as a target for Nietzsche's parodies. In this section the entire *chorus mysterius* is parodied.

Yet Roger Hollinrake (*Nietzsche, Wagner and the Philosophy of Pessimism* page 155) claims the parody is superficially aimed at Goethe, and hits Wagner instead. Hollinrake's arguments and evidence are unconvincing, and he himself retreats to the more measured claim that Wagner is included in the attack.

109. Nietzsche probably means Hegel in connection with the phrase *vox populi vox deus*; one example of the romantic model is Schiller's *On Naive and Sentimental Poetry*, translated by Julius A. Elias (New York: Ungar Press, 1966).

110. The role of misinterpretation of the poetic inspiration experience in the creation of superhuman fantasies is explored in Feuerbach's works, for example, at *Saemtliche Werke* Volume VII, pages 262-63.

111. See comments and notes to II.2.

112. Ludwig Feuerbach provides an extensive analysis of *das Uebermenschliche* in precisely this sense in *Das Wesen des Christentums, Das Wesen der Religion*, the Heidelberg lecture series, et al.. Nietzsche may have been aware of this analysis as early as 1865.

113. Extremely important here is *Zur Genealogie der Moral* II 24 (*KSA* V 335-36).

114. See II.2.

115. The original title of this section was "On the Firehound." Closely related sections are Prologue 6, I.11, II.6, and II.7.

116. C.G. Jung discovered this source in 1901. (See *Psychiatrische Studien*, Zuerich/Stuttgart 1966 page 92. See also Charles Adler's *Nietzsche, sa vie et sa pensee*, Paris 1958 Vol.III page 258f) The sea captain's journal is *Blaetter aus Prevost* by Justinius Kerner. My translation of Kerner's entry, as found reprinted in *KSA* XIV page 305, follows: "The four captains and a business man, Mr. Bell, went ashore to shoot rabbits. At 3:00 they called their party

together, in order to board their ship, when they saw to their inexpressible astonishment two men appear, who flew past them very fast through the air. One was dressed in black, the other had gray on, they came by them with the greatest haste, and to their greatest consternation, ascended into the middle of the burning flames, into the terrible volcano, Mt. Stromboli." Nietzsche employs the reworked story to return to the motif of mixed identities between the devil and Zarathustra.

117. See comments to II.13 for the resolution of this very important image.

118. The Soothsayer may be identified as Schopenhauer, as Hollinrake, for example, insists, but his *character type* is more important than a definite identity: this type is generalizable beyond the figure of Schopenhauer. Still, it is very odd that Naumann does not make the connection between the Soothsayer and Schopenhauer. The character of the Soothsayer reappears in IV.2, where his cry changes. Naumann (II page 138) identifies the cry as that of Solomon.

119. This ash image is separate from the image in the dream, which *does* relate to Prologue 2, I.3 and I.17.

120. Naumann (II page 138) identifies the "evil moon" "evil eye" and corrupt wine as images of superstition: Messer (page 91) identifies them as Italian superstition.

121. Concerning the nonsense word "Alpa," Naumann (II page 143) speculates the word is "probably an oriental cry, similar to Sela." (My translation.) Messer (page 92) writes, "Knocks at the door frighten him. He expects that someone is coming again to bury his former life (to carry his ashes to the mountain . . .); the "Alpa, Alpa!"—recalling the first letter of the Greek alphabet—probably occurs only because of the solemn side-effects thereto." (My translation.)

But Montinari (*KSA* XIV page 306) finds the key to the word: "Nietzsche related a dream with the words "Alpa! Alpa!" in the Summer of 1877 to his friend Reinhardt von Seydlitz: "Nietzsche related laughing, having to climb up an endless mountainpath in a dream; way at the top, just below the peak of the mountain, he wanted to pass by a cave, when out of the dark depth a voice called to him: Alpa! Alpa,—who carries his ashes to the mountain?"—" (My translation of *KSA* XIV 306. See also Reinhardt von Seydlitz, *Wann, warum, was und wie ich schrieb*, (Gotha, 1900, page 36.))

The image of carrying ashes to the mountain occurs in Prologue 2, I.3 and I.17. Fire is the burning love of the overman, whereas ashes symbolize a burnt-out love (=contempt) of man. The horror of the cry in II.19 is born of the terrible weariness with man threatening Zarathustra.

122. Here is another example of perpendicularity tropes (see comments to I.4). Here perpendicularity is not contrasted to centripetality, however, but rather to the horizon.

123. See Matthew 15:30.

124. See II.3.

125. This critique of modern man is reminiscent of Feuerbach's and Marx's criticism of industrial man. Nietzsche's critique does not connect the compartmentalization and specialization of man to division of labor and taylorism. Nietzsche's anthropology in general does not inquire into the economic, political or social basis of man.

126. Hollinrake (page 14) suggests that the ear parodies Richard Wagner, based on a caricature of Wagner by Gill (1869), showing Wagner hammering a musical note into a gigantic ear. Wagner's head was disproportionately large to the point of deformity, making him an easy object of parody.

     Both Messer (page 93) and Naumann (I 150) give an alternative interpretation of the ear favored here.

     As a symbol of overly-developed receptivity without creativity, the ear image fits squarely into the ongoing major theme of Part II concerning giving and receiving. The ear also could be connected to the criticism of poets, scholars and "immaculate perceivers."

127. Nietzsche was a field attendant in the Franco-Prussian war. One of his recurring haunting visions therefrom was the scene presented to him after the Battle of Woerth. Nietzsche, by his own reports, was haunted by such visions for many years.

128. See II.3.

129. Important here is a note from the *Zarathustra* notebooks: "The ego first in the herd. Opposite thereto: in the *overman* the You of many I's of millenia has become One. (Thus the *individuals* have become One)." (My translation of *KSA* X 165. See also *KSA* X page 430.)

130. The attentive reader will notice that Zarathustra's ideal for man resembles the Greek and Renaissance ideals of the physically and spiritually disciplined and educated man. Nietzsche himself recognizes the existence of his ideal in the past. Yet the overman's unique feature of affirming the eternal return finds no parallel. In the *Zarathustra* notebooks, Nietzsche seems to waver about the existence of overmen in the past. (See *KSA* X pages 181, 422, 581 et al..)

131. The thrice-repeated "Willing liberates" originates in II.2, one of the most important sections of Part II. The section "On Poets" is virtually a commentary to II.2. (See also III.12.16.)

132. The term "facticity" comes from Martin Heidegger and is employed here to mean the completeness, unalterability and irreversibility of the past.

133. See comments and footnotes to the passage from I.22.2: "Not only the reason of millenia, but their madness too, breaks out in us. It is dangerous to be an heir. Still we fight step by step with the giant, accident; and over the whole of humanity there has ruled so far only nonsense—no sense."
There are a number of passages in the *Zarathustra* notebooks to the point that the development of the overman is a long steady process requiring patience and disallowing radicalism. (See e.g., *KSA* X 482, 497, 524, 525.)

134. The term "true believer" is Eric Hoffer's, not Nietzsche's, expression. His understanding of the "true believer" as frustrated fanatic functions here *in pace* Nietzsche.

135. The passage "Everything passes away; therefore everything deserves to pass away" employs Goethe's *Faust* (I 1339-1340): "for all that comes to be deserves to perish wretchedly" (Kaufmann's translation.)

136. See comments and footnotes to the gravedigger scene in Prologue 8.

137. "All "it was" is a fragment, a riddle, a dreadful accident—until the creative will says to it, "But thus I willed it"."

138. According to folk-wisdom, hunchbacks are especially sharp-witted. Source: Messer page 95.

139. This section was originally entitled, "On Calculating Reason" (*Von der kuehlen Vernunft*). Important sections for comparison are Prologue 6, I.6, I.17 and II.22.

140. This is the meaning of the oblique phrase, "I should be swept up and away too easily." Zarathustra had previously lost his love of man, resulting in the adoption of an afterworldly madness. (See comments to Prologue 2, I.3 and II.2.)

141. The "good actors" of II.21 are strongly related to the Jester of Prologue 6 and the "great man" of I.11 through the generic qualities of 1) showmanship, 2) vanity, 3) entertainment value and 4) popular, mass orientaion. In addition to the figures mentioned, Richard Wagner is also almost certainly included, as he fits all the above categories in Nietzsche's mind. The vain man, when threatened, becomes "the mother of all tragedies": the metaphor of life as a

play suggests Wagner: and the pleasure of "looking at life" recalls the criticism of Wagner in II.15.

142. Tragedy as a "physician of melancholy"—i.e., as an aesthetic justification of life allowing one to "remain attached to life as to a play"—is the major theme of *Die Geburt der Tragoedie*, out of Nietzsche's wagnerian period.

143. Very important to compare is I.17 and III.10. The motif of evil and the confusion of identity between the overman and devil is a major theme throughout the book. For the connection of the higher man to fear of the devil, see comments to Prologue 6.

   For an idea of what is meant by evil, see comments to I.1, I.17 and III.10.

   Concerning the phrase, "many things are now called grossest wickedness and are yet only twelve shoes wide and three months long," Naumann (II 165) writes, "The phrase "twelve shoes" probably refers to one of the older civil punishments; and the sentence to imprisonment up to three months makes the distinction of offenses tried by jury from the crimes refered to a judge, according to German law." (My translation.) Montinari (*KSA* X 307) accepts this interpretation: Messer remains mute. Of course the combination of length and feet is intended to conjure images of a great dragon, in keeping with the previous imagery. If Naumann is correct about the length of jail sentences, then the image of "twelve shoes wide" may well refer to the space occupied during this time, i.e., the jail cell itself.

   Concerning evil and its symbols, Nietzsche's use of animal imagery is somewhat uneven, taking species from India, North America and the Middle East. The lesser animals (=toads, wildcats, snakes) represent man's relatively domesticated and diminutive nature. The more dangerous beasts (=crocodiles, tigers, dragons) symbolize man's increased capacity for *evil*. The image of "hunter and overdragon" probably refers to Wagner's *Siegfried*. For Nietzsche's use of snake imagery, see comments and sources in footnotes to Prologue 10.

144. This image comes directly from I.14. Kaufmann in his mini-notes seems to miss the existence of this fourth prudence, though this hardly seems possible. (Viking Press edition of *Zarathustra* page 82).

145. *Allusions to previous sections*: Zarathustra as bear (Prologue 2), the stillest hours (II.8), valleys/peaks (I.6), teachings as dew (II.7), commanding/obeying (II.12), lion's voice of commanding (I.1), overman as shadow (II.15), child without shame (I.1), overcoming youth (I.21), tearing laughter (II.19) and teachings as seeds (II.1).

   Allusions to Bible: See Deuteronomy 15:7, Matthew 3:11, Exodus 4:10 and John 16:12.

   There are as well a large number of *allusions to later passages*, especially Part IV. Special sections to compare with II.22 are I.6, I.21, II.20, II.21 and Prologue 6.

Prefatory Remarks to Part III

After completing Part II, Nietzsche travelled to visit his scattered friends and then sojourned for the winter in Nizza.[1] There he wrote Part III, in January, 1884, during a short spurt of creativity and "involuntary bliss." This brief respite from problems with his anti-semitic sister and publishers (Fritzsch and then Schmeitzner) afforded Nietzsche sufficient time to pen another Part for *Zarathustra* (in a mere ten days). Further, Nietzsche's famous relationship with Paul Reé and Lou Salomé was to take a sudden, disintegrative and final turn during this time of great personal woes. True to his message, Nietzsche suceeded in creating one of the finest pieces of philosophical literature while confronted with his greatest personal challenges.

Part III builds directly upon the major themes of the Prologue and first two Parts. Zarathustra is "one who crosses over" to the overman. Thus he faces all the dangers to the higher man detailed in Parts I and II. Further, *he must summon, master and survive the doctrine of the eternal return of the same.* This notion is discernible as early as the Prologue,[2] and rises triumphant in "The Drunken Song" at the book's end. Thus the eternal return is the "central concept" not only of Part III, but also of the book in its entirety.[3] Everything hitherto, in a sense, has merely led to the Part at hand.

Zarathustra's trials and tribulations do not end with Part III, however: once he has succeeded in his quest to command the notion of eternal return, Zarathustra is tempted by pity in Part IV, threatening his gains. And indeed, it is not enough that Zarathustra summons, masters and survives the doctrine, for he must also *teach* it. This does not transpire until IV.19. Part IV, then, must be seen as ultimately decisive to the elucidation of Part III.

It is very important to note that the doctrine of eternal return is given in Part III in several versions by Zarathustra and in several versions by the animals.[4] Later, in Part IV, one of the higher men formulates his own version of the notion as well.[5] Thus the notion only gradually unfolds throughout Parts III and IV. *My final interpretation of the notion therefore does not occur until the penultimate moment of the book*, i.e., "The Drunken Song." It is only there that any "finalized" version may be rendered.

Notes

1. A moment's reflection shows the similarity between Nietzsche's actions and those of Zarathustra in Part II.

2. See comments to Prologue 10.

3. See *KSA* VI page 335.

4. See Part III sections 2, 13 and 16. An abbreviated account of the action in Part III is given in Appendix I.

5. See IV.19.

Commentary to Part III

You look up when you feel the need
for elevation. And I look down because I am elevated. Who among you
can laugh and be elevated at the
same time? Whoever climbs the highest
mountains laughs at all tragic plays
and tragic seriousness.

(Part I sec.7)

Part III

1. The Wanderer[1]

In broadest outline, Zarathustra's life may be divided into nine phases.[2] With the beginning of Part III we enter into the penultimate phase, i.e., his struggle after the doctrine of the eternal return of the same. A last phase will occur in Part IV when Zarathustra consolidates his victory by surviving the final temptation of pity.

"The Wanderer" finds Zarathustra completely confident and conscious of his destiny to affirm "the eternal return of the same." This doctrine, the "basic idea of the work,"[3] is the recognition and affirmation of the perpetual recreation of the lowest elements in man.[4] Zarathustra's second phase created the ashes of extinguished love for man: the overman however rekindles the flame of humanism only for the highest elements in humanity. Zarathustra, having gone among the lowest examples of mankind (—the rabble, priests, pitiers, etc.,), has proven his mettle, but has not restored his original humanism. The "eternal return" marks the greatest maturity of an idealism: love of the highest without disgust, *ressentiment* or will to the destruction of the lowest. Thus the greatest test of all is that Zarathustra stand at his highest (=peak) and yet reach down to the smallest man (=ocean), affirming the eternal meanness and sublimity of human existence. (This is the primary image of II.21.) The great terror of this journey downward is not the sorrow and misery of life, but its meaninglessness. (Schopenhauer's pessimism sees only the "sublime," miserable and tragic elements of life. This is easily overcome by Zarathustra:[5] it is rather the *small man* who represents the greatest argument against the value of human existence for Zarathustra. That man remains in his lowest element for eternity is the thought that brings Zarathustra, visionary of the overman, to disgust.) This journey involves the deepest loneliness and bitterest melancholy,[8] but its ultimate end is a justification of

human life. Hardness, not sentimentalism, is virtue along this path
to completion and perfection. Zarathustra's restless spirit climbs
and descends but seldom sits. A personal destiny now shapes his
every move and casts all things after an image of his inner essence.
"The time is gone when mere accidents could still happen to me."
This destiny is not a fate *from without* but rather the unfolding of
personal essence *from within*; or, in an oxymoronic expression, destiny is to "become what one is." This conversion of chance into
destiny was prefigured in I.17 and I.22. The solar Zarathustra casts
himself into the depths of undifferentiated humanity, an undergoing accepted with complete confidence, but also with *Sturm und
Drang* emotionalism.[6] Thus the stage is set for the notion of eternal
return to manifest itself in a surrealistic vision/riddle of Zarathustra's *psyche*.

2. The Vision and the Riddle[7]

An oblique mixture of childhood dreams, visions, riddles and
dark mysteries, this section, the most important since the Prologue,
marks the earnest beginning of Zarathustra's path to the notion of
eternal return.

Scene 1. On the sea-like level of undifferentiated humanity, separated from his friends, standing at his destiny's doorstep,
Zarathustra relates undergoing a surrealistic experience[8]—"the
riddle I *saw*, the vision of the loneliest"—which lays bare the innermost torments of his *psyche*. Among those who live dangerously, he
offers his riddle for interpretation. The image of sailors recalls the
value-creators of II.12, who sail over undifferentiated humanity in
the same fashion. Those on board are "higher men" in this sense.
(A riddle was also offered to higher men in II.19.) As the vision begins, Zarathustra is climbing the mountain path of despair and nihilism through scenery reminiscent of the dream in II.19.
(Similarities between the dream and vision include: climbing of a
mountain path; confrontation with a voice/figure; dread of death
and nothingness; a door/gateway; and emotional stress and loneliness.) Objectified as the small, noisy and annoying stones under his
feet, the small man is crushed by the spiritual progress of Zarathus-

tra. (Throughout Part II the small man was portrayed in imagery of pointedness, annoyance, distraction, triviality; e.g., spiders, thorns, flies.) On Zarathustra's shoulders rides the personification of nihilism and despair; the "spirit of gravity."[9] This figure tortures Zarathustra with the devaluation of all values—a nihilism that would bring all higher men to their downfall. (The leaden thoughts of the dwarf allude to the medieval torture of dropping molten lead into the ear of the unfortunate. This torture is portrayed in Shakespeare's *Hamlet*. The thoughts themselves are the nihilistic doubts, depairs and sublime realizations borne of life's dionysian insights. Their serious ("grave") nature would cause the downfall of the higher man, as thoughts of the devil caused the downfall of the Tightrope Walker in Prologue 6.) Zarathustra's teachings would crush him as they return to haunt him in his imperfection. All those who would raise themselves above the lower man succumb to a grave sense of responsibility to ideals. All higher values created by the higher man, however, devalue themselves and fall victim to the nihilism of the small man. Zarathustra's "wicked torture" is not stilled by the thought of the overman (=dream), whose distance and abstractness create "a more wicked dream." (Mention of torture turning into dream anticipates the dream occuring in the next scene.)

Assembling his courage, Zarathustra overcomes nihilism in himself, for *courage to attack the lowest is itself the path to self-overcoming and to the height of the overman.* Though great overcoming is achieved only over great sorrow, human courage has raised man above all animals. Dizziness from the dangers of elevation (=abysses) is cured only through courageous exertions of the will. (This image returns to the figure of the Tightrope Walker and his dizziness in Prologue 6. Above all, the higher man must not become an object of pity in his trials. Compare Zarathustra's reaction to the downfall of the Ropewalker, whom the gravediggers refer to as a "dog.") All life involves pain,[10] and progress requires sorrow: pity stops before pain and sorrow and therefore before life. Courage overcomes pity and allows progress of the higher man. Without pity, the sorrows of life are not the focus of life, death is not feared, and the higher man raises himself above life in one motion to survey life as a whole, affirm its goodness and decisively call for its recurrence (=Was *that* life? Well then! Once more!). Such self-overcoming and elevation is festive (=playing and brass) and initiates the dionysian celebration of life. (The dionysian cults of ancient Greece celebrated the goodness of life and, in the myth of Dionysus-Zagreus, taught the cyclical rebirth of life.)

Scene 2. Zarathustra's final notion has been prefigured by verbal evocation of recurrent life. Thereafter, Zarathustra feels confident to confront even the most nihilistic elements of his spirit in a battle of wits. (This is the inverted image of II.20, in which a hunchback wins a battle of wits concerning eternal return.) Within Zarathustra's vision, his innermost awareness of time is objectified as a gateway connecting two lanes, one representing the eternity (i.e., infinity, unlimitedness) of the past, the other the eternity of the future. The gateway itself is the smallest perceivable increment of time (=Moment), serving as the reification of all individual moments, i.e., it does not represent one particular moment. Within the immediate Here and Now (=Moment), the facticity of the past and the inevitability of the future exist in dynamic tension (=contradict each other): the future threatens to turn the present into nothingness, while the past annihilates the entire future (i.e., all future becomes nothing as time passes, and all past becomes nothing in the future). The dwarf joins in the dialectic, disdainful of Zarathustra's apparent sophistries; indeed, admits the dwarf, past and future form a circle within the present, but only in a sophistical sense.

Zarathustra then bares the innermost thoughts he conceals and espouses a fully articulated version of the notion of eternal return of the same. He gives two deductions to this purpose. First, since the past is infinite, all possible events must have been actualized, and indeed an infinite number of times:[11] the future is a recurrence of the past such that the path of time has no proper Alpha and Omega. Second, since all events bear within themselves their antecedent causes and consequent effects, events must contain within themselves the conditions for their own recurrence.[12] All events

that have occurred are possible events which are eternally actualiz-
able and which therefore recur eternally an infinite number of
times within the infinity of time, selfsame in every detail. Zarathustra is *not* suggesting that the same *type* of events recur, nor that
similar events recur, but rather that the *same* events recur. That is,
the immediate Moment does not pass away but is eternal.[13]

Though these proofs seek to establish an apparently cosmological doctrine implying the eternal existence of the self,
Zarathustra in fact wants to establish the infinity of the Present
without any such doctrine as personal immortality.[14] As a cosmological doctrine, the eternal return is taken seriously only as a
touchstone for those who can(not) accept the sublimity of life and
yet justify it in an affirming judgment of universalization.[15] This
universalization includes *affirmation of permanent death* rather
than a continuous self-identity.

Having given an articulate preliminary explication of his notion,
Zarathustra becomes anxious before the ultimate consequences of
the doctrine. His vision of dwarf and gateway suddenly changes to a
vision of deep night and howling dogs under the moon. Like the
Ropewalker of Prologue 6, the dog believes that what is "over him"
(=the moon) is supernatural and evil (=ghost and thief): the
overman (=moon) appears as the devil to the anxious and faltering
Ropewalker (=dog =Zarathustra in crisis).[16] As the dog howls,
Zarathustra pities him: this is the pity of the higher man criticized
in Scene 1. This terrifying howl, based on a dream from Nietzsche's
childhood relating to his father's death,[17] is the bad dream which
does not still nihilism, but replaces bad with worse.[18] The utter
dread of eternal return following Zarathustra's explication of his
notion causes a retreat into a subconscious projection of his innermost feelings. But his subconsciousness also provides an image allowing for the overcoming of his deepest fears of death and nothingness.

This image of overcoming is provided by the image of the shepherd locked in struggle with a serpent. The shepherd, has swallowed the vision of the eternal return of the small man (=black
snake).[19] *He who would create new artistic justifications for the*

world (myths, religions, values) is seized by a dreadful nausea at the eternal existence of the lowest elements in human existence; namely, the small man. Zarathustra attempts to rescue the shepherd (=himself) by ridding him of the notion *by force* (=tearing out with hands), but when this fails, he finds the solution in *facing and accepting the nauseating consequences of the notion* (=biting down). Zarathustra's entire nature (=all that is good and wicked) partakes in this affirmation in one yell; namely, "Bite!"

The symbolism of this section relates directly to *Die Geburt der Tragoedie*. Both the apollinian dream artist of Nietzsche's first book and the shepherd of this section fall asleep under a tree at noon to wrestle with dionysian knowledge of the world. Both characters create an aesthetic justification of the world in order to overcome this knowledge (the tragedies and eternal return, respectively). Nietzsche portrays Homer and Archilochus as falling asleep at noon under a tree, dreaming the tragedies which were later written down. The counter-image of the shepherd is to be found at IV.10, when Zarathustra experiences the beautiful without the nausea of the sublime.

Hollinrake[20] suggests the shepherd scene is a parody of the Siegfried-dragon scene in Wagner's *Siegfried*, or possibly Apollo and the python. The only similarity between the shepherd scene and *Siegfried*, dramatically or symbolically, is that both contain a human battling a serpent (—in Wagner it is indeed a dragon, not a snake). Apollo and the python is a better suggestion, and connects favorably with the apollinian overcoming of dionysian nihilism running throughout the notion of eternal return.

The final image of the vision is *the transformation of man into the overman*. As the shepherd breaks the nausea of eternal return, he raises up from his horizontal position to stand perpendicular to the earth, "no longer shepherd, no longer man—one changed, radiant, *laughing*!"—namely, the overman. Never yet has there been such an overman, but his image in Zarathustra's *psyche* gives Zarathustra a burning desire for his the overman's actualization. This is the sea in which the Soothsayer may drown, the lightning to set fire to the dry grass of mankind, the reason Zarathustra does not die a "free death."

Thus the three questions posed to the sailors are answerable for the reader. The shepherd is Zarathustra himself; the snake is the great disgust at the eternal return of the "last man" foretold in the Prologue; the overman is the one who bites the head from the snake of disgust. The vision, however, remains a riddle to Zarathustra, for his *psyche* has not yet allowed the deepest consequences of the notion to rise to a conscious level. The overman is as yet an alienated, removed, object outside of Zarathustra: the realization of the overman within Zarathustra must await the full and final pronouncement of eternal return and its consequences in III.13.

3. On Involuntary Bliss[21]

After the extraordinary events of III.2, Zarathustra delivers a monologue in the blissful, still cool of a philosophical afternoon. Though without great revelations, this monologue is important for interpretation of sections II.18 to III.2.

Reflecting on recent events, Zarathustra finds himself in the middle of his lifework (=afternoon), unrestrained by doubts and fears, blissful before the task, in an "hour of quiet light." The task in whose service he spares no self-overcoming, is the accumulation of companions (=trees)[22] into a future community (=living plantation, garden) —the fraternity of higher men he collectively denominates "the overman." Whereas such men have not yet existed, Zarathustra has found it necessary to create his own companions. So that these men of the future be individuals, rather than another herd, the zarathustran virtues of solitude, defiance and caution are necessary. When enough such individuals are cultivated, they will be brought together in the collective "overman." As a final touchstone of those who could carry on his creative heritage, Zarathustra must first prepare a "last test and knowledge," i.e., the notion of the eternal return. This "abysmal thought" is the weight the overman can carry, but the one that would crush the small man.

Zarathustra then clarifies in rapid sequence the most oblique scenes of sections II.18 through III.2. The mystifying cry of the Shadow in II.18 and IV.2 (i.e., "It's high time!") and the door/wind image of II.19[23] were both allegories of an unfulfilled destiny and of a ripeness to fulfill it. The corpses of II.19 staring at Zarathustra were the sorrows of the past, sleeping but not yet dead, buried alive, awaiting resurrection.[24] Thus all his thoughts, dreams and visions have called allegorically for Zarathustra to confront his destiny, be it his "going under" or not. But only when the dreadful thought of recurrence (=the snake of III.2) "bit me" did he respond. Though he explicated the notion under this prodding in III.2, Zarathustra is not yet ripe enough to teach it without dread: as yet, he *obeys* the thought, but cannot *command* it.[25] His "seal of perfection" will come only when he can wilfully teach "the perfection of all things." The men of the future (=children) "write my will on my tablets to contribute to the greater perfection of all things." That is, they raise his thought of eternal return to a tablet of self-overcoming through an act of will to power.

Zarathustra *wants* now to face the sublimity of life in its most terrible forms, and yet he experiences only the bliss of his own fulness. Like a woman, who is attracted only to him who does not chase her, so his happiness comes to him only when he does not seek it. (Montinari notes that the original ending to this section parodies the parable of Christ stilling the Sea of Galilee: Zarathustra desires rough waters, but finds only "smooth sailing.")

4. Before Sunrise

Still mellow in his "involuntary bliss," Zarathustra addresses what is "over him" (=sky)[26] in a monologue contrasting his own worldview with that of religion.

As a god is cloaked in a veil of beauty, so the overman (=star) is surrounded by the deep darkness of the night sky. Zarathustra stands under the dome of night and yearns for the overman with a desire previously reserved for the gods. In the darkest nihilism, the stellar hope of the overman lightens and enlightens Zarathustra's path through life. Like the night, Zarathustra knows the sublimity of human existence, and yet, just as the night contains stars, so his nihilism is illuminated by the stellar overman. In parallel fashion, the darkest message (the eternal return) contains an unbounded affirmation of all existence: the overman is in fact none other than he who accepts and overcomes the meaninglessness of existence by affirming the eternal return of all things. A pure blue sky symbolizes the "uncanny, unbounded Yes and Amen" within the acceptance of eternal recurrence: the overman is the man who "smiles cloudlessly" and thereby learns to ascend beyond good and evil. All moral concepts and judgments are clouds which *limit* affirmation: what one deems evil one cannot also approve. Zarathustra rejects the moralists' notions of good and evil and so affirms existence in all its reality, whether "good" or "evil." His spirit—objectified as the sky and projected "over" him—demands a clear, full, nonmoral but blissful affirmation illuminated by a single inner source of willpower (=sun).[27]

Since all things are to be affirmed as perfect, judgments of good and evil becomes a Yes-*and*-No-saying that puts constraint on the will (=clouds, shadows). Beyond good and evil stand *chance, innocence, accident and prankishness*. These are the new dimensions of Zarathustra's worldview replacing *purpose, guilt, contrivance and seriousness*. Zarathustra would fight world-renunciation and constraint in order to teach the perfection of each thing, giving man an example of what his relation to life can become. The instantaneous present is eternal and perfect, and consequently all things share in this perfection beyond good and evil. Judgments of good and evil are shadowplays casting doubt and dread over man's existence. Accident, chance, innocence and prankishness, as the ultimate characteristics of the universe, destroy not only the crushing gravity of christianity but also the panlogism of idealism and rationalism.[28] If the universe is organized only by *chance*, and all time is unlimited, then all possible events must eternally recur. There is no christian "providence," no idealist "endpoint of world history," no rationalist "purpose" for man's existence. Further, man has not been placed into earthly existence as punishment, nor is man by nature *guilty* of an original sin. Human volition becomes an innocence beyond good and evil, existence itself an accident and the moral character of existence, as a whole, prankish.

Zarathustra wants man to once again look upon life creatively and to give it an aesthetic justification. His own justifying myth, the eternal return, is not far from fruition, for he has already pronounced the fifth and sixth strokes of the "Other Dancing Song": "the world is deep/ and deeper than the day had ever been aware."[29] That is, the ultimate nature of the world is irrational, instinctual, random, hidden from the simplifying abstractions of reason (=day),—an insight Zarathustra finds in the dark and loses with the dawning of the small man's "rationality."

5. On Virtue that Makes Small[30]

Section 1. In his absence from the mainland, Zarathustra's teachings have been ignored, and modern man has become even more petty and limited (=smaller) than before. Zarathustra looks to the future man, "into the distance," and contemplates the reason for man's self-diminution.

Section 2. Later that day, Zarathustra reveals the ground of man's pettiness: namely, *modern man's doctrine of happiness and virtue.* The small man wants only to be comfortable and cozy—a "little happiness"—without care or concerns. His overcomings (=forward advancing) are trivial and small (=jumps), and so, like the Tightrope Walker, he is overcome by all those in a hurry. Many who have worldly pleasures nonetheless seek the afterworld as a goal.

Most small persons hide their own pettiness, though not well. The all-too-many are false and deceptive, either against their better judgment or against their will, in pursuit of happiness: they are disingenuous in every way, except as genuinely disingenuous. Modern man, without genuine expression of an inner self, is thus emasculated, cosmeticized, made acceptable, false and superficial.

In democracy, everyone becomes another's indistinguishable servant: the danger of democracy comes forth when the leaders become servants to the wishes of the masses—jesters for the crowd.[31] Justice, pity and civil virtues, without a higher purpose, become only weaknesses which make man petty: the bourgeois man relates to himself and others as undifferentiated grains of sand in a pile. The highest goal is simply that no one hurt them, and cowardice is heralded as virtue. Virtue is none other than not making waves. Man's instinctual, animalic nature becomes thereby not only civilized, but also domesticated—yet this is not to say cultivated, but rather denaturalized, stifled, impotent. In all things the eudaimonist and hedonist wants measure, for anything in excess implies a threat to happiness. Measure, though, is a euphemism for mediocrity.

Section 3. The small man's complaint against Zarathustra began with the latter's attack on bourgeois virtue and happiness: now the strife intensifies as Zarathustra is found to be an enemy of the faith.[32] Entirely without bad conscience, Zarathustra revels in his godlessness and asks only to become more so. The faith of the people coincides with their doctrine of happiness and virtue: in love of neighbor and the theological virtues lies the cause of undifferentiatedness, unproductiveness and noncreativity. Thus the content and mediocre man takes away from the future man by not expanding the present possibilities of man. Man has forgotten how to will for anything other than coziness: he must still learn how to will. Man's love of neighbor is simply wanting to be left alone: thus he cannot even truly love himself. Zarathustran love is for the possible, higher, future man, not for mankind immersed in creature comfort without deeper insight. But, as previously lamented, his teachings have not found their time, and must await "the Great Noon." At that time, the small, unproductive and unmotivated man will perish in a drought of nihilism. This "Great Noon" is an age of total nihilism that would scorch all but the most robust, resourceful and willful man, i.e., the "overman. It is the terrifying period in which god "dies," the last man "goes under" and the overman is "born."

6. Upon the Mount of Olives[33]

Primarily a personal testimony on Nietzsche's lifestyle,[58] this monologue also develops the two aspects of Zarathustra's persona—his hardness against severe, adverse conditions (=winter) and his joyful, celebratory enthusiasm (=solar will, sun, warmth). Zarathustra's Mount of Olives, in contrast to that of Jesus, is the winter mountain of snow, ice and wind.[59] Zarathustra "runs away" from the severity of the completely hardened personality, and yet he "runs *well*," for he retains hardness against adversity while remaining joyful and affirmative. Jesus, on the contrary, prays for a future peace in heaven.[60] This Mount of Olives represents a joyfulness in adversity, a celebration in the presence of challenges—in short, it objectifies the dual personality of Zarathustra.[61]

Adversity (=winter) rids Zarathustra of the petty complaints of the comfort-seeker (=mosquito), for the latter avoids the former at all cost. Where hardness is required, those who depend on others vanish (=moonlight is afraid of the night). Zarathustra also praises adversity for separating him from those who seek comfort and refuge in god and other artificial consolations (=pot-bellied fire idol). (The image of people rubbing hands together before a stove gives the approximate visual affect of prayer. In this, and in the preceding and following, section the image of prayer occurs frequently. Zarathustra's "grudge" alludes to Nietzsche's own physical reaction to humidity.) Though Zarathustra himself has small pleasures (=winter bed), he does not avoid adversity, and even seeks it out (=cold bath in winter). The warmth of the winter bed brings back good spirits to Zarathustra, revitalizing his malice against comfort-seekers. His desire for material poverty is most easily satisfied when he is faced with the hardships of winter.

The winter sky, an objectification and projection of Zarathustra's spirit, is the external hardness (=wind, ice,snow) hiding his dionysian joy and celebration (=sun). His inexorable solar will is the principle of triumph over adversity, overcoming in hardship. This duality of joy behind hardness is also the substance of his "bright silence." Zarathustra's insights are so deep that he need not pursue obscurantism to be profound. Words cannot communicate the depth of his world,and so his brilliance remains silent. Like ice water, his thoughts are invisible and silent, but deep. (This recalls imagery of Italy and Sils-Maria, where even the clearest of water, from the Alps, is opaque in its depth.)

In his cultivation of hardness and severity, Zarathustra does not avoid misfortune and adversity (=he suffers innocent accidents). And so his loneliness, material poverty and tribulations cause pity for Zarathustra within the soft-hearted comfort-seekers. (Nietzsche's friends, family, reviewers and critics took a very pitying stance to his lifestyle, which is alluded to here. Though of no great philosophical import, such remarks were occassionally included by Nietzsche, perhaps to communicate his true feelings to others.) Though this pity be anathema to him, Zarathustra allows the small man's indulgence in it and shows only his external severity: for to reveal the great joy concealed behind such loneliness would attract the jealous and vengeful.[35] Loneliness, alas, may be either escape *for*, or *from*, the sick: Zarathustra's solitude is the latter, and thus is not an appropriate object of pity. The concealment of great joy behind great severity is the cultivation and synthesis of great capacities, and is one example of the overman's deceptive "prankishness."

7. On Passing By

Nietzsche returns in this, and the next, section to the problem of *followers*.[36] Zarathustra's "Ape" has adopted some of the phrases, cadences and ideas of his exemplar, yet without possessing the spiritual superiority and insight necessary to understand them. Thus his wild diatribe against the Great City mimics Zarathustra's style to some extent, without exhibiting the direction and control of the master.[37]

Zarathustra is quick to note that the Ape's diatribe stands in contradiction to his actions: "if you warned me, why did you not warn yourself?" The fool has indeed become one of the reprehensible "scream-throats" he criticizes, and he does not take his own advice to flee the city for solitude. Zarathustra's question, "Does not the sea abound in green islands?" refers to the Blessed Isles: in other words, he asks "Are there not enough small groups of like-minded individuals with which to live?"

But the greatest objection Zarathustra lodges against the Ape is that the latter criticizes man not out of love of the overman, but rather out of wounded vanity and revenge. Not sufficiently flattered by his fellow man, the Ape adopts Zarathustra's words to level a resentful attack on man.

Very interesting to compare here are the figures of Timon and Apemantus in Shakespeare's *Timon of Athens*. Timon, from wounded vanity and a desire for revenge, leaves Athens for a mountain cave. There he foreswears mankind, finances an army to destroy Athens and succumbs to an all-embracing misanthropy. Apemantus, the local cynic, condemns mankind in every way at every opportunity, yet never leaves Athens and remains always in the company of those he detests. Apemantus' hypocrisy does not escape Timon's attention when the former seeks refuge with the latter.

Nietzsche owned Shakespeare's *Timon of Athens*, was familiar with it, and alludes to it in the published works.[38] Yet this copy contains no marginal notes and so a definite connection is unverifiable. In any case, Nietzsche's Zarathustra is neither Timon nor Apemantus. Zarathustra does not foreswear mankind out of nihilism. In fact, this is the very misanthropy that occurs *before* the beginning of the book.[39] Nor is Zarathustra an Apemantus, for he practices the isolation he teaches, and is no man's fool. It is clear that Apemantus has not truly lost his love for man. But Zarathustra is honest about his love and overcomes apemanthusian cynicism to arrive at his love of the overman.

This section serves as a before-the-fact condemnation of Elizabeth Foerster, who adopted just enough of her brother's stylistics to (poorly) falsify many letters,[40] as well as Alfred Bauemler et al., who sought to use Nietzsche's words to lend credence to Nazism.[41] Totally *a propos* of them is the passage: "And even if Zarathustra's words *were* a thousand times right, still *you* would *do* wrong with my words."

Zarathustra's disgust with the fool and the Great City reaches a pitch as he calls for the incineration of both—an event presumably tied to the great wars preceding the period of great nihilism called "the Great Noon." Destruction of the Great City as a precondition of the Great Noon appears here for the first time. The *Untergang* of mankind, as I have often pointed out, implies, in one connotation, the total destruction of the human race. Nietzsche had in fact predicted unprecedented wars: a great holocaust from nuclear war is one possible scenario for a period of great nihilism that puts mankind to the test.

8. On Apostates

Sub-section 1. Zarathustra's first companions were the totally dependent corpse and the violently opportunistic Jester.[42] But after the fiasco of the Market Place, he awakened in Prologue 9 to the necessity of finding proper companions. Though he felt safest among his animals, the "loneliest one" began to assemble about him a group of human followers in the Motley Cow, whom he left at the end of Part I only reluctantly, for the sake of solitude and meditation. In Part II he travelled from the mainland to cultivate new companions on the Blessed Isles.[43] With the onset of Part III, Zarathustra wanders back to the Motley Cow and to the first group of friends. Underway he finds that man has ignored his message, or has "become smaller," and that the Ape uses his manner and messages as a pretense for vicious attacks on the people. In this section, Zarathustra finally arrives in the Motley Cow, only to discover that the first group of believers have reconverted to the old faith (=have become pious again), seeking to avoid the hardships and responsibilities of atheism and showing themselves to have become "weary, ordinary and comfortable." Their thirst for a non-christian knowledge has vanished, and the courage of atheism derived from Zarathustra is now dissipated and even defamed. The disappearance of the "godless one" has created in them a fear of god and punishment,[44] intensified by Zarathustra's inability to offer anything as attractive as eternal reward. "Did their ears perhaps listen longingly long, *in vain*, for me and my trumpet and my herald's call?" Zarathustra of course does not intend to give such consolation. Already in II.5 the new disciples were warned that they still seek reward for their behavior.

Even among the radically atheistic there exists a majority who
are too weak, too ordinary, too cowardly to leave their faith decisively. His companions of Part I were seasonal followers
(=springtime, meadows) who wilted with the onset of adversity
(=winter).[45] Their reconversion, however, does not sadden Zarathustra, for those who are not strong enough for his teachings deserve no pity, nor does he want the half-and-half as followers. This
is once again an example of Zarathusra's unconditionality: he wills
that men either decisively "harden" themselves or "go under."

Sub-section 2. Some of the "reborn" are in good faith, some in
bad.[46] In either case, those who have discovered an intellectual
conscience at any time return to prayer in shame: only the ignorant
and uninitiated may pray without disgrace. The inner fear of retribution, however, convinces the weak that god *does* exist, involving
them in an endless spiral of irrationality. Piety seeks fulfillment of
wishes born of fear and meekness, not the dangers of self-overcoming.[47] For the pious, the mousetraps of emotionalism are set by
the Church. Organized religion (=trap) seeks to play on the deep
psychological wants of the meek (=mouse). Everywhere sects arise
to pamper the petty emotions of man and to dazzle his gullibility
with rite and mysticism.

Childlike innocence, nurtured by the pious, is the incessant
pleading for sweet rewards for faith, even to the point of spiritual
nausea (=upset stomachs). The pious man listens to evangelists,
who have material interest in the prosperity of the flock, and who
teach the cleverness of combining material and spiritual interests.[48] Spending countless hours attempting to glean wisdom where
none is to be found, the believer, far from profound, is in fact the
fool. Some approach religion as an indirect method of satisfying
earthly desires,[49] while others seek spiritualists and other charla-
tans in pursuit of the unearthly.[50] Still others become theologians
and pious philosophers who entertain ancient and irrelevant matters surrounding a god already dead.[51] The pious watchmen begin
with an anthropomorphic conception of god which degenerates to
deism, then scepticism, followed by pietism and finally cynicism. By
an inner logic, their highest value devalues itself to a matter of ni-

hilism and emptiness. This spectacle only humors Zarathustra, for their god is already dead, and their debates only remnants of the age of faith.[52]

The "death" of the gods came not as a great contest between Divinities and Promethean men, as in Wagner's *Goetterdaemmerung*, but as the effect of an inner logic resulting in the transition from polytheism to Judaeo-christian monotheism. This monotheistic concept of god is the *reductio ad absurdum* endpoint of religion.[53] "There is one god" is the absurd conclusion reached by all theology. That the entirety of all good and perfect things are contained in a single superhuman being residing in a supernatural realm outside of all materiality shows the complete poverty of religion: namely, its gods and afterworlds are mirror reflections of earth and body, selected capriciously with prejudices of good and evil.[54] Polytheism contains the truth that there are many goods in the world not assimilatable into one Divine Personality, not to mention one of such dubious moral character as the jealous, grave "old grimbeard."[101] The anthropomorphism of both mono- and polytheism show the further truth that the divine is in fact the perfection of *man*: creation of One Perfect Man is precisely what is *not* godly. What is divine is the human essence raised to its highest development, though this is possible only in many individuals. "Is not just this godlike that there are gods but no god?" This should be compared to Feuerbach's statement that precisely what the religious man has taken as god is *not* god, and what he has taken as not godlike precisely *is* god. Mankind, the non-divine, is now revealed as the truly divine. Thus there are many gods—but no transcendent Being. The humanization of the concept of god is the highpoint (=noon) of man's self-knowledge.[55]

9. The Return Home

After the two day journey from the Motley Cow, Zarathustra finally arrives at his cave and once again finds himself in solitude. Amid a wealth of allusions to previous sections ranging over the entire book, he summarizes his hard-earned lessons on solitude, followers and leaders, the dangers of crossing over, giving and receiving, virtue, etc.,[56] Above all he has learned that he is forsaken not in solitude, but when he is among his fellow man. With the full treasure of his insights assembled, he has reached the maturity to fulfill his destiny.

The line "consideration and pity have been my greatest dangers and everything human wants consideration and pity" warrants special commentary. From Prologue 6 the lesson had been derived that the higher man, in "crossing over" to the overman, would undergo a series of dangers. Here Zarathustra has already "passed by" the pitying (in II.5) in their various forms. Even after he succeeds in Part III, Zarathustra will undergo another trial of pity in Part IV. *Consideration and pity for man would keep him from his task, i.e., to use mankind as a means to something higher.* In this cause, man must be "overcome." Hardness in the creator is essential for the dionysian type: dionysian joy in creation of the overman requires a *No-doing* and *annihilation.* Pity would stop far short of Zarathustra's "hardness."

10. On the Three Evils

Sub-section 1. In a dream Zarathustra weighs the value of existence. For Zarathustra, like the Greeks, the world is finite, but time infinite: these are the premisses necessary for the notion of eternal return. Force (=number) propels the wheel of eternal return. Thus Zarathustra's upcoming message is preformed here in a passage otherwise out of place in this speech. Zarathustra finds the world, in a number of self-altering dream images, to be not only complete and perfect *in itself,* but also perfect *for humans* (=humanly good). The full, ripe cool, soft apple represents the perfection of the world in its finitude: the bent tree symbolizes the beckoning of the world to man, strong enough to support him in his deepest weariness: the shrine represents the world as a holy, sacred object relieving human nihilism by its very beauty. A complete evaluation of the world, though, would include weighing those features most often found objectionable by religion and moralities; i.e., sex, lust to rule and egoism.

Zarathustra's conclusions are stated immediately. Whereas sexuality makes the future man possible, whereas the lust to rule brings the lower man under control of the higher and whereas egoism is the drive for ever-higher development, these three "evils"—the opposites of the three monastic virtues—are pronounced virtuous (i.e., advantageous for life) by Zarathustra.

Sub-section 2. Sexuality is a torture for the "despisers of the body," the constant drive they cannot bear, turning them against all things bodily.[57] It is, in its pleasures, the sufficient refutation of the "afterworldly." To the pleasure-rabble, the "all-too-many" of humanity, sexuality is a consuming passion, a poison for those already wilted on life. And yet it is at the same time the innocent joy of life's connoisseurs, the ecstatic enticement of the future, refreshment for those who break the tablets of the good and just, a bodily parable of joy in creativity.

Lust to rule is the all-consuming passion of the power-insatiable tyrannt, fanatic and martyr, the collective madness of peoples and their opportunistic leaders, the disruptive force overturning all order, the malformed question concerning a master race, the will to tyranny making man slavish and subordinate, the gruesome cruelty turning man against life.[58] And yet the will to rule is also the drive bringing a new nobility to power as masters of the earth, the drive giving order and rank to the chaos of man.[59]

Selflessness—elimination of will and desire, denial of world and body, defamation of humanity—is the goal of the world-weary christians and schopenhauerians.[60] For such types virtue becomes death-like inactivity toward this end. The "good reasons" for this thinly disguised death-wish are fundamental weaknesses of the body making the world pain and sorrow.[61] The zarathustran man, the "powerful soul," practices a "wholesome, healthy selfishness" by the exercise of will, enjoyment of body and earth, and development of the higher self. This powerful soul requires "the high body," i.e., the powerful, instinct-rich, maximally developed body in touch with itself and in control of its desires as connoisseur, not as suppressor. Dionysian celebration of the praiseworthy self—"self-enjoyment of such bodies and souls"—is a new virtue Zarathustra sets over man.

Thus, in his weighing, Zarathustra has shown the three "evils" to be "humanly good," and has shown their disadvantages to be mere slanderings from the world-weary. Old "evils" are the "goods" of the new nobility, and the "virtues" of the good and just are revealed as "bad" (=disadvantageous for life).[62]

11. On the Spirit of Gravity

Sub-section 1. Though his language can become crude and blasphemous, his messages unwelcome and anarchistic, his path a satanic *tour de force*, his ideas nurtured on a diet of "evil" and irrationality, Zarathustra is nonetheless *proudly* the archenemy of Jesus Christ (=the spirit of gravity)—a self-styled Antichrist attacking the faith at every turn. Unlike that of the evangelist, Zarathustra's enthusiasm is not a showmanship rooted in a will to popularity: his atheism comes rather from a spiritual necessity.

Sub-section 2. He who finally teaches man innocent lightheartedness will remove "boundary stones" of "good and evil" from man's consciousness. (Boundary stones represent artificial limits on mankind, as did the chalk streaks in I.6.)[63] Christ warned that those who laugh on earth will cry and howl in Hell:[64] Zarathustra however wants man to enjoy life and love himself. This self-love is neither hedonism nor egoism, but the hard-earned self-appreciation of those who have created a higher self. (Nietzsche of course does not glorify man in just any condition: present man is something that must be overcome. Yet the self-created individual must be "high" enough to become a substitute for god after the Great Noon.) Christianity promotes the doctrine of original sin, emphasizes the evil in man's character and seeks to attract man's attention to an afterworld, i.e., it leads man away from human life: "we must even be forgiven for living."

Notions of "good and evil" give an alien seriousness to life, loading man down with Thou Shalt, Thou Shalt Not, guilt, sin, conscience, self-contempt, the will to death. (This passage concerning the camel trope is the source of my interpretation of the camel in I.1. The camel is laden with *alien* notions of good and evil, and their overwhelming weight makes life a "grave burden.") Much in man is indeed nauseating, but he has great unfulfilled potential. Christianity has placed a limit on man's self-expression by imposing an absolutist morality (=good/evil for all). Here the dwarf-mole imagery of III.2 is clarified and supplemented. The Dwarf-mole represents an absolutist morality and seriousness about life. A dwarf that says "Good and evil for all" was already identified with the spirit of gravity.[65] The last thing an absolutist morality allows is moral autonomy and individuality.[66] True self-creativity begins only when one discovers oneself as one's own moral legislator (=saying "*my* good and evil"). Man's ideal must *become realized in himself,* in flesh and blood, not a past hero (=mummy) nor a god removed from life (=ghost).

Zarathustra has *learned* to cultivate his higher self over great lengths of time, step by step, along a variety of paths and methods, until he acquired enough wisdom to gain an overview of that higher self. His path was really a variety of discontinuous and twisted paths: he did not follow a single, pre-determined, prescribed way. In a stepwise self-creation he has *learned* to love himself with a love deeper than that of the neighbor. "Love of the neighbor" sounds like a basically philanthropic notion, but when it blocks individual self-expression and development, it turns misanthropic: "with this phrase the best lies and hypocrisies have been perpetrated so far, and especially by such as were a grave burden for all the world." Throughout his self-creation Zarathustra seldom sought wisdom from others, but instead preferred trial and error. The final product is a self and a wisdom of his own, of which he is proud, and which stands over man like a light to lost and forsaken individuals. (The image of "shipwrecked sailors and castaways" clearly indicates *individuals* who "live dangerously" but have come on bad times. A similar message is given to sailors in I.6: "I am a railing by the torrent: let those who can, grasp me! Your crutch, however, I am not.") This beacon beckons, however, by virtue of its elevation, not from a will to attract the many. Any absolutist, searching for the "One Way," receives from Zarathustra only the retort, ". . . *the* way— that does not exist."[67]

12. On Old and New Tablets

In this monologue, Zarathustra attempts a grand summary of the Prologue and first three Parts. Only IV.13 is comparable in comprehensiveness and precision. Perhaps the single most philosophically interesting speech of the entire book, it provides a compact synopsis of many major motifs in Nietzsche's philosophy. Sections 4-28 comprise an attck on old values; sections 29-30 are a paean to new values. I will divide them according to subject matter.

Sub-sections 1-3. The first three sections comprise a unity consisting of Zarathustra's reflections on his own life project. Sitting triumphantly before his cave among broken tablets of morality, he patiently awaits for a sign to descend among man a final time. His "broken old tablets" are the moral codes of the past. Nietzsche's phrase here alludes to Exodus 32:19. Like Moses, Zarathustra has "broken" the law, but to an opposite purpose. The "new tablets half covered with writing" are the incomplete teachings Zarathustra codifies in this section. His "hour of going down and going under" is the hour of his death, greatest maturity and the final journey among men. He has yet to receive the sign signaling his completion and perfection (=laughing lion and flock of doves). This occurs at IV.20.

Previously Zarathustra had awakened mankind to the narcoticism of morality and had shaken the belief that mankind already knows the meaning of good and evil. The great danger to life from pessimism, nihilism and spiritualism had also been exposed. Man, relieved of the grave burden imposed by christianity,[68] will strive for individual goals and create a generation of over*men*. Such overmen are the "distant futures" of which Zarathustra dreams. These godlike types of the future, *as individuals*, are "overmen" and as a whole form the *overman*. What is to be stressed here is the *plurality of human ideals* replacing the supernatural Yahweh. These overmen will stand over the grave man as gods over mortals.

In pursuit of his own highest ideal, Zarathustra invented the words "overman," "Great Noon," etc., seeking to synthesize into himself one great individual, who redeems the accidents and setbacks of his life, affirming the past and future return of the small man. Zarathustra's ideas of overman, Great Noon, will to power and self-overcoming were created in his cave before the beginning of Prologue 1. His new values were hung over man as a tent of laughter, for example, in III.4. He taught redemption through becoming whole in II.20, and taught redemption of the past in III.2. Now that Zarathustra nears his death, he must present man with his greatest gift—the message of eternal return.[69]

Sub-sections 4-7. The tragedy of the higher man is summarized in three short sections. Though Zarathustra has proclaimed *his* goal of the "overman," others are free to pursue their own ideals, step by step, unconstrained, unafraid of eternal punishment, ready to command as necessary. That "there are many ways of overcoming" leaves humanity a plurality of personal ideals to adopt and consequently there are many possible *overmen.* In overcoming oneself, one will adopt ways violating deontological "rights" of fellow humans: but public morality is subordinate to Zarathustra's individualism. Thus the neighbor need not be protected at the price of rejecting a personal destiny. An ideal must be pursued step by step, because a violent, single leap to a worthy goal is the illusion of the frivolous.[70] Constraint by conscience and fear of eternal punishment must be overcome, if a personal destiny is to be realized at the expense of public morality.

He who strives higher must not seek happiness, comfort or joy, and yet paradoxically it is precisely to him that the highest joy comes.[71]

In his struggle to "cross over," each higher man is a "firstling" in some way; as pioneer, inventor, artist, revolutionary, etc., they come forward as "firsts." Various idols of the masses will seek to spell the undergoing of all higher men. Thus "firstlings" are frequently "sacrifices" at the altars of tradition. "Good and just" men preach harmony from an inability to do otherwise: the tragic man must however bring together all things "evil" in order to overcome the good and just man.[72] This of course requires that the higher man conquers the voice of conscience emanating from echoes of idols and their priests.[73] New knowledge is achieved only by breaking old limits, and so all new insights into man will be accomplished with a bad conscience. That, however, is something to be overcome.

Sub-sections 8-10. In the next three sub-sections, the nature of good and evil are outlined. All great notions seem eternal in their truth and validity, and so it is with "good and evil." He who sees the flow of history, and its rise and fall of the highest values, understands the impermanence of all loci of hope and consolation. Zarathustra is one who would seek to hasten the advance of values by calling for the breaking of today's tablets.

Soothsayers and stargazers of the past have speculated about, and falsified, the nature of the universe, disguising the voluntaristic, perspectival nature of values. (One of these stargazers and soothsayers was the historical Zoroaster, whose worldview, of good and evil as the two great poles of cosmic struggle, is the dichotomy that Nietzsche's Zarathustra seeks above all to collapse.) Hitherto, values have been used as weapons in a world-historical war between law-givers: today's values were set by those seeking to turn man against the world and himself. Thus apparently philanthropic values hide misanthropic goals.

Sub-sections 11-12. Nietzsche introduces one of his most characteristic ideas in these sub-sections; i.e., *the new nobility.*[74] This section in fact reads like a before-the-fact renunciation of Hitler and fascism. The greatest danger to mankind is that from the Great Dictator, who interprets world history as a process culminating in his own *Reich*, who is supported by the rabble, and who interprets all society racially. As a counter-balance, a new nobility of free-thinkers is needed to combat tyranny and collective madness. Such a pluarality of individuals, beyond good and evil, stands as gods above mass movements and "great men." Notice the text phrase, "noble men of many kinds": this pluralism of human ideals was central to III.12.4 and runs throughout the book. This future group of men, who replace the gods by themselves, form a community of overmen. Here Zarathustra decisively intercedes for my interpretation of the phrase, "Precisely this is godlike, that there are gods, but no god."[75]

This nobility is not an elite capitalist class, nor an aristocracy of race, nor a privileged social class, nor a theocracy[143]—all of which look to the past for their justification rather than the *future*. Instead, the new nobility is a radical aristocracy of the spirit, redeeming past failures by securing a new age and a new goal over man.

Yet Nietzsche's "new nobility" has taken on virtually every one of these meanings at the hands of misinterpreters. Ayn Rand identifies his "masters of the earth" as the capitalist "producer" class: the Nazis misinterpreted Nietzsche as meaning a racial nobility: many marxists take Nietzsche to mean a privileged social class (junkerism). No one has taken him to mean a theocratic class, however, unless it be the negative theology of anti-semitism.

Sub-sections 13-18. In these sections, Zarathustra launches a prolonged attack against schopenhauerian resignationism. The introductory proverb "all is vanity" is not a parody of the Bible, for once, but is rather a direct quote from Ecclesiastes 1:2. By "vanity" Solomon means "that which is empty, without permanent value, that which leads to frustration." Vanity is *not* foolish pride but rather the emptiness of all life apart from God. "Vanity is futility. It is to be born, to toil, to suffer, to experience some transitory joy which is as nothing in view of eternity, to leave it all, and to die."[76] "All is vanity" is the theme occupying most of Ecclesiastes. Thus old testament wisdom shares the following indictment with Schopenhauer. Pessimism, denouncing life as sorrow, vanity and futility, is a disease of the spirit preventing man from enjoying the fruits of the world.[77] Indeed, there is much objectionable about life, but this is itself not a decisive indictment of existence. For the most despicable foulness on earth is the pessimist himself, who seeks to turn the world's treasures into the despicable. Paradoxically, his sickliness repels the healthy man and drives him to a final overcoming of pessimism: " . . . nausea itself creates wings and water-divining powers."

In the afterworldly, renunciation of self and life becomes conscious and a matter of conscience. Those who slander the world preach a quietism of the will: Zarathustra takes *superactivity* of the

will to be the ultimate cure for this schopenhauerian resignationism. The pessimist does not commit suicide, but only contemplates the sorrows of the world in bad faith.[78] From this half-
and-half voyeurism, the two outcomes are either final fulfillment of
the death-wish or rejuvenation.[79] With all his will, Zarathustra
would force man to decide the issue of sick pessimism versus
healthy optimism.

Pessimism may stem from inner loss of will or it may come from
weariness in a great task.[80] The former is to be crushed at every
turn. He who is weary from a great task, though, is the "one who
would cross over" and so is heroic. But his final victory must come
from within himself, not from aid out of pity.[81]

Sub-section 19.[82] Zarathustra's "overman" is the dionysian
spirit—the man of great contradictions brought together in a great
tension—comprehensive yet vast, sensing destiny yet seeking adventure, the complete and self-perfected man who strives for
change yet always finds former selves, possessing great wisdom yet
involved in great folly; in short, the man of great good *and* great
evil. This great spirit attracts the small man, curious and jealous,
who seek to steal something of his greatness. This parasite, though,
is no deterrent against striving for creation of an overman in oneself. (The *necessity* of the smallest man, or parasite, here prefigures
the soon-to-be-proclaimed doctrine of eternal return.)

Sub-section 20. Zarathustra's life project is not to heal the sick,
but to create a value system bringing them into a desperate nihilism, that they may show their true mettle and flee the earth by
fulfilling their own death-wish.

Sub-sections 21-23. Nietzsche's thoughts on war and warriors receive some clarification here. Brute militarism is not Nietzsche's
suggestion: wars of nationalism are the follies of peoples without
higher motive than vanity and conquest. In such wars, non-participation is better than war for war's sake.[83] Class wars, as well, do not
prove spiritual superiority, but only material preponderance.[84] Nietzsche's preferred type of "war" is a spiritual battle of ideas and
ideals for the minds of men.[85] A war of weapons and material is the

brute force found in nature.Man's "wars" must not be abolished, but rather "spiritualized."

Man's spirit must become more masculine *and* more feminine: stronger and more fit for battle, more creative and fruitful in the creation of *ideals.*[86]

Sub-section 24. Marriage must become more than a relation of convenience, if higher beings are to arise. Future man (=child) requires the parentage of two *individuals.* Wedlock as a divine covenant simply locks two unfortunates together for eternity.[87] Instead, Zarathustra suggests "immoral" relations—cohabitation outside wedlock and, if wedlock has failed, divorce.

Sub-section 25. Peoples and civilizations rise and fall just as wells are unearthed and reburied. The going under (*Untergang*) of one people due to an upheaval of values may give rise to a new people with new values. The peoples of the earth today are not the materials of Zarathustra's new age: they must be brought under, that new peoples and a new age may be generated.[88] A people is the raw material of commanders: only power relations, not "social contract," determine rulers and subjects.

Sub-sections 26-28. Though the immoralist would bring destruction to the *status quo*, and though the afterworldly turn away from life itself, it is rather the good and just man himself who presents the greatest danger to human life, for he seeks to block all change and advance.

In a rare but insightful moment, Zarathustra identifies Christ as a revolutionary who had fought against the "good and just" men of his own time.[89] The small man's conscience prohibits undertaking any action breaking the tablets of society. And Christ's revolution did precisely this. (Jesus was, of course, tried and convicted under normal jewish and roman laws against heresy.) As a defense of their own mediocrity and contentment, the small man—the pharisee of all ages—deftly misconstrues and ignores the revolutionary messages of great human beings. As Zarathustra said in III.9: "the stupidity of the good is unfathomably shrewd." Those who *follow* values must persecute, belittle and crucify those who create *new* values, for creation implies breaking old values.[91] Anyone who seeks more than the *status quo* is an enemy of the people and faith, and must be crucified. So it was with Christ.

Despite Christ's flaws, he is, in Zarathustra's eyes, a relatively higher man, persecuted, belittled and brought under by the "good and just" (i.e., pharisees). "Good and just" men would sacrifice the revolutionary higher man for the sake of their own comfort. They are thus always the greatest threat to higher culture and are the greatest proponents of a final stasis.

Setting oneself against the herd, as it were, creates a deep disgust with mankind, coupled with a dread of immoralism. But the vision of something over mankind inspires and fortifies. Fighters for a new age must learn to remain true to the earth and body, learn to survive, and then thrive, on the raging storm of social unrest in order to steer the ship of man to higher ground.

Sub-section 29. The immoralist, if he is to become a *fighter*, must learn the virtues of the soldier. He who would create the future man in himself must *become hard* with himself and with all those who stand in his way. Forces of immoralism must achieve overwhelming pressure, if a lasting effect on man's history is to be achieved.

Sub-section 30. Zarathustra breaks into a paen to his own will power. His higher ideal, *over* himself and *in* himself, is now totally incorporated into his being. As the overman,[92] he now stands ready to deliver the message of eternal return to man and survive this notion that would "break the good and just." This "*one* great victory"[93] is his great task, his destiny, to which all events have led. His will is now driven to this greatest moment in the following speech.

13. The Convalescent

Subsection 1. Zarathustra has nearly been driven mad by the notion eluding him, and he attempts here in a melodramatic act of will to finally command the idea of eternal return. In a scene parodying Wagner,[94] Zarathustra attempts to "awaken" his most abysmal thought. He succeeds in projecting, objectifying and personifying his deepest subconsciousness, but fails to withstand its appearance, i.e., fails to affirm all its consequences.

Sub-section 2. Immediately upon failing his test, Zarathustra lapses into a deathlike trance, as in II.19, remaining so for seven days. His only companions are the ever-faithful eagle and snake.[95]

As Zarathustra regains consciousness, his attendant animals bid him to go to the garden-like world outside his cave, but he instead breaks into a paen to the faculty of speech, whose refreshing qualities heal him. Here he feels at one with reality and has overcome all alienation from it,[96] and he waxes poetically in his bliss. The animals revel in the animated language of Zarathustra, and use the occasion to give the first of four statements of the doctrine of eternal return. Here the notion is cosmological. The universe is viewed as a single, self-moving, deterministic substance (=the wheel of being).[97] Within the relentless revolutions of this "wheel," life is enacted in its entirety endless times without the slightest variation.[98] Time and space become relative notions in an einsteinian sense: "In every Now, being begins; round every Here rolls the sphere There. The center is everywhere." Past, present and future are perspectival: each moment is simultaneously beginning, middle and end of time. The animals giving this variant are, as before, Zarathustra's wisdom and knowledge, objectified and animated. (Confirmation of this comes at IV.15.) Thus this scene counts as the first successful pronouncement of the notion by Zarathustra himself—and thereby the fulfillment of his destiny—though the animals themselves speak. Indeed, the animals here, as elsewhere, read Zarathustra's thoughts.

After confirming the animals' discovery of his innermost thoughts, Zarathustra launches into a paen to cruelty and evil without any apparent connection to the previous subject, only to conclude "man must become better and more evil." The ideal synthesis of great good and great evil has previously been called "the overman." Zarathustra's lament is precisely that the greatest men are all-too-similar to the small man: there has not yet been an overman. This is his "great disgust with man" and is symbolized in III.2 as the snake caught fast in the shepherd's throat, and makes its first appearance as early as Prologue 3.

The Soothsayer's pessimism about man has tortured Zarathustra since II.19, making him weary and demoralized, misanthropic and nihilistic. But the decisive indictment of existence in Zarathustra's mind, despite his words, has been the ineradicability of the multitudinous, petty, myopic, monadic, limited or partial, dimwitted man of the masses.[99] Zarathustra now recognizes the eternal return of the all-too-many as a consequence of eternal return of the same, and moreover does so without being broken by it. *Thus he passes the test of the overman.*

Once again the animals bid him to greet the world and sing a song of convalescence, fulfilled later in III.16, but before their exuberance fades, they proclaim him *teacher of the eternal return of the same* and thereby confirm the completion of his destiny. They give a third version of the notion immediately thereafter—once again cosmologically, but containing the crucial consequence of the return of "what is greatest as in what is smallest."

Zarathustra's animals show anxiety about his approaching death and give a fourth statement of the notion disguised as a hypothetical deathbed speech. The dream sequence of II.19, the vision/ riddle of III.2 and this formulation of the eternal return hang together as a unity and unlock the real meaning of eternal return at a personal level. This final version recognizes the *total real annihilation of the individual*, body and consciousness. This confirms my previous claim that Nietzsche does not want to substitute one kind of personal immortality for another. But as causal parts of the "wheel of being," each individual *always comes back into being* with every revolution of becoming and being. Thus there is no personal immortality, no Nirvana-like escape from the wheel, no rebirth into a new, different life, no christian resurrection, assumption or eternal life. There is only eternal life and death in the eternal return of the only possible world. Zarathustra's undertaking has been to cross over man, teaching his doctrines, and thereby giving man something higher to esteem. Since Prologue 1 this has been his "going under" (*Untergang*)—his personal life and death struggle.

Concerning the phrase, "thus *ends* Zarathustra's going under": it is clear from the context preceding this scene that *personal downfall and death* are meant here by "going under" (*Untergang*). It is therefore clear that Zarathustra's going under is *not yet finished*, but only *prefigured* by the animals' speech. And since the animals deliver this speech as a hypothetical death-bed speech, their pronouncement would be true only in the hypothetical case of his death.

But Zarathustra does not hear this last version of the notion, and lies meditating. He has fulfilled his destiny, and so convalesces. In the remaining sections of Part III he will grow to his full stature as Dionysus, or the "overman."

14. On the Great Longing

Still meditating in the sleeplike trance ending III.13, Zarathustra joyously recounts his many victories in a monologue with his own soul—projected, objectified and personified as Ariadne of Greek mythology. The original title of this section was in fact "Ariadne." Zarathustra's "soul" was already personified and feminized as Ariadne in II.13. This identification works at a number of levels: 1) as referring to the character of Greek mythology, the trope is a natural companion to Dionysus, 2) as a feminine trope, it stands interchangably with the other women of the book—Truth, Life, Eternity and Wisdom, 3) as a trope of Nietzsche's personal life, Ariadne is Cosima Wagner, expressing a not-so-secret longing for Richard Wagner's wife.

Zarathustra now fast metamorphizes into his "overman"—Dionysus—as reflected in the imagery borrowed from various Dionysus myths. The general sensual overtones of this section are entirely appropriate to Dionysus. Wisdom as *wine* recalls Dionysus' role as god of wine: Ariadne is described as a growing vine and her gifts are described as grapes. A "vine's urge for the vintager and his knife" is a trope for "the great longing": i.e. the longing of those who are ripe and fruitful for harvest, the longing of Ariadne for Dionysus. One ancient myth portrays Dionysus appearing from a mist to sailors on high seas, who attempt to bind him. He turns the sailors into dolphins, the boat begins to sail itself and the mast grows vines and grapes to provide an umbrella over the god. An Attic *kylix* from circa 540 B.C. portraying this scene survives to this day. Nietzsche of course knew this myth and may have worked its imagery into this section. The *kylix* shows Dionysus yielding a vintager's knife, for example. The "many great and small animals and whatever has light, wondrous feet for running on paths blue as violet" could refer to Dionysus and the dolphins: the "great deliverer" is of course Dionysus, one of whose epithets in mythology is "liberator": the "future songs" giving his name may allude to a series of poems Nietzsche himself wrote entitled "Dionysian Dithyrambs."[100]

In the Dionysus-Zagreus myths, Dionysus is torn into pieces as an infant, only to be eaten, made whole again and reborn by Zeus. Dionysian religion taught a cyclical repetition of birth and death typical of harvest gods, and so Dionysus appropriately serves as *deliverer of the message of eternal return.* Closely associated female deities—Persephone, Demeter and Ariadne—share this mystery of cyclical birth and death. Zarathustra has given all within his power to Ariadne and awaits thanks. Ariadne, now overrich, feels the pain of one who wants to give but finds no receivers, and so is ungrateful. Turning from Zarathustra, Ariadne wants the harvestor god Dionysus to relieve her superabundance by gleaning her wisdom for the benefit of mankind. (As one of the two chthonian gods—Demeter being the other—, Dionysus never leaves earth to join the olympians. He is considered a friend of man, as are all harvest gods.) Dionysus, the overhero, has overcome the hero (Zarathustra), and approaches Ariadne in a dream, fulfilling the prophesy of II.13. Her overhero arrives in a self-piloted bark, ringed by leaping dolphins, brandishing the vintager's diamond knife, to collect her wine-like wisdom.[101]

15. The Other Dancing Song[102]

Sub-section 1. Life, already personified as a beautiful woman in II.10, returns to flirt with Zarathustra, attracted by his dionysian bliss.[103] Ecstatic in his own wisdom, Zarathustra throws abandon to the wind and seeks to dance with, then possess, Life herself, only to be slapped. "In my face two red blotches from your hand itch." Ariadne portrays various qualities of life in this section: playfulness, elusiveness, danger, incalculability, but especially *command and obedience*.

Sub-section 2. Zarathustra regains his senses and his prior wisdom: Life, like happiness and Wisdom, are attracted only to the non-seekers and indifferent. Tamed by Zarathustra's whip,[104] Life confesses jealousy of his wisdom and accuses him of infidelity—alluding to his nearing death. The meaning of Zarathustra's "thinking about leaving" life is that, having now reached his greatest height, he considers "free death." Since I.21 it has been a theme of the book that one must *die at the right time*. And as in II.10, Zarathustra wonders if now might not be the right time. He is aware of his mortality, but his wisdom is still friendly to Life, for his wisdom includes knowledge of his own eternal return. (It is of course knowledge of his own eternal return that he whispers to Life.) And indeed, Life remains dearer to him than Wisdom.

Sub-section 3. This is the song requested by the animals in III.13, sung with the intermittent tolling of the bells of eternal return. On the day of Nietzsche's death, this poem was set into stone on Chasté Peninsula, in the vicinity of Sils-Maria. It is remembered as one of Nietzsche's finests poems. Since this song is extensively analyzed at IV.19 by Zarathustra himself, consideration of it is postponed until that section.[105]

16. The Seven Seals (Or; The Yes-and-Amen Song)[106]

In this final section, Zarathustra reaches his greatest stature as the Yes-saying Dionysus. He says Yes! to all existence and Amen! to the past, i.e., "so I willed it!" Thereby he seals the seven solitudes of his undertakings.[107]

Seal 1. Both the "Soothsayer" and Zarathustra are prophets of man's future: the former is a pessimist, the latter the optimist of the overman. It is Zarathustra's destiny to deliver the doctrines distinguishing weak No-sayers from strong Yes-sayers.[201]

Another female figure, Eternity, is the highest feeling of joy, and is the only source of future values (=children) Zarathustra desires.

Seal 2. Once Zarathustra has destroyed christianity in his own heart—"killed god"—and has set the stage for its demise *in toto*, it is inevitable that the Yes-sayer would come to desire an eternal value of his own (i.e., eternal return). Having totally affirmed one Moment, he affirms all Time.

Seal 3. Zarathustra is a value-creator who casts lots with even the gods for the attention and will of man. He would harness man's esteeming faculties and will power to bring about the Great Noon—the destruction of the christian-bourgeois world order—so that a future type may repopulate and develop the earth. To this end, love of an eternal value is necessary.

Seal 4. The two sides of human nature, "good and evil," are to be mixed together into one strong drink[108]—the overman—and Zarathustra is one who would use even the greatest evil to create a *whole, full, vitalic, eternity-desiring, great human being.* He is to be a mixture of the farthest and nearest, fire and spirit, joy and pain, great evil and great grace. That this great synthesis *thrive*, the doctrine of eternal return is necessary.

Seal 5. Searching and attempting are the great joys of Zarathustra's spirit. Plotting new courses in a storm of conflicting values, he pays no heed to the resistance of the small man, and seeks instead to discover the new lands of future man.[109] His adventurism demands the dissolution of all moral limits and religious chains, but this itself is a hardship. And if he who lives dangerously is not to drown in nihilism, he must be wed to the inspiring, driving, luring vision of eternal return.

Seal 6. From beginning to end, Zarathustra has fought all burdens of the spirit, sought to give a new higher meaning to body and earth and taught wisdom to man's spirit, making it gay and refreshed. That dancing replace praying, the uplifting doctrine of eternal return must become the greatest love of man.

Seal 7. Time after time, Zarathustra has projected and objectified himself in countless images. Within his own imagination, he has a boundless world, void of moral orientation and gravity, where his spirit may fly and sing and celebrate. He has overcome the panlogism of words, and has rediscovered the irrational and the non-discursive. In this way he is akin to the laughing Buddha. Joy in eternity is the emotional seal to his hard-won spiritual development.

Zarathustra has said Yes and Amen! not only to one great Moment, as did Goethe's Faust, but to the eternal return of every Moment. This life, on *earth* in this *bodily* constitution, is pronounced *holy* without the sanction of a transcendental deity. The essence of the celebrated "eternal return" doctrine, the final seal, is a super-temporal joy, a state of dionysian spirit, saying and doing Yes! to the challenges of life. As such, it deserves a place in the pantheon of great religious and spiritual ideas.

Notes

1. The figure of the Wanderer in this section, along with the Shadow of II.18, alludes to the second division of the second part of Nietzsche's book *Menschliches, Allzumenschliches*. Section III.3 also contains these figures. The Shadow's cry, "It's high time!" from II.18 recurrs in III.3 and IV.2.

2. See "Nietzsche's Zarathustra" in my Introductory Essay.

3. See *KSA* VI page 335.

4. Nietzsche's concept of eternal return has sparked a large literature. Most important are Karl Schlechta's *Der Grosse Mittag*, (Frankfurt: Klostermann, 1954) and Karl Loewith's *Nietzsches Philosophie der ewigen Wiederkehr*, (Frankfurt: Kohlhammer, 1954). For shorter articles, see M.C. Sterling's "Recent Discussions of Eternal Return" in Volume VI of *Nietzsche-Studien* and Bernd Magnus' "Eternal Recurrence" in Volume VIII of *Nietzsche-Studien*. For an interesting essay on the connection between overman and eternal return, see Wolfgang Mueller-Lauter's *Nietzsche* (Berlin: de Gruyter, 1971), chapter 7.

5. See I.7.

6. German for "storm and stress." I do not refer here to the *Sturm und Drang* movement in German literature, which placed great value on overflowing emotion, individualism and nationalism. Although Nietzsche bares superficial resemblance in some ways to this movement, he reacts strongly against this movement, and should not be confused with its writers.

   The great tension in this section between "being hard" and sentimentalism remains a major motif for the remainder of the book. Resolution of this tension occurs only at the end of Part IV as Zarathustra survives his final temptation.

7. The original title of this section was "On the Vision of the Loneliest," a phrase occuring several times in the text. According to Montinari (*KSA* XIV page 309), it is possible that this section was originally intended to be bound with III.13. An important forerunner of the dwarf-mole scene occurs at *Froehliche Wissenschaft* 341 (*KSA* III page 570). This section is intimately linked with II.19 and III.11.

8. If indeed this section was linked with III.13 (see previous footnote), it was probably meant as a dream experienced in Zarathustra's death-like coma. As it stands, it should be interpreted as an hallucinatory projection of the *Sturm und Drang* in Zarathustra's soul.

9. The spirit of gravity is the topic of III.14, where it is written, "He, however, has discovered himself who says, "This is *my* good and evil"; with that he has reduced to silence the mole and dwarf who say, "Good for all, evil for all."" In III.2 the mole/dwarf is the embodied principle of seriousness and responsibility, a broader concept than ethical absolutism, though of course closely connected. The mole imagery relates to a narrow (=universalizing) nature; the image of the dwarf represents the diminutive stature of those who act only out of responsibility. As well, the human figure, when compressed (as by gravity), results in the dwarfish shortening of the entire being.

10. "as deeply as man sees into life, he sees into suffering."

11. "From this gateway, Moment, a long, eternal lane leads *backward*: behind us lies an eternity. Must not whatever *can* walk have walked on this lane before? Must not whatever *can* happen have happened, have been done, have passed by before?"

12. "And are not all things knotted together so firmly that this moment draws after it *all* that is to come? Therefore—itself too?"

13. A very important forerunner to this section, *Froehliche Wisenschaft* 341, contains the variant: "dieses Leben, wie du es jetzt lebst und gelebt hast, wirst du noch einmal und noch unzaehlige Male leben muessen; und es wird nichts Neues daran sein, sondern jeder Schmerz und jede Lust und jeder Gedanke und Seufzer und alles unsaeglich Kleine und Grosse deines Lebens muss dir wiederkommen, und alles in derselben Reihe und Folge—und ebenso diese Spinne und dieses Mondlicht zwischen den Baeumen, und ebenso dieser Augenblick und ich selber. Die ewige Sanduhr des Daseins wird immer umgedreht—und du mit ihr, Staeubchen von Staeube!"

14. This claim may only be forwarded here: its proof may be developed only underway to the completion of the notion.

15. This is my counter-thesis to an entirely cosmological interpretation. *Froehliche Wissenschaft* 341 makes my position much clearer, as do notes from the *Zarathustra* period and later.

16. This image relates as well to the youth of I.8, the higher men of II.21 et al..

17. See Elizabeth Foerster-Nietzsche's *Das Leben Nietzsche* I pages 20-21: "Very curious was a dream of my brother Fritz, which he wrote down in the small biographical notebook mentioned above. "I dreamed at that time that I had heard an organ like that at a funeral. When I looked to find what the cause would be, a casket suddenly raised itself, and my father in burial clothes emerged from it. He hurried into the church and came back with a small child in his arms. The gravemound opened itself, he climbed back in and the lid sank back into the grave. In the morning I related this to my dear mother; soon thereafter little Joseph [Nietzsche's brother] became ill, got convulsions and died within a few hours. Our sorrow was tremendous, my dream was fulfilled completely." (My translation.) On page 21 Foerster-Nietzsche relates the text under consideration directly to the scene as the Nietzsche family left Roecken. This dream bears even greater resemblance to that of II.19. This lends some additional credence to the interpretation of this section as ultimately concerned with death and nothingness.

18. "I was like one sick whom wicked torture makes weary, and who as he falls asleep is awakened by a still more wicked dream."

19. See III.13: "The great disgust with man—*this* choked me and crawled into my throat; and what the soothsayer said: "All is the same, nothing is worth while, knowledge chokes." . . . my sighing and questioning croaked and gagged and gnawed and wailed by day and night: "Alas, man recurs eternally! The small man recurs eternally!" . . . And the eternal return even of the smallest—that was my disgust with all existence. Alas! Nausea! Nausea! Nausea!" Section III.13 is the primary test for any *Zarathustra* interpretation.

20. Hollinrake (page 95).

21. Originally entitled "On the High Sea," this section was intended as III.1 in early drafts.

22. As Montinari (*KSA* XIV page 310) notes, from now on Zarathustra speaks of "my children" and no longer of "my friends."

23. See comments and footnotes to II.19.

24. See II.11: "And only where there are tombs are there resurrections." Here the corpses awaiting resurrections are once again past sorrows. It is of course highly appropriate that Nietzsche would use the imagery of his childhood dream in II.19 as a symbol for sorrow generally.

25. See comments to II.22 and I.1. The image of the lion as commander is the penultimate symbol of the book (IV.20).

26. Zarathustra objectifies and projects his spirit over himself in numerous other passages, most notably Prologue 1. The passage, "And when I climbed mountains, *whom* did I always seek on the mountains, if not you?" inverts the position of Zarathustra relative to the sun as found in Prologue 1.

27. The image of sitting in a barrel under closed heavens recalls Diogenes the Cynic. Zarathustra forces the decision between timonian misanthropy and zarathustran superhumanism.

28. The passage, "A *little*, to be sure, a seed of wisdom scattered from star to star . . ." recalls the early essay "On Truth and Lie in an Extra-moral Sense," and his critique of hegelian panlogism in "Vom Nutz und Nachteil der Historie . . ." Here Zarathustra reacts to the rationalist and idealist notion that the ultimate nature of the universe is knowable to reason.

29. See III.15.

30. Other sections important for comparison are Prologue 4 and 5, I.2 and II.5. This section was originally entitled "On Self-reduction" or "On Making Oneself Smaller."

31. "woe, if the first lord is *merely* the first servant!" alludes to a quotation from Frederick the Great.

32. This section contains a number of biblical allusions (Matthew 19:13, 22:39 and Jes. 5:24). Zarathustra has of course shown himself to be an enemy of the faith at every turn.

33. Originally entitled "The Wintersong." For relevant biblical passages, see Luke 22:39-46 and Luke 21:37-38.

34. This section is loosely styled upon Nietzsche's everyday life in Italy during winters. For some idea of his sufferings, see the "Translator's Preface" to Kaufmann's translation of *Also sprach Zarathustra* in Viking Compass Press.

35. Nietzsche dreaded the intrusions of the curious and of parasites into his personal life. Kaufmann's "Translator's Preface" to *Zarathustra* (Viking Compass) is interesting in this connection.

36. This theme was introduced in the Prologue and plays a central role in Prologue 6-10, I.4, I.22, II.1, II.21 and later sections.

37. Naumann (III 61-68) argues that the Great City is Berlin and the Ape is modelled after Eugene Duehring. No notes confirm this, however.

38. See (*KSA* III 631-32).

39. See my comments on Nietzsche's Zarathustra in the Introductory Essay to this commentary.

40. Elizabeth Foerster, as curator of Nietzsche's literary estate after the onset of his insanity, forged a series of spurious letters from Nietzsche and placed them in the *Gesammelte Briefe* edition of his correspondence with co-editor and co-conspirator Peter Gast, in a pathetic attempt to cover the deep schism between herself and her brother concerning personal relations, morality, christianity, racism, anti-semitism and nationalism. For a (partial) list of falsified letters, see Karl Schlechta's *Nietzsche-Chronik* (Muenchen: Carl Hanser, 1975). For an extremely interesting expose of another attempt to alter Nietzsche's works after his breakdown, see M. Montinari's *Nietzsche Lesen* pages 120-169. Also fascinating is H.F. Peters' *Zarathustra's Sister* (New York: Crown Publishers, 1977).

41. It has been the unseemly task of post-World War II Nietzsche scholarship to disassociate him from the Nazis. For a decisive refutation of the myth, see "Nietzsche zwischen Alfred Baeumler und Georg Lukacs" in M. Montinari's *Nietzsche Lesen* (Berlin: de Gruyter, 1982).

42. See Prologue 6-8.

43. The dream of II.1 foretells their denunciation of Zarathustra. It is alluded to in this section with the passage, "your cowardly devil within you, who would like to fold his hands and rest his hands in his lap and be more comfortable-- this cowardly devil urges you, 'There *is* a god.'"

44. "Did their hearts perhaps grow faint because solitude swallowed me like a whale?" alludes to Jonah 1:17, often cited as an example of God's vengefulness, and not Jonah 2:1 as cited by Colli and Montinari.

45. The corpse and Jester are dismissed as true companions, for the corpse does not have *autonomy*, and because the Jester is not *serious* and only sways in the breeze of public opinion.

46. I.e. those who are ashamed are in bad faith (in Sartre's sense of *moi fau*), those who are unashamed are in good faith, yet not in a good faith.

47. I.e. a "prayer-muttering chase," not a "wild chase."

48. The cross-marked spiders were already met in II.7 associated with *ressentiment*. Naumann (III page 74) interprets this passage *in pace* my analysis. "So the cross-spiders carry the sign of Christ on their backs, spin their webs espe-

cially well crisscross on crossed wooden pieces and nevertheless have nothing other than prey-catching in mind. It lives like one in a church and thereby has a material interest in its well-being." (My translation.)

49. This may well allude to Wagner, whom Nietzsche often psychoanalyzed in terms of eroto-religious feelings.

50. Nietzsche means spiritual mediums here. See *KSA* X pages 16-17 and a letter to Peter Gast of October 3, 1882 for his thoughts on mediums. These sources are listed at *KSA* XIV page 316.

51. The nightwatchmen may allude to the dream sequence of II.19, but more likely symbolize the gravekeepers of the dead god. The inclusion of pious philosophers here is not capricious, as Nietzsche, like Feuerbach, considered philosophy to be disguised theology. (See *KSA* I page 445 for an allusion to Feuerbach's formulation, and *KSA* XIV page 85 for confirmation of the source.)

52. The sad horn-playing of the watchmen symbolizes nihilism at the death of god. Wagner was previously connected with this trope (see comments to II.11). The awakening of "old, sleeping, light-shunning things" refers to Wagner's *Siegfried*, which Nietzsche often parodied. (See Hollinrake, chapter 5, for background.)

53. For elucidation of this point, see the important *Froehliche Wissenschaft* section 143 (*KSA* III page 490). The absurd conclusion come to by all theology is "there is one god."

54. This is the important point made against christology by David Friedrich Strauss in *Das Leben Jesu*.

55. See for example, the important *Froehliche Wissenschaft* 285 (*KSA* III pages 527-28) 103 (III 459-60) and 125 (III 480-82).

56. Zarathustra had left his solitude "like a storm" in Prologue 1: that man wants above all consideration is a theme in III.5: he was forsaken the first time ("in a forest, undecided where to turn, near a corpse") in Prologue 10: he was foresaken among the drunken in II.19: he was foresaken in his "stillest hour" in II.22: he learned to "pass by" in III.7: he became nauseated by the unclean rabble in II.6: the spiritual poverty of the shopkeepers was lamented in I.12: "everyone talks and nobody listens" in III.5: the temptation of pity occurs in Prologue 6,7 and II.3 and elsewhere but, unknown to Zarathustra, is not yet behind him: the necessity to disguise himself is the theme of II.21 and III.6: the smallness and maliciousness of the small man is a theme throughout the book: the stupidity of the small man becomes the theme in III.12: stiff sages

are to be found in I.2, I.3, I.4, I.9, II.3, II.4, II.8, II.17, II.19 et al.: the "grave-diggers" were encountered in Prologue 8 and II.14 (see especially my comments to Prologue 8).

57. See I.4.

58. Tyrant, fanatic, martyr=hardest of the hard-hearted. Collective mad-ness=malicious gadfly. Opportunistic leaders=riders of every horse. Disruptive force=earthquake. Question of master race=lightning-like question. Will to tyranny=glance making man lower than snake and swine. Gruesome cruelty=teacher of great contempt.

59. Zarathustra's "gift-giving virtue" here takes on a new meaning: the *giving* of order and rank from above onto passive peoples is a *virtue* of the future creator. To *take* power was pronounced "wholesome and holy" in I.22—but this type of selfishness is in direct contrast to the power-taking of the impoverished. When one has higher goals to offer, taking power is giving: when one takes power to satisfy revenge alone, taking is a type of degeneration. (See comments to I.6 and I.11.)

60. "And "selfless"—that is how all these world-weary cowards and cross-marked spiders wanted themselves, for good reasons." Allusions to christianity are obvious throughout the speech. Schopenhauer is alluded to as the promoter of "wisdom that blooms in the dark, a nightshade wisdom, which always sighs: all is in vain." Schopenhauer is also a promoter of "all wisdom that is all-too-mistrustful." Schopenhauer may also be taken as the european representative of buddhism and oriental scepticism. Nietzsche's critiques here, as everywhere, seeks to hit generalizable targets, not merely individual faiths or philosophers.

61. See comments to I.21.2 for an explanation. (See also comments to I.6.)

62. Here appears Nietzsche's famous distinction between good/evil and good/bad, though only in outline. The master's aristocratic value equation judges good=noble=powerful=beautiful=happy=loved-by-god. He judges *himself* as good while the plebian is judged to be *bad* (=powerless=ugly= unhappy=overlooked by god). The slave's value equation, on the contrary, is *reactive*: the slave first judges the noble man as *evil* (=powerful=happy= beautiful, etc.,) and secondly judges himself as *good* and *beloved by god*. Nietzsche contends that the value equation of the aristocrat precedes that of the slave, and that slave morality is reactive and dependent. (See *Zur Genealogie der moral* First Essay (*KSA* V 257 ff) for the best exposition of this distinction.

63. See III.12.2.

64. See Luke 6:24-25.

65. See comments to III.2, II.19 and II.20.

66. "For whatever is his own is well concealed from the owner; and of all trea-sures, it is our own that we dig up last: thus the spirit of gravity orders it." And therefore one suffers little children to come unto one—in order to forbid them betimes to love themselves . . . . " (this parodies Matthew 19:14). "Man is hard to discover—hardest of all for himself: often the spirit lies about the soul. Thus the spirit of gravity orders it."

67. The recent christian phrase "One Way" was of course unknown to Nietzsche, though it would hardly have surprised him. The text parodies the saying of Christ, "I am the way, the truth, the light."

68. I.e. "the spirit of gravity, and all that he created: constraint, statute, necessity, and consequence and purpose and will and good and evil."

69. "dying, I want to give them my richest gift." It is clear from I.21, IV.20 and Nietzsche's notes that Zarathustra's death is intended to coincide with the highest point of his maturity.

70. See comments to Prologue 6 and I.22.2 for the passage, "But only a jester thinks: man can also be *skipped* over."

71. See III.3, III.4 and III.6.

72. See II.20 and III.10.

73. Concerning the barrier of conscience to immoralism, see esp. I.6, I.8, I.17 and I.19.

74. Especially important in this connection are Part 5 of *Menschliches, Allzumen-schliches* the first Essay of *Zur Genealogie der Moral*, the ninth Part of *Jen-seits von Gut und Boese* and a series of notes collected and translated by Kaufmann as Book IV section 3 of *Will to Power*.

75. (See comments to II.8.)

76. *Holy Bible. New Schofield Reference Edition*, page 696 footnote 1.

77. The imagery of eating prevalent in sections 13-18 clearly marks Schopen-hauer as the target, as has previously been the case (see esp. comments to II.15). Schopenhauer was an infamous friend of food. The imagery is based

upon the identification of spirit and the stomach. Schopenhauer the pessimist is unable to enjoy the world because his spirit is "upset." (Note the materialist imagery.)

78. "No one of you wants to embark on the bark of death. Why then do you want to be world-weary?" My term "bad faith" here is intended in the sense of Sartre's *moi fau*.

79. "and if you do not want to *run* again with pleasure, then you should pass away . . . . But it takes more *courage* to make an end than to make a new verse: all physicians and poets know that."

80. I.e. "tablets created by weariness" and "tablets created by rotten, rotting sloth."

81. The "raving vermin of the "educated"" are the historians, philologists, biographers, etc., who feed off of the higher men for thoughts, inspiration and the like. (See the gravedigger figure of Prologue 8 and II.16.)

82. The second half of section 19 is quoted almost *in toto* by Nietzsche in *Ecce Homo* (see *KSA* VI 344), indicating its significance in his own eyes.

83. " . . . therefore go away in to the woods and lay your sword to sleep." "Go your *own* ways! And let the people and peoples go theirs—"

84. Wars for the "smallest advantage from any rubbish" are wars for class interest. The shopkeeper class is of course not the masters of the earth.

85. "Thus they should become better beasts of prey, subtler, more prudent, more *human* . . . . "

86. See comments to I.20 and I.10.

87. See esp. II.20.

88. For Nietzsche's distinction between peoples and states, see I.11, II.15 and III.10.2.

89. This view of Jesus is maintained in Renan's *Life of Jesus*, a book Nietzsche highly respected. As Renan points out, the pharisees were the target of all Jesus' attacks. (See page 112 of the Diogenes Verlag edition of Renan's book.)

90. Jesus was of course tried and convicted under the normal jewish and roman laws against heresy.

91. See the highly interesting *Froehliche Wissenschaft* 143. (See *KSA* III pages 490-91.)

92. As shown in *Ecce Homo* (*KSA* VI page 344), the overman is indeed embodied in the figure of Zarathustra. This occurs only when Zarathustra is able to speak the word of eternal return without breaking. He succeeds in doing so in the following section.

93. The emphasis on *one* occurs in the German, though not in Kaufmann's translation.

94. See "And once you are awake, you shall remain awake eternally. It is not my way to awaken great-grandmothers from their sleep to bid them sleep on!" This parodies Wagner's *Siegfried* Act III Scene 1, in which Wotan awakens Erda for no apparent reason. For the story behind this parody, see Roger Hollinrake's *Nietzsche, Wagner and the Philosophy of Pessimism*. Hollinrake makes the exaggerated claim that this two line parody is the nub of *Zarathustra*'s construction.

95. The image of eagle aiding convalescent occurs at Kings 17:6. This scene strongly recalls the imagery of II.19 and III.10.

96. "For me—how should there be any outside-myself? There is no outside."

97. Other symbols of the substance: year of being, house of being, ring of being.

98. "Everything goes, everything comes back; eternally rolls the wheel of being. Everything dies, everything blossoms again; eternally runs the year of being. Everything breaks, everything is joined anew; eternally the same house of being is built. Everything parts, everything greets every other thing again; eternally the ring of being remains faithful to itself."

99. "All-too-small, the greatest!—that was my disgust with man. And the eternal recurrence even of the smallest—that was my disgust with all existence. Alas! Nausea! Nausea! Nausea!"

100. I wish to thank Bill Stouffer for bringing this to my attention.

101. See also III.12.3: "For I want to go to men once more . . . . From the sun I learned this: when he goes down, overrich; he pours gold into the sea out of inexhaustible riches, so that even the poorest fisherman still rows with golden oars. For this I once saw and I did not tire of my tears as I watched it."

102. The original title of this section is "*Vita Femina*. The Other Dancing Song."

103. The leading image of a golden boat recalls III.14 and III.12.3, both being dionysian images.

104. The whip, made (in)famous in I.18, symbolizes here once again the interpretation of life as command and obedience. (See also II.12.)

105. This poem has also been exclusively discussed in the Nietzsche secondary literature. (See Roger Hollinrake's and M. Rutler's "Nietzsche's Sketches for the Poem "Oh Mensch! Gieb Acht!"" in Volume IV of *Nietzsche-Studien*.

106. The title of this section in the rough drafts was "The Sealing" (*Die Besiegelung*): in the fair copy of sub-section 1, "Yes and Amen": in the fair copy of sub-section 3, "Dionysus": in the fair copy of sub-section 4, "On the Ring of Rings." (See *KSA* XIV page 324.)

107. From the notebooks it is clear that these seals correspond to Zarathustra's seven solitudes. Since these solitudes result in anti-christian thoughts, the seven seals are likely also related to "the seven devils" of I.17. For the "seven seals" of christianity, see Revelations 5:1. And for "Yes and Amen," Rev.1:7.

108. Heraclitus had compared the world to a mixing bowl: Plato used the opposite image of a winnowing basket. The image of drafts occurs nowhere else in the book. The synthesis of these opposites clearly occurs at III.12.19.

109. Imagery of sailors is rampant: see e.g., II.18 and III.2. The seawaves fight the keel of the creator in II.12. For jubilating in the boundless, see III.12.2.

Prefatory Remarks to Part IV

Nietzsche finished writing Part III on January 18, 1884. By the end of April it was printed and in distribution. Thereafter Nietzsche paid a series of visits to friends. From July to September he sojourned in Sils-Maria, the "holy spot" of *Zarathustra*. During August he was visited by Heinrich von Stein, who may have been influential in the design of Part IV. By November Nietzsche was writing again, this time in Menton, Italy. The result, Part IV, took several weeks to write and was under publication (privately) by 1885. From the first "flash of lightning" in August, 1881, to the finalization of Part IV in December 1884, the entire *Zarathustra* project took a mere three years and four months to complete. Only the first three Parts came immediately to the public eye: Part IV was distributed privately to a select group of friends at Nietzsche's own expense. The commonly accepted explanation (e.g., Walter Kaufmann) is that Part IV was suppressed out of fear of confiscation on grounds of blasphemy.

There were many outlines to Part IV with a variety of plot twists and endings. Yet in all of them, Part IV was seen as a "bridge," or "intermezzo," to a subsequent Part or Parts portraying the Great Noon and other events. Thus, even in four Parts, *Zarathustra* is an incomplete work. Though Nietzsche writes of it as complete and final, from a purely structural perspective, much remains to be done. At the end of Part IV Zarathustra stands ready to descend a final time but this itself does not occur. The result, as he descends, would presumably be another Part of many speeches. The Great Noon must still occur in yet another Part, followed by a final Part chronicling Zarathustra's death, according to one plan. Thus Part IV is far from the "final" Part of *Zarathustra*, and much less is the book complete in *three* Parts, with Part IV somehow superfluous.

Commentary to Part IV

Alas, where in the world has there been more folly than among the pitying? And what in the world has caused more suffering than the folly of the pitying? Woe to all who love without having a height that is above their pity! Thus spoke the devil to me once: "God too has his hell: that is his love of man." And most recently I heard him say this: "God is dead; God died of his pity for man." (Part II Section 3)

Part IV

1. The Honey Sacrifice

At this moment in the book, we stand before a great vista: the bizarre and densely symbolic events of the ascent through Part III are years past, the highpoints and ridges of Part II now stand as foothills below the rarified atmosphere of Zarathustra's cave, and the great trials and tribulations of crossing over the mass of humanity encountered in Part I were enacted in the arabesque and now remote Motley Cow. The events of the Market Place now lie as far removed from him as the earth's center from its highest peak. At this awesome height, Zarathustra is "as one having overmuch of the good." His solar will radiates beams of supreme happiness, a golden cup running over with honey.[1] Though he playfully attempts to hide his happiness from the animals, they return his jokes, verbalize his inner states and find the proper metaphor for his spirit.

Zarathustra is in the twilight of his years, and though he is dying, happiness has finally come to him as fruition comes to all things organic. He jokingly suggests that happiness itself is the cause of his coming death.[2] The sobering accuracy of his imagery ("blood thickens and soul calms") is verified by the animals,[3] who divert his thoughts of death to the perfection of the world and who bid him to climb even higher than the cave. It is at this highest elevation that Zarathustra performs the "honey sacrifice."[4]

His mystical manner of speech is, of course, a "mere cunning and, verily, a useful folly." True, his bliss may be poeticized as "honey" to catch "growling bears and queer, sullen birds,"[5] but Zarathustra's real message could equally well be allegorized by Jesus' parable of discipleship as fishing.[6] Indeed, "even the gods might covet" the higher types swimming in the human seas of the earth. *Behind both images stands Zarathustra's desire to gather disciples around him. His happiness is a love of mankind compelling him ever again back among men.* Now, in his last years, Zarathustra desires to assemble his proper companions.

It is clear from the context that Nietzsche alludes to Jesus' self-description as a "fisher of men." Such a comparison was anticipated as early as Prologue 7. Some elements of this imagery relate to III.10, but the real allusion is to III.12 (3). That section contains the image of a fisherman floating in sunshine, as in IV.1. The fisherman of III.12 was already identified as Dionysus, the "overman." Zarathustra had "seen" the overman as a fishing Dionysus—now Zarathustra is the fisherman enveloped in sunshine, Dionysus himself, the overman.[7] By claiming a sort of divinity, Zarathustra completes his counterposition to Christ and sets the stage for a systematic blasphemy against the Gospels.

Zarathustra's promethean love of man is the solar happiness of the overman (=sun). The relation in Prologue 1 between the main character and the sun undergoes a copernican revolution in meaning here. Zarathustra now finds the solar overman *within* himself: previously the overman was an external attraction for him. Now Zarathustra is the force attracting all who are "the queerest human fish" in order to satisfy "the most sarcastic of those who fish for men." But fishing is his essence and so search he must for his proper companions.

Though he is old, Zarathustra has not forgotten the lessons of the Market Place. Rather than erring in haste, he awaits his time in great bliss and patience. If Zarathustra is to go among men only once more, he must choose his time and audience carefully, awaiting the "sign" of IV.20. Thus his idea is to attract the higher man to Zarathustra, rather than go out among the masses. His disciples seek him out beginning with the next section. But the "queer fish" found in sections 2-9 are nonetheless only *isolated, projected, objectified, humanized and animated aspects of Zarathustra's own person.* "And whatever in all the sea belongs to *me*, my in-and-for-me in all things—*that* fish out for me, *that* bring up to me." All imagery in *Zarathustra* is *a projection of his inner states, thoughts and feel-*

ings. This has been shown in many cases. The general rule is verified in III.1: "in the end, one experiences only oneself." Part IV exploits this mechanism to portray a depth-psychological view of Zarathustra in the form of seperate *persons*.

As with Zarathustra and Jesus, so the "great men" of power politics—the rabble-rousers of mass movements promising "great events"—also seek followers. But such waves of humanity and their strong men crest and then are gone: they are surface water.[8] Zarathustra wants a *spiritual* movement in the spirit of mankind deeper than any political movement, a "great *Hazar*: that is, our great distant human kingdom, the zarathustran kingdom of a thousand years." This is, of course, a parody of Revelations 20:1-6, i.e., one of innumerable antibiblical counterposes. Yet there *is* a real soothsaying spirit in Zarathustra[9] who prophecizes a future man— the overman—arising after the period of total nihilism called the "Great Noon." (There is, of course, a pervasive ambiguity between the Great Noon as a world historical occurence and as a psychological event: this very ambiguity is characteristic of Nietzsche's prophetic thought.) *Hazar* is simply another label for the epoch following the fall of christianity ushering in a rise of new strength and optimism.[10] Yet it must be asked how Zarathustra's Ape would misinterpret this speech.

Genuine dionysian optimism wants Yes-saying only after the greatest contempt and so Zarathustra fishes in the black waters of melancholic mankind. Indeed, Zarathustra is himself truly a Yessayer much changed from Part III. Previously he had barely been able to accept the mere existence of the small man, albeit into eternity. Now he overflows with a love of man and a full appreciation of the "dawning human futures" he foresees. His bliss is total and his love of himself as overman overflows.

2. The Cry of Distress

The first higher man to be attracted by the honey sacrifice is the soothsaying "growling bear" of II.19. His message—"All is the same, nothing is worthwhile, the world is without meaning, knowledge chokes"[11]—anticipated in Prologue 3 as "the great contempt," has worked an oppressive effect upon Zarathustra, as schopenhauerian pessimism had worked upon the young Nietzsche. This effect was acknowledged at III.13: "The great disgust with man—*this* choked me and had crawled into my throat; and what the Soothsayer said: "All is the same, nothing is worthwhile, knowledge chokes."" Indeed, this character is the personified schopenhauerian aspects of Zarathustra's personality. The Soothsayer embodies the weakness and pessimism Zarathustra has opposed in himself and others, including, if not especially, *pity*. He is one of the "sublime," an "immaculate perceiver," a "despiser of the body," an "unconditional" and a "teacher of opiate virtues." He suffers from a great disgust with man, but he sees no redeeming justification for life. *One might well say that his message—"knowledge chokes"—encapsulates in two words the great struggle surrounding the eternal return.* But unlike Zarathustra, the Soothsayer has no overman, no notion of eternal return, i.e., no self-created ideals: he is the lion caught in a nihilistic desert of his own making. Thus he is associated with the Pale Criminal, youth on the mountainside and other higher men who lose their courage to overcome the lion stage of spirit.

This "proclaimer of ill tidings" introduces the plot structure for the teaching of eternal return—now he must secure his victory by passing a last temptation, beginning in this section and lasting until IV.20. The entirety of Part IV occurs during one day of Zarathustra's life.

In III.9 Zarathustra confides, "Consideration and pity have ever been my greatest dangers . . . . " He comes into danger from pity here as the Soothsayer prophecizes a great weariness in man, a rising tide of nihilism that would engulf the higher man and even Zarathustra. As if on cue, a long and eerie cry of distress floats up from the valley like a flood of despair. This pitiful cry of higher man is the oblique utterance of the Shadow in II.18; namely, "It is time! It is high time!" *This cry is the temptation to pity the higher man.*[12] It announces the hour of Zarathustra's final descent, threatening to lure him prematurely from his cave. The true "sign" of his final descent does not come until IV.20. By means of a contagious pessimism, the Soothsayer nearly succeeds in trapping

Zarathustra with pity. After mention of the Blessed Isles, however, he regains his courage and braces for the search for the higher man. As Zarathustra said in III.2: "Courage is the best slayer: courage slays even pity."

3. Conversation with the Kings

The two kings are spokesmen for what George Brandes called "Nietzsche's aristocratic radicalism."[13] Their companion, the ass, symbolizes official state philosophy and in IV.18 becomes the object of worship in a blasphemous ceremony. As the caravan arrives, the kings launch into a thinly veiled diatribe against wilhelminian society from the vantage point of the disenfranchised aristocracy. But as previously seen, Nietzsche's "new nobility" is a purely non-political vision.[14] The social and political arena of bourgeois society—the moneyed classes against the rabble—allows no place for thinkers. This is, once again, the lesson of the Market Place from the Prologue. A rising tide of social nihilism—democratic or socialist sentiment—forces a retreat of aristocratic spirits from the leadership roles of society, leaving them to the crude and bungling; and so a crisis of imbalance, ignorance and bravado is created. Indirectly commenting on Prologue 6, Zarathustra says, "Man's fate knows no harsher misfortune than when those who have power on earth are not also the first men." Yet this radicalism is one entirely of spirit: Nietzsche in no way endorses the resurgence of a political aristocracy.[15] His "overman" and "higher man" form no political parties nor do they indulge in political adventurism and opportunism. At most, Nietzsche is guilty of sword-rattling, anti-socialist sloganeering or waxing poetic for a spiritual "aristocracy" without social reality. Laughing at himself, Nietzsche portrays the kings more as funny old men than as militant reactionaries.

Zarathustra well recognizes the possibility of misinterpretation by those with "long ears," and yet he nonetheless entertains an insipid Junker romanticism and speaks in martial proverbs. Given consequent historical misassociations, the reader may well question the pride behind the statement, "I have long become unaccustomed to any consideration for long ears."

4. The Leech

In this section, Zarathustra's intellectual conscience is personified as a man lying prostrate in a swamp. He is depicted as the modern scholar or scientist whose will to truth drives him ever further into specialization. This is the meaning of his study of the leech's brain: not only must he specialize to knowledge of the leech, he must further restrict his knowledge to its brain. The leech-bitten man, in his own type of extremism, has a will to honesty that is "hard, strict, narrow, cruel and inexorable." And so the Conscientious Man is meticulous in all things, bringing many pains onto himself, always seeking foundational truths, even if they are of microscopic scale.

This character reappears in IV.15 in a minor role. Both sections are low points of Nietzsche's stylistic experiment in Part IV. The imagery of these sections may well rest upon a pun on Zarathustra's proverb, "Spirit is that which cuts into itself."

5. The Magician

Sub-section 1. Shortly after the schopenhauerian Soothsayer arrives, the wagnerian Magician appears, who, like the other higher men, attempts to induce pity in Zarathustra. After flailing about in "piteous gestures," the Magician delivers a melodramatic, wagnerian monologue aimed at fostering sympathy for the "ascetic of the spirit," i.e., the poet-magician who at last turns his spirit against itself.[16]

Sub-section 2. Though temporarily deceived, Zarathustra recovers and exposes the Magician's deception as *a trick of an artist disgusted with himself.* (This allegorizes Nietzsche's image of Wagner in one elegant stroke.) The artist-who-becomes-showman must above all attract a following, not unlike the singers of III.11, "whose throats are made mellow . . . only by a packed house." But a lack of substance, of *truth*, plagues the Magician: he is *all show*—a one-man theater of masks, poses, mirrors and frills. Thus he is also linked to the "man of great events" and the Jester of the Prologue. Though he is advertised as a great man, the wagnerian artist falls far short of his own expectations. (This recalls the Tightrope

Walker of Prologue 6 and the speech on the higher man at Prologue 4.) He leads a genuine life only when he admits failure.[17] Thus he is disgusted with himself and the entire charade. To elicit pity, he deceives and flatters Zarathustra: "Did I seek you? I—merely seek." But this is plainly a lie: and so he reverts immediately back to his deceitful ways after being momentarily genuine.

Zarathustra must fight back pity for the Magician, but he succeeds and instead lashes the Magician with barbs against so-called "great men" and their cults of genius. It is Zarathustra's lot in life to expose and attack (=stab) men of great events and their mass followings, be they politicians or artists, such as Wagner. But when the Magician is out of sight, Zarathustra jubilates in his new acquaintances.

6. Retired

This section begins the earnest presentation of one of Nietzsche's most famous dicta; namely, that *god is dead*.[18] As early as Prologue 2, this idea is anticipated when Zarathustra exclaims, "Could it be possible? This old saint in the forest has not yet heard of this, that *god is dead*!" (The same hermit is mentioned later in this section.) In II.13, Zarathustra relates being told by the devil that "god is dead: god died of his pity for man." (This quote is also Nietzsche's choice for the introductory quote to Part III, stressing its importance.) In III.8 the gods *laugh* themselves to death at the pretentiousness of christian monotheism. We meet in the present section the only witness of god's death, as a narrative tool for deeper investigation of the notion.

On the surface, the Last Pope operates as a representative of the priestly psychological type. At a deeper level, though, this figure personifies *piety without a savior*: the Last Pope is religion without belief in god—religiosity in the abtract. More precisely, *the Last Pope is a personification of Zarathustra's faculties of religious esteem and emotion divorced from an object*. Paradoxically, the Pope is piety incarnate when belief in god is no longer possible.

The Last Pope was under way in search of the Hermit from Prologue 2, whom he calls "the most pious man." But, like god himself, the Hermit is dead, without hopes of resurrection. And so the Pope must settle for *the most pious atheist*. Though god is an unbelievable hypothesis for Zarathustra, he still has not lost his ability to esteem with religious intensity. Indeed, this intensity of devotion, with the ideal of Dionysus as its object, is the *love of the overman* promoted throughout the book. Nietzsche consistently distinguishes between the general concept of god (*Gottesbegriff*) and the specifically christian notion, and honors the former while rejecting the latter.

When belief in god becomes impossible, it is the truly pious man who suffers the greatest, for his entire being has been directed to the service of his lord. In his sufferings, the Last Pope is a higher man whose sorrows entice great pity: once again Zarathustra is tempted by pity for "those who would cross over." Pity is one of the theological virtues Zarathustra has repeatedly cited as detrimental to life. And yet everything about the Last Pope is pitiful. His sorrows elicit pity; he worships a god who pities man; he pities god on the cross, who pities mankind even as he suffers. Indeed, the essence of christianity, for Nietzsche, is the depth psychology of sorrow, pity and *ressentiment* working at cross-purposes with life.[19]

In the image of their god, the pious see an inverted image of themselves. In their religious imaginations, those who pity imagine a suffering god, whose pity for mankind drove him from body and earth. These sorrows are multiplied in the spirit of the pitier as he is unable to fight back his pity. When the priest looks for metaphysical comfort, he sees a mirror of himself in the clouds. Christ pities man, as does the priest, and then he seeks to alleviate human sorrow; this makes the man-god adequate to the emotional needs of the priestly type. God dies on the same cross as the pious man—pity born of love for man. But pity, for either god or man, "always offends the sense of shame."[20]

As the last believer, the Pope knows of the circumstances of god's death. And as the lifelong servant of his lord, he claims to have certain damning evidence surrounding the conception of Jesus. This blasphemy signals an attack on the very moral character of Jehova himself. In judaism, the god Yahweh (=Jehova) is the

judgmental father figure. In christianity, Jehova becomes a grandfatherly figure of great love, and even more so a grandmotherly
figure of overconcern, puritanism and nagging. As the senile god of
German deism and pietism, he chokes to death on his overindul-
gent pity.

God's death has already been portrayed in a number of conflicting images, and there are more to follow. This very multiplicity of
images suggests multifarious and contradictory interpretations of
the dictum, as is typical for the notions contained in *Zarathustra*.
And we should bear in mind what the Shadow exclaims much later
in IV.17: "in the case of gods, *death* is always a mere prejudice."
There are indeed many ways in which god(s) may die: there are
many paths to atheism. This is already evidenced in the types of
rejection portrayed: e.g., from the theological motives of the
gravediggers to Zarathustra's sense of taste to simple revenge (as in
the next section). And indeed, god's death is a mere prejudice,
since the difference between belief and doubt is human choice.

As he frequently remarks,[21] Zarathustra's loss of faith was determined by judgments of *taste*: the moral character of God in
christian mythology offends his most basic sense of beauty and sublimity: the "old grimbeard" of christianity could no longer *inspire*
belief. Though his reasons seem based on theology reminiscent of
God's gravewatchers in III.8, his real basis for rejection of christianity is one of aesthetics; more precisely, the aesthetics of religio-
mythical vision. Yahweh is no justification whatsoever for the
world. Thus Zarathustra concludes, "Away with *such* a god! Rather
no god, rather make destiny on one's own, rather be a fool, rather
be a god oneself!"

As previously seen, the death of god is closely associated with
"birth of the overman" (here detected in the phrase "rather be a
god oneself!"). When the faculty of religious emotion and feeling is
returned from god to man, from whence it came, the rekindled
flame of love for man will provide the guiding light over man, i.e.,
the overman. This diversion of consciousness from the concept of
god to the future man spells the dissolution of all religious consciousness, emotion and substance. Before such promethean hu-

manism, the Last Pope stands in awe. Zarathustra has given direction to the Last Pope's enormous capacity to esteem, saving him from the nihilism of atheism.[22] Now seeing the dionysian overman as *the aesthetic justification of the world after the death of god*, the Last Pope declares, "some god in you must have converted you to your godliness." That is, Zarathustra has not replaced the dead god with despair, but rather has redirected his religious impulse toward rediscovery of man, his body and earth.[23]

The Pope does not detect residual christianity in Zarathustra, but instead discovers a new orientation for man. Now Zarathustra attempts to set man perpendicular to the earth again: "And I wish that I could put everyone who is sad back on firm land and firm legs." Perpendicularity here, as elsewhere,[24] allegorizes the naturalist orientation to the earth, in contrast to the centripetality of swooning religious emotion. Man should stand on his own feet and reach for the stars; that is, be earth-oriented but striving after goals harmonious with the earth. Zarathustra would gladly be the overman to reinspire man, but he finds himself waiting for the "sign" to descend. Given that he is still unable to answer the Soothsayer's demand in II.19 to *see* the overman, it may be premature to announce the death of god. Yet such momentous truths require gestation, and so the death of god is slow to dawn in the consciousness of man at large. But convinced that the fate of christianity is a *fait accompli*, Zarathustra the godless revels before the Last Pope in the knowledge that "this god lives no more; he is thoroughly dead."[25]

Another level of meaning to the Last Pope lies in the history of nineteenth-century German atheism. Two "Young Hegelians," David Friedrich Strauss and Ludwig Feuerbach, figure prominently in the history of atheism. Strauss delivered a blistering exegesis of the Holy Scriptures and related documents in *Das Leben Jesu, kritisch bearbeitet* (1835), while Feuerbach attacked the theological and metaphysical underpinnings of christianity in *Das Wesen des Christentums* (1842). Yet, according to Nietzsche, both remained all-too-similar to the churchfathers whom they assailed.[26] Rather than spend his lifetime reexamining the works of evangelists, the-

ologians and metaphysicians, as did Strauss and Feuerbach, Nietzsche rejected christianity from an aesthetic perspective.[27] Yet Nietzsche shared the (super)humanist and naturalist tendencies of
Feuerbach and respected Strauss greatly. Indeed, Zarathustra's
wish to put melancholic spirits ". . . back on firm land and legs" may
well allude to the feuerbachian dictum made famous later by Karl
Marx: "Hegelian philosophy of religion *hovers in the air*, mine
stands firmly with both legs on the familiar soil of earth."[28] This
section, then, may well reflect Nietzsche's (limited) admiration of
his forerunners in atheism, since his own initial turn from religion
was fueled by readings of Feuerbach and Strauss, a formative impe-
tus he was not likely to forget.

7. The Ugliest Man

As in the myth of Oedipus and the Sphinx, Zarathustra is met by
a monster of nature in a forbidden and terrifying place, to be confronted by a riddle incarnate: "What is revenge against the witness?
Who am I?" Zarathustra correctly surmises the following identities.
The "witness" in the riddle is God himself; "revenge against the witness" is the murder, or death, of God; and the transgression revenged is God's witnessing of man's basest elements, thus offending
man's sense of shame. The Ugliest Man is therefore surmissed to
be the *murderer of God*, introducing another contradictory image
to God's death.

In a note to this section, Nietzsche describes this character as
"the ideal of world-renouncing ways of mind."[29] The Ugliest Man
has lost the natural human desire to find himself beautiful, whether
his own person or his overimage in a god. The note continues:

> But religions are also results of this drive for beauty . . . : the final conse-
> quence—to grasp the absolute ugliness of man, existence without god, reason,
> etc.—pure buddhism. The uglier, the better.

The Ugliest Man no longer has the drive to esteem himself and to
protect an image of his own higher elements over himself as an
ideal. Thus he is the most pitiful of the higher men, and *Zarathustra succumbs to an attack of pity.*

But Zarathustra quickly rebounds from his pity and shows his respect for god's murderer, whom he calls "the indescribable one." Avoidance of pity is what has driven the Ugliest Man to the Valley of Snake's Death, for the all-too-many have offended him in his shame. Zarathustra showed shame even in his pity, and so has avoided offending the ugliest of all men. This "unspeakable one" proceeds to level an aristocratic rebuke of the "good and just," including heavy blasphemy concerning Jesus before Pilate. Above all, the Ugliest Man joins Zarathustra in his fight against the christian-schopenhauerian-wagnerian virtue of pity.

An affront of pity is the motive for the "murder of god," as it is told here. God, in his omniscience, became the "curious, overobtrusive, overpitying" grandmotherly type as bemoaned in IV.6. Recalling Raskolnikov and the Pale Criminal, he laments, "The god who saw everything, *even man*—this god had to die!" But the transgression of witnessing man's basest nature is of great import, only if a sense of shame is offended. The Ugliest Man feels a great shame in his own humanity, and so seeks to murder the omniscient god who is his own image. He is the man who cannot overcome his great contempt for man. Zarathustra has overcome nihilistic atheism in his new ideal, Dionysus. In language reminiscent of Prologue 4, he praises the "great despisers" whose great contempt is a kind of height. *But contempt, like all things about man, is "something that must be overcome."*

8. The Voluntary Beggar

Zarathustra next stumbles upon "a peaceful man and sermonizer on the mount," who, like the hermits of Prologue 2 and 8, disavows mankind to go among the animals for solitude. The Voluntary Beggar's personal history reflects that of Gattama Buddha and indeed Nietzsche gives to this character a sort of oriental wisdom. Nietzsche had read a short biography of Gattama Buddha shortly before writing *Zarathustra*. Elements of the biography appear as early as Prologue 1. Through the voice of the Beggar, Nietzsche seeks to balance his "aristocratic radicalism" with a critical stance against consumer society and materialism. This hyper-critical stance, however, results in a political resignationism: "mob above and mob below! What do "poor" and "rich" matter today?"

Zarathustra draws two analogies: first, between the Beggar's resignationism and vegatarianism; and second, between the Beggar himself and the cows. But the underlying question of happiness—animal, human or superhuman—is, however, postponed for the festivities of the evening.

9. The Shadow[30]

As the last of the "queer fish" foretold in IV.2, Zarathustra's own Shadow comes to life to (meagerly) embody the main character's adventuresome, risk-taking and nomadic nature. His Shadow was already seen in a brief but dramatic appearance in II.18, as he flew through the air screaming, "It's time! It's high time!" only to land in a volcanoe. This call was later interpreted as the call for Zarathustra to teach the eternal return, though still later it becomes the "cry of distress" tempting Zarathustra into pity for the higher man.

Zarathustra's Shadow personifies the nietzschean motto, "Live dangerously!"[31] He leads a life of risk-taking and wandering, daring to "cross over" man, issuing a call for self-overcoming. Thus he is like the sailors, wanderers and adventurers with whom he is constantly associated. He is one of the higher men lauded in Prologue 4 and personified by the Tightrope Walker in Prologue 6. And yet he is the higher man who has *failed*, for he is, alas, still only Zarathustra's Shadow—dependent, goalless, a follower as much as any corpse. (All the higher men of Part IV, in fairness, may be said to embody great failures of various types, and necessarily so.) Above all, the Shadow lacks his own goal, his own overman, that it might give him substance.[32] Thus he sinks into a deep nihilism with his cries, "Nothing is true, all is permitted! ... Nothing is alive anymore that I love ... O eternal, in vain!"[33] Yet he will reemerge from nihilism in IV.16 in the role Nietzsche had originally cast for him; namely, *the good european*. (The Shadow was intended as a symbol of the "good european" in *Menschliches, Allzumenschliches*. This underdeveloped figure was meant there as a counter-image to european nihilism and German nationalism.)

10. At Noon

Having found the last of the higher men, Zarathustra rests under a tree at this "perfect noon hour." What then unfolds offers us a counter-image to the nightmarish vision and riddle of III.2. Zarathustra, who is compared to a shepherd, rests at the hour when shepherds do not play their pipes, i.e., at noon, when Pan was said to sleep.[34]

At this "perfect noon hour" Zarathustra undergoes a state of altered awareness, which he describes as sleeping with open eyes. In this dreamish condition, Zarathustra watches as the world of the waking transforms into a vision of perfection. First, he projects and personifies his own spirit as the mythical Ariadne, slowly reclining as she is overcome with sleep. Second, he projects his dionysian happiness into the vision of a god (Dionysus) lying under the sun in the shade, drunken and overflowing with laughter out of an over-abundance of happiness. "The old noon sleeps, his mouth moves: is he not just now drinking a drop of happiness . . . ? It slips over him, his happiness laughs. Thus laughs a god." By the postures and attributes of these mythic figures, one sees that these visions are mirrors of Zarathustra's own satiation and bliss. But even when seeing visions, Zarathustra reaffirms his love of mother earth, for Ariadne and Dionysus rest on solid ground even in dream and intoxication, "near the earth, faithful, trusting, waiting, tied to it with the softest threads."

A final transformative vision occurs as the world of the waking becomes objectified and perfected in the vision of a "golden round ball." This is in fact the counter-image of III.2. (Neither Naumann nor Messer recognize this.) In that section, the shepherd/Zarathustra was unable to withstand the vision of eternal return, and so it turned venomous, biting fast and choking him. But Zarathustra now receives a totally ecstatic image in his "involuntary bliss." The symbol of the "golden round ball" incorporates the metaphor of recurrence as a ring, gold as the highest value and the global shape of the solar overman. In this one image, then, eternal return, will to power and overman are grasped as one simplified unity.

Not only does Zarathustra's vision here counter-pose that of III.2, it also alludes, once again, to Nietzsche's portrayal of the ancient Greek tragedians in *Die Geburt der Tragoedie*.[36] Just as the tragic poets had used their myths and legends as an "aesthetic justification" of the tragic nature of the world, so Zarathustra finds his own aesthetic justification in the transformative vision of the overman who can affirm the eternal return of every moment. By "aesthetic justification of the world," Nietzsche means a redeeming vision, myth, notion, etc., which raises the sublime and tragic in life to a beautiful appearance, making the former worthwhile, i.e., reaffirming the value of existence.

Upon seeing the overman/shepherd of III.2, Zarathustra described him as

No longer shepherd, no longer human—one changed, radiant, laughing! O my brothers, I heard a laughter that was no human laughter; and now a thirst gnaws at me, a longing that never grows still.

Zarathustra now satisfies his thirst for the overman as he fulfills his own admonition in IV.7 to "become a god oneself" in a spontaneous moment of ecstasy fit for the gods. His laughter is spontaneous and born of overabundant happiness, for only "thus laughs a god." And yet the laughing overman is none other than the man who can murder god and survive the pangs of conscience, for, as the god-slaying Ugliest Man notes in IV.18, "whoever would kill most thoroughly, *laughs*." God's death, the overman's birth and laughter become ever more indistinguishable events.

But this involuntary bliss does not last long, and Zarathustra steps outside himself to awaken himself to "ordinary" reality. The entire vision lasts but a moment, and yet it is such moments that reward his many years of spiritual struggle.

11. The Welcome

This section confirms a number of crucial identifications made in this commentary on the first half of Part IV. First, it is indeed the "cry of distress" from the higher man which signals Zarathustra's temptation to pity.[37] Second, the higher men Zarathustra assembles are indeed the first signs of a *rising disgust with man*.[38] Third, Zarathustra has in fact assumed the stature of the overman, for he is now portrayed as the sea in which the storm of nihilism will be quenched.[39] Fourth, the higher man does not represent the "sign" for Zarathustra's final descent for the Great Noon. Rather than go down to man, Zarathustra has *pulled up* the higher men to his mountaintop. The final descent, with consequent death of the main character, never occurs in *Zarathustra*. Thus, even in four Parts, it is an incomplete work.

Though relatively long, this section is only a summarizing inter-mezzo, setting the stage for the final scenes of *Zarathustra*: i.e., the blasphemous parody of the Last Supper (sections 12-19) and the next morning (section 20).

The higher men have been analyzed as the disparate elements of Zarathustra's evolving higher self. Indeed, it is important to note that Zarathustra uses only the singular "higher man"; it was their *unified* cry of distress that Zarathustra mistook as a single voice. And when he enters his cave he exclaims, "So it was *your* cry of distress I heard? . . . *the higher man*" though there be a number of men in the cave.[40] This underlines the ambiguity between unity and division among the higher men, an ambiguity Nietzsche leaves in tension.

All in all, though, the higher men are only *great despisers*. In his own persona, Zarathustra has drawn together the *highest* elements of his spirit in order to overcome the disgust experienced by the higher man. And though Zarathustra stands far above his guests in stature, he sets a mood of frivolity by laughing at himself and his seriousness.

12. The Last Supper

The ravenous schopenhauerian Soothsayer demands dinner, signaling the beginning of a parody of the Last Supper to occupy the next several sections. Zarathustra begins the comedy by posturing as a conqueror exhibiting a booty of "the best food, purest sky, the strongest thoughts, the most beautiful women." This is, of course, self-derision: the food is meager; there is no sky, only a cave ceiling; their thoughts soon turn to idol-worship; and there are no women present. The Kings are not slow to exploit the chance to poke fun at Zarathustra. The ass, which soon becomes the new idol, parodies Zarathustra's "Yes-saying" with an asinine "Yea-Yuh," playing the straightman for the Kings. Thus even here the ass fulfills his duty as the representative of state philosophy, i.e., the "yes-man" of the (disenfranchised) ruling class. The higher men lose their melancholy for several sections, though they, like their host, are not yet safe from their respective temptations.

13. The Higher Man

The "higher man" is a type encountered in the Prologue as the Tightrope Walker, whose trials and tribulations became the major theme of Part I. After taking on a variety of masks, the higher man is seen again as Zarathustra's shipmates in Part III, who "live dangerously" and "attempt to cross over." Attempted rescue of the higher man drowning in despair has been the structure of Part IV, an undertaking culminating in the present section.

Under discussion here are topics of greatest concern to the higher man: human inequality, the "overcoming" of mankind, courage, evil, sacrifice, prudence, limitations, self-formation, failure, overestimation of the self and the value of laughing and dancing. It is in this section, also, that Zarathustra finally solves his *problem of the proper audience* begun in the Prologue, for he here addresses the higher man concerning the higher man. Given this unique feature, and the speech's position as the last major summarizing section of the work, we should give higher priority to this speech than others in any interpretation of *Zarathustra*. Though Zarathustra does not provide the necessary clarification for the notion of the "higher man," this section is nonetheless valuable as a summary and as a source for validating previous comments on the higher man.

Sub-section 1. Although he recalls the Market Place of the Prologue after several decades, Zarathustra's opinions of public life and mass movements remain unchanged. In the spheres of modern political life, the notion of human equality holds absolute power.

Public arenas of power remain inappropriate domains of the higher man. Zarathustra's doctrine of the overman is a totally *anti-political* notion, and so has no interests in common with power politics.

Sub-section 2. Human equality is claimed on the basis of a theological equality of all souls before god. But when belief in god dies, belief in human equality is shaken from its foundation. It is only when god is foresaken (=murdered) that the higher man will take over as master of his own destiny (=becomes—master).

Nietzsche's phrase, *nun wird der hoehere Mensch—Herr*, contains a deadly ambiguity. The German word *Herr* may mean, among other common meanings, "lord" or "master" in a religious sense, or it may mean "lord" or "master" in a (feudal) political sense. Whether Nietzsche means this phrase as part of a systematic inversion of christianity, or in an aristocratic-political sense, is a question of great import. Naumann, for example, comments: "The Great Noon nears, at which the higher man becomes lord over the masses and the overman assumes the position of God."[41] Naumann then associates the Hellhound with "revolutionary democracy," giving the entire section a suspiciously anti-parlimentarian, reactionary, i.e., fascist, tone. Naumann also does not explain what he means when he says the higher men will be "breeders" (*Zuechter*). Naumann, it should be noted, wrote in 1905, was one of Nietzsche's editors and is perhaps still the foremost *Zarathustra* scholar in any language. He not only never accomodated the nazi appropriation of Nietzsche, but had in fact battled Elizbeth Foerster over contested manuscripts, which Nietzsche had sent to Naumann personally. Thus it is somewhat startling when Naumann gives such a fascist tint to a section capable of many more fruitful interpretations. (It is also extremely interesting to note who Naumann takes Nietzsche to be concerned about in sections 5 and 7: according to Naumann, it is the *criminal class* who worries Nietzsche. Elsewhere it is more clear that Nietzsche rather feared expropriation by the right-wing Junkers. Messer, who wrote in 1922, i.e., after World War I, remains silent on whom Nietzsche means here.) This section illustrates how ambiguities in the text, if not approached carefully, may lead to unintended and surprising misinterpretations.

Man is his own master when the biting voice of conscience, the grandmotherly nagging god, is silenced. God's death signals man's ascent, for as the emotional esteem formerly directed to god is redirected to its source, mankind will (gradually) climb in stature with renewed courage, commitment and love.[42] But renewed "master morality" in the higher man brings with it an aristocratic rejection of the doctrine of *human equality*, an idea so deeply rooted that its rejection is registered first emotionally, and only later intellectually.

Today's higher man signals the advent of a *future man* to bear Zarathustra's legacy, but the assembled higher man is not yet the overman.[43]

Sub-section 3. All social concern, be it of whatever form, seeks either the improvement of man's material circumstances or the alleviation of strife. Yet Zarathustra does not seek the *preservation* of the species—a mere continuation of the all-too-human—but instead the spiritual surpassing of the brutish in man's nature. Rather than evangelical "peace on earth, good will toward man," he foretells great wars spelling the destruction of modern man, for man is alas only a "bridge" to something beyond historical precedent.[44]

The word *Untergang*, as often noted, denotes *decline* when applied to civilizations. And as noted,[45] every overcoming (*Ueberwindung*) requires a going under (*Untergang*). Thus the surpassing of man requires the decline, if not the total destruction, of modern man. Naumann comments that "the all-too-many must be brought to extinction."[46] He ends his comments to the sub-section by saying, "It doesn't become them [the higher men] to mingle with the herd, the average: better to enter into struggle (*Kampf*) against them." *Contra* Naumann, I suggest the great wars are endorsed only as inevitable and that Zarathustra does not condone participation in them.[47] There is no more enthusiasm or *Shadenfreude* (—roughly translatable as "joy in another's sorrows") in this doctrine than in the eventual failure of the higher man. Further, these great wars are certainly not the higher men at war with the all-too-many, but rather the all-too-many at war with themselves.

Nietzsche's vision includes the extinction of man as a species due to a diremption into higher and lower forms. Man is thus torn into two successor species; first, by *degeneration* into lower types, and second, by *generation* of a higher type upsetting the status of the species.[48] Nietzsche would hasten the process of conflict and division, not out of malice, but out of a sense of inevitability. Western civilization is built on a set of absolutes which devalue themselves and which result in nihilism. Ultimately, european nihilism will manifest itself in a series of degenerative crises, mass hysteria and wars.[49] This soothsaying side of Zarathustra offers no sign of *Shadenfreude*, a fact easily overlooked in the horror of the vision. Nietzsche expresses no delight in war for its own sake, but did consider war as an inevitable feature of all-too-human existence. Wars based on false values, like all things about man, is "something that must be overcome."

Sub-section 4. Pride in one's challenges and courage before the fearsome are the marks of the higher man.

Sub-section 5. The value of evil in the higher man's ascent is continuously recommended, but not to the exclusion of great good. Capacity to do great good grants power to do great evil, though the Church denies this and attempts to disprove it. Those who have not turned out well—the rabble, men of great events and Zarathustra's Ape, for example—would falsify Zarathustra's words, or link them to actions alien to their meaning.

Sub-section 6. As was clear from the Prologue and Part I, Zarathustra recognizes the grave dangers to those who "cross over." Yet he has not withheld from urging hardness and preparation for great sacrifice. Indeed, Zarathustra speaks here, at least in part, of literal perishing and widespread destruction. Only from a great disgust with modern man can Zarathustra envision, and affirm as necessary, the image of man's decline. Those who are not ready for sacrifice have not yet suffered from man's imperfections sufficiently and maintain their concepts of "hope," "progress" and "peace" against the dynamics of the species. When man ascends high enough to endure the greatest sufferings, lightning will strike, and the overman will evolve as the overpowering counter-movement to the last man. This is Nietzsche's unique brand of "optimism" about man.

Sub-section 7. Nietzsche's brilliant style and esoteric notions blind the average man to the meaning of his message. In aiming to exclude the "rabble" from his audience, the author attempts to stipulate his own readership, in order to circumvent opportunistic misreadings and other mischief. It is a circumstance fateful to the reception of *Zarathustra*, that while Zarathustra could eventually limit his audience to that of the higher man, Nietzsche himself could not do likewise.

Sub-section 8. Achievement of a radically transformed being, the overman, is not within the powers of those assembled before Zarathustra. It is within their capacity, however, to prepare the conditions for the overman, and so it is the latter that Zarathustra recommends.[50]

Sub-section 9. Reason is not the dominant force operative in the arenas of public life; madness is an exception in the individual but is the rule with the masses. The higher man cannot compete in the arenas of democratic ideas, and so he must hide his inner reasonings. Reason is indeed the exception in the Market Place, not the rule; and where reason prevails, it is only in concert with accident.

When the ultimate foundations of ideas are examined, they begin a long process of devaluation eventuating in moral bankruptcy. Scholars promote the devaluation of all values and would deplume the feathers beautifying all higher values and higher men. The scholar's inability at poetic thought is compensated by a *will to expose*, which is far removed from scientific objectivity. Poetic inspiration is preferable to sophistical scepticism as a basis for belief.

Sub-section 10. Self-formation requires autonomy: dependence is a tragic flaw for the higher man.

Sub-section 11. The higher man must give first priority to his creation (=child=higher self), as in analogy to the mothering instinct. Love of the neighbor is a torturous misrouting of priorities. Regardless of the neighbor's value, creation is individual. Love of oneself necessarily precedes loving another.

Sub-section 12. Creation is a trial of errors, evils and mishaps resulting in a great deal of failures (=filth). He who would "cross over" must be willing to face his own failure, but also must be able to have done with failure and attempt to create once more.

Sub-section 13. Nietzsche's lamarckianism comes to the fore as he embraces the dubious notion of inheritance of acquired characteristics. One's heritage limits the individual by determining strengths and weaknesses. But it as well provides a kind of personal destiny when the individual drives his acquired virtues and vices to their extremes.[51]

Sub-section 14. When higher individuals "go under," it spells their personal demises. But if mankind "goes under," it means the surpassing of man in the birth of a higher type. That is, the species does not cease to exist altogether, but rather dirempts itself into higher and lower forms.[52]

Sub-section 15.   Failure is an inevitable part of higher man's nature. In the face of failure, Zarathustra commends that the higher man "be of good cheer, what does it matter?" Higher man is not defined by his success, but rather in his "attempt to cross over." When the attempt fails, life remains worthwhile. But such a type, sensitive to his own tragic flaws, finds failure difficult to bear, and so must learn to laugh out of necessity. And could it be any other way, since the very project of the higher man is faulty? By aiming at the overman as an *external* goal, the higher man is doomed to failure, i.e., already "half-broken." But the drive pushing him to create something over and beyond himself is pregnant with man's future: man's fate must be in the hands only of those who "attempt to cross over." Although they eventually fail, the higher types are symptomatic of a healthy human spirit. There have been many individuals who have failed and yet, when taken collectively, represent a relatively higher type. The proliferation of well-turned-out individuals should inspire he who strives to create something within himself. Despite their tragic flaws, the higher men teach hope to those underway.

More generally, Zarathustra teaches that the higher man must come to rediscover the beauty and perfection of "ordinary," "mundane," reality. All beings are perfect in their own uniqueness and irreplacability. Higher men see life itself as a failure all-too-easily. If only their vision would transform itself, the perfection of existence *as it is* would make itself evident. And if they were to see the world differently, would they not then see themselves differently too?

Sub-section 16. Jesus' pity for man excluded any happiness, and *a fortiori* any laughter.[53] The innocent man and the lover find ample happiness in the goods of the earth in order to laugh; but Jesus, seeing the world as sorrow, could not laugh. His lack of real love caused him to disdain laughter and all worldly gaiety. Rather than pass by, Jesus cursed the happy and damned them, exposing an inner hatred.

Sub-section 17. Higher man represents progress toward the overman not in success, but in his *failures*. His happiness comes in his pouncing chases: his attempt to cross over, rather than its results, must be the source of his laughter.

Zarathustra's gait is a dance. He has found the "unbearable lightness of being," to use Milan Kundera's nietzschean phrase, in "becoming what one is." This lightness overwhelms him in song and dance and lifts him over the swamps of melancholy. In order for the higher man to dance, he must first *rediscover the prefection and delightfulness of the seemingly mundane*. When one does so, *laughter* overwhelms the newly enlightened one. In this connection, the "laughing Buddha" of zen provides a fruitful comparison.

Sub-section 18. Nietzsche's philosophy is the first and foremost recognition of the value of humour for life. Zarathustra's antics of self-coronation and holy pronouncements are a comical celebration of the triumph of zarathustran lightness over rival nihilistic and desperate philosophies.

Modern man is melancholic and a stranger to lightheartedness. He is weighed upon by the grave concerns of the day, be they great or small. He does not know celebration and even those who are the jesters of the crowd must attract attention with matters of life and death.

Sub-section 20. The transformative vision expressed in the impulse to dance and laugh is alien to the average man and to those concerned with his preservation. Artistic man, detached from the gravity of world events, is scorned. But celebration and gaiety are vital necessities for the higher man, lest melancholy after his own failures be his undoing. *For melancholy is the great temptation of the higher man.* The zarathustran legacy integrally includes *humour* as the "saving grace" of the higher man. That saving grace is put to the test in the following section.

14. Song of Melancholy

Sub-section 1. In IV.13 Zarathustra finally finds the proper audience for his doctrines, i.e., the higher man. Yet even the higher man does not still his nausea from the human, all-too-human. Only his animals—vital lifeforces—share in Zarathustra's appreciation of simple, clean, refreshing, unconscious nature (=air). Even the higher men still smell of convention, reason, false depth and ritual.

Sub-section 2. The Magician of IV.5 declares his real master to be Zarathustra's archenemy, "the spirit of gravity," and would now lead the assembled guests into temptation. Just as Zarathustra epitomizes *laughter*, so the tempter here is the spirit of *evening melancholy.*

Sub-section 3. In his song, the Magician reminds himself of a period in his life when a burning nihilism—caused by the death of god—left him thirsting for relief by means of a new wisdom from a god yet to appear, i.e., Dionysus.[54] Weary of life and his thirst for knowledge, the Magician was haunted and taunted by the scorching glance of the overman,[55] a reminder over him of what he is not, i.e., not a wise man, not a god worthy of ultimate truth. He is not *merely* a fool poeticizing his experience, but one incapable of capturing truth.

Man is the rational animal, yet rationality is a mere device of simplification necessary for understanding. To live in the world, one *must* simplify, *must* falsify. Every human is a mere poet who must simplify and falsify to live: in doing so willingly and knowingly, *man is a liar.* In his language one finds only artificial structures giving foreign colors to a world completely unknown to him. His knowledge of the gods is falsifying poetry: his knowledge of earth is pragmatic simplification. Man thus sits in an inescapable dilemma between religious and secular untruths.

As a seeker of platonic Truth—eternal, immutable, lifeless—man hopes for various extra-natural realms. But man thirsts unto death in expectation of such Truth. The world is instead a heraclitean swirl of life and death, change without rest, a jungle of drives, lust and fleeting perceptions. In such a world, only the vital lifeforces within man receive a chance to participate fleetingly in life, able to discern the intricacies and dangers in life. Man thus desires a camoflage enabling him to hunt in the primeval jungle of good and evil for "truths" which destroy all rationality, defy all schemata, all worlds, all human knowledge. Vitality thus replaces the thirst for knowledge in the man who is truly in contact with nature and its sublimity, i.e., the overman.

Dionysus, the overman, searches and destroys all elements within himself that are virtuous, tender, banal and benign (=lambs). He thereby cultivates his predatory, eagle-like nature that all remnants of *dead truths* be devoured.

Will to truth is the poet's human desire to get to the bottom of truth, of the world. Yet dionysian wisdom is precisely the insight that truth is only surface, only appearance, only non-Truth by platonic standards. Investigation into truth reveals that *there is no underlying truth*. All truths, great and small, of gods and men, are torn asunder by dionysian inquiry. What the "suitor of truth" finds is that his own ego has been splintered into mere appearance and that he no longer even knows himself. Dionysian bliss comes from the *process* of destroying all truth, including that of the knower himself. Dionysian man looks deep into the world to discover only surface: for him the daylight rationality of apollonian man is drowned by the night-like destruction of all Truth.

As the ideals of Truth, Knowledge and Being are destroyed, the seeker of old Truth undergoes an emptiness of the greatest extremes, sinking into nihilism, disenchanted with Knowledge and all ideals, weary of trying and living, nauseated by Reason, totally scorched by the terrible dionysian wisdom that there is no Truth.

By means of this ploy, the Magician leaves the guests in a state of schopenhauerian despair without the means to overcome it. Without hope of self-redemption, all humans are damningly indicted as "only fools, only poets!"

15. On Science

The Magician has successfully tempted the higher men to melancholy, except the leech-bitten Spirit of Science from IV.4. Scientific Spirit is repelled by the Magician's pessimism: science demands a sense of value-neutral objectivity. To the Scientific Spirit, the Magician is "like those whose praise of chastity secretly invites to voluptuous delights," for in his message of melancholy lies a secret delight in the defamation of world and self. And like the "immaculate perceivers" of II.15, the Magician is "like men . . . who have long watched wicked, dancing, naked girls," for in his contemplative withdrawl from the world, the Magician still lusts for the object beyond his will.

Scientific man, with his will to truth, demands the most secure foundations available for knowledge.[56] And so the Scientific Spirit is attracted by Zarathustra, for he has broken many illusions and overturned many past errors. In contrast, the wagnerian Magician wants mysticism, illusion, theater, deception, i.e., greater uncertainty. In the face of such irrationalism, science withdraws out of *fear of ignorance and error*.[57] In this role, the Scientific Spirit embodies the positivist changes Nietzsche underwent after abandoning Schopenhauer and Wagner.

Upon reentering the cave, Zarathustra shows the limitations of the so-called "will to truth" and the fear of error. Zarathustra has already long discounted any "will to truth," interpreting it as one of many expressions of the will to power.[58] And concerning science as fear of error, it is rather the *courageous* man who strives after the ultimate foundations of the universe, though there be in fact no truly ultimate foundations. The characterizing mark of the higher man is indeed the courage shown in the face of adversity. For that reason, the Magician is a truly higher man: he courageously attempted to dominate the higher men by subtrefuge, and nearly succeeded. In harshly scolding this higher man, Zarathustra has "taken revenge on his friends," and so lowers himself. Thus Zarathustra makes a concilliatory gesture to the Magician before taking leave of the cave again.

16. Among the Daughters of the Desert

Sub-section 1. Even the Shadow joins in the buffonery, singing a ballad to ward off the "feeble feminine spirits" of "melancholy old Europe."

Sub-section 2. The "doubt-addicted" European sits in the shelter of his tiny oasis, barely guarded from the nagging knowledge (=sun) of his growing nihilism (=desert). But his nihilism has grown until only the smallest shade protects him from a total loss of values. (Remember the desert of nihilism from I.1.) "European dignity" is a facade that the man of position must maintain against the realities of growing despair. "European fervor, european ravenous hunger" is no more than the "virtuous howling" of a lion without substance, a mere paper tiger. And so, despite all of the eloquently lauded values he holds, the impotent former member of the ruling class cries amid his broken institutions, "there I stand even now as a European; I cannot do else; God help me!" Here the allusion is, of course, to Luther's phrase "Ich kann nicht anders. Gott hilfe mir!"

Nihilism grows: he who harbors nihilism will be scorched by his own doubts at "the Great Noon."[59] Until then, the Shadow's parody of Europe's ruling class has furthered the recovery begun by the Scientific Spirit.

17. The Awakening

Sub-section 1. Already sensing victory over his archenemy (the spirit of gravity, or Christ), Zarathustra begins to realize the full significance of the day. He has long pursued a conscious strategy of pitting *laughter* against *melancholy*, relying on its powers of convalescence to cure the higher man's sorrows. After decades have passed, the strategy has finally succeeded, or so it seems.

Sub-section 2. Like David Friedrich Strauss, who "killed god" for a generation of German intellectuals only to reconvert later to christianity, the Ugliest Man, the very "murderer of god," turns apostate and delivers an asinine litany. The assembled higher men reverently look on in an hilarious, if pitiful, apotheosis of spiritual asininity.

This scene indicates the floundering point of Zarathustra's entire project: for if the higher man turns back to christianity in any form, there will be no "overman," no "crossing over," no "children's land," and *no future*. Zarathustra has already lost successive waves of disciples to the "old faith," or as they see it, a "new faith." Within Nietzsche's near contemporaries one may point to a large group of atheists who had diverted to asinine idolatries—Stirner's egoism, Wagner's germanism, Schopenhauer's pessimism, etc.. And in fact it is these very men who populate Part IV in caricature.

Now higher men are attracted back to worship god in his most asinine form in the very hour of their triumph. That the very murderer of god now gurgles a litany to the Yea-braying ass suggests that Zarathustra is still greatly hampered by the same problem facing him at the very beginning of the speeches; i.e., bringing the higher man safely over the crises of the leonine phase of the spirit.[60]

Analysis of the litany.[61]   The Ugliest Man, lying on the floor of the cave at the hooves of the ass, gurgles the entirety of Revelations 7:12 as an invocation to adoration of the "new idol." The phrase "new idol" comes from I.11, meaning the modern democratic or socialist state, which Nietzsche considers to be by, of and for, the average man. As if it understands what is about to take place, the ass brays a confirmative "Yea-Yuh." The consequent litany becomes comic by a persistent ambiguity. The description of "our god" could fit either the ass or the man of the masses. Using imagery from various biblical passages, Nietzsche also draws a parallel in imagery between the ass and Christ.[62] The slave morality of the christian, democrat and socialist is personified in Christ, whose attributes are those of the beast of burden. (Thus the ass and Christ are tied to the camel trope of I.1, as per comments thereto.)

The ass says "Yea-Yuh" in fulfillment of his "never saying No" to the small people who believe in him.

The third stanza of the litany compares the detachment of a deist god to the dumb silence of the ass, except for occassional asinine brayings. God's wisdom and ways are thus conveniently hidden from the perusals of mortals, and the ass can rarely be wrong with his unintelligent "Yea-Yuh."

In the fourth stanza the ass is compared to the average man of the masses. Thus the new idol is seen as a reflection of the democratic, socialist and christian sentiments of the times. And he is likewise a reflection of the impoverishment of modern man—his featurelessness, powerlessness, moderation in all things, spiritlessness in its most asinine form. Though no one sees them, the state agents of the new idol are omniscient, as was the old god. As if certifying the information with a veiled threat, the ass brays again "Yea-Yuh."

As a mere image of the small man, the new idol, the state, is adequate to the needs of the all-too-many. The idolization of the masses is a religion by, of and for, the people, and so bares their trait of being "as stupid as possible." And as if to confirm his unconscious wisdom, the ass brays unconsciously "Yea-Yuh."

The new idol is the man of the masses who reflects and obeys the every whim of the majority. Just as man sets an image of himself over himself in religion, so man sets his own image over himself in the seat of power and judgment. One man of the masses who sets himself over the masses, only to play their every tune, is the Jester of Prologue 6. This opportunism is a sort practiced beyond good and evil, but which asininely claims its own innocence out of ignorance. With another "Yea-Yuh" the ass concedes the insubstantiality of this new idol.

Since the new faith forms its "new idol" as a projection of itself, i.e., in the image of great men of the rabble, it makes no distinction between higher and lower humanity, and uncritically takes man as *already perfected and fully developed*. There is nothing problematic about man for the ass: he is complete and already fulfilled. And since the ass *cannot* say No, it says "Yea-Yuh" once more.

This new idol has a ravenous appetite: it will not refrain from picking up even the smallest advantage. When the state becomes dissatisfied with its share of world power (=hungry), it grows violent (=thorn in its heart). This political gargantuanism is the "wisdom" of the new idol. And the ass cannot deny it.

18. The Ass Festival

Sub-section 1. Several of the higher men are challenged by Zarathustra for the reasons behind their adoration of the ass.[64] As religious esteem and emotion incarnate, the Last Pope can claim a superior understanding of the value of worship for life.[65] Those who would worship god as a supernatural spirit, however, would cheat man of a *concrete representation* of his esteem. The new idol, the ass, objectifies the man of the masses in the form of an ass. Though it be the epitome of paganism, it is better to express the religious drives in service of this image than none at all.

It is interesting in this connection to remember Feuerbach's *Wesen des Christentums*:

> Hence the historical progress of religion consists in this: that what by an earlier religion was regarded as objective, is now recognized as subjective; that is, what was formerly contemplated as god is now perceived to be something *human*. What was at first religion becomes at a later period idolatry; man is seen to have adored his own nature. Man has given objectivity to himself, but has not recognized the object as his own nature: a later religion takes this step forward; every advance in religion is therefore a deeper self-knowledge.

The ass is not a blasphemous image of the judeo-christian Yahweh, but rather the image of the highest value to replace god, i.e., the average man. Since man now gets the love hitherto given to god, his new self-love is a deification of the essential (i.e., average, common, shared) traits in human nature, depicted as an ass.

The wanderer's Shadow evades responsibility for the ceremony and reminds Zarathustra that in the case of religious (dis)belief, all decisions are based on the unreason of aesthetic preference (=mere prejudice).

In a rare act of honesty, the Magician admits the folly of abandoning his free spirit for the supplication of worship. As previously noted, the Magician is genuine only when he admits his disingenuousness.

Spinning a tongue-in-cheek theology, the Scientific Spirit argues that god, being eternal, must be the slowest and stupidest of all beings, or an ass. He also reminds Zarathustra—one suspects out of revenge—that his own doctrine of eternal return is *no less irrational* than worship of the ass. (Zarathustra has chastised the Shadow for his overprudence and lack of adventurism in IV.15: now the Scientific Spirit shows where such adventurism can lead.)

After these "explanations," the real question remains, "Why has the very murderer of god now taken the instigating role in adoration of the ass?"[67] Whether the Ugliest Man's belief in god had ever died, or was resurrected, or is now "thoroughly dead," is a matter of *uncertainty*: belief is based on man's choice and folly. As noted by Zarathustra in I.7, the most certain way to kill belief in god is a blasphemous non-seriousness at its most solemn moments. (It is precisely this which is underway in the text.) A vengeful antichristian fanaticism is not nearly so fatal to the faith as instructive comedy.[68] In matters of god's death, Zarathustra is the more expert of the two.

Sub-section 2. Like Moses disrupting the golden calf festival, Zarathustra bursts into a tirade against the ass worshippers.[69]

Sub-section 3. Insofar as the ass festival is a celebration of the earth and laughter, though, Zarathustra would have it done "in remembrance of *me*," obviously parodying I Corrinthians 11:24. This brings to a close the blasphemous and comical mood of Part IV. Now the higher men regain their solemnity before Zarathustra and come to enjoy their true happiness, thus fulfilling his promise to the Involuntary Beggar in IV.8.

19. The Drunken Song[70]

Sub-section 1. After the bufoonery of the evening, Zarathustra and the higer men stand "in silence, old people all of them, but with comforted brave hearts," feeling the happiness made possible by

their host. At this still hour occurs "that which, on the whole
amazing day, was the most amazing thing of all," for now the Ugliest Man denies the Soothsayer's previous cry "Nothing is worthwhile" and gurgles his own maxim, "living on earth is worthwhile."

But the Ugliest Man goes still further and gurgles a formulation
of the eternal recurrence without previous instruction from
Zarathustra.

> "Was *that* life?" I want to say to death. "Well then! Once more! My friends,
> what do you think? Do you not want to say to death as I do: Was *that* life?
> For Zarathustra's sake! Well then! Once more!"

It is important to note that the Ugliest Man expresses himself in
terms of *facing death*,[71] for this most fearsome and most mysterious
of all phenomena is the heart and soul of the eternal return:
Zarathsutra's most central doctrine is, at the most personal level,
an answer to the question, "How should the higher man conduct
himself in thought and deed concerning his own death?" This topic
was central in I.21. The overman is he who answers this question
with the doctrine of eternal recurrence.[72] Since the assembled men
are all "old people" and zarathustra himself is nearing death, this
topic is of intense shared interest. Once the Ugliest Man has overcome fear of death and can affirm all of life, the assembled men
burst forth in thanks to Zarathustra. Now the "spirit of gravity"—Christ—is "thoroughly dead"; now the overman is born, or
more precisely, another higher man has "crossed over"; the Soothsayer is now shown "a sea in which he can drown," thus fulfilling
prophecy in II.19. The Soothsayer also fulfills Zarathustra's
prophecy at IV.2 that the Soothsayer would soon dance with joy.

Though Nietzsche momentarily breaks his own veil of
authorship to jokingly question the reliability of "the chroniclers,"
in the end he can only ask, "What does it matter?" (Incidentally, the
ass *could not dance*, but it could *follow* just fine!)

Sub-section 2. It is "high time" for Zarathustra to fulfill his destiny, but this time it is Zarathustra himself, rather than his Shadow,
who announces "the hour has come!"[74]

Sub-section 3. The remainder of this section is a type of mini-commentary on the song of III.15. It is not so much the infinitely many interpretations of this song that defies commentary as it is the inexpressible beauty, compactness and simplicity of this song. What one finds in the "Once More Song" is an expression of Nietzsche's highest vision. Though it consists of only eleven short lines, every notion and image in *Zarathustra* may be brought into relation therewith. What Zarathustra himself offers here is one of an infinite number of variations on the poem's theme. To alter one of Zarathustra's sayings from III.11, "*the* interpretation—that does not exist."

"*Oh man, take care!*" The first bellstroke summons the higher man to receive the ominous message of the midnight clock. Midnight is associated with depth, stillness, profundity, secrecy, ominousness, unreason, instinct; i.e., the dionysian. Its teachings are perennial, timeless and eternal and are drawn from the accumulated experience of countless generations. Though its ominous bells are slow to resonate, the clock's message announces the destiny of mankind.

Sub-section 4. "*What does the deep midnight declare?*" Zarathustra remembers the terribleness of the eternal return in imagery from II.19 and III.2, which this commentary has continuously linked to attitudes about life and death. Here he narrates his own death. The question, "Who shall be lord of the earth?" challenges him to speak the terrifying notion of eternal return. Instead, the eternal return is declared by the deep, still and terrifying midnight.

Sub-section 6. "*The world is deep.*" Many would become "masters of the earth," but few spirits are light enough to survive the tests of dionysian truth. The higher men are still unable to rekindle their lost hopes and aspirations, or "redeem the dead."[75] Man's awareness of his own mortality eats at him like worms through a coffin, robbing him of values and making life pass by as if one were a nightwatchman at a tomb. In its woes, life is an internment in deep anxiety and sorrows, awaiting the end of imprisonment in final death. This is, of course, also the worldview of the "preachers of death," "afterworldly," "despisers of the body," et alia.

Sub-section 6. "—deeper than the day had been aware . . . "
Zarathustra's notion of eternal return brings a dionysian joy for overcoming life's sorrows and dread of death. With this destiny nearly complete, Zarathustra turns "ripe" and ready for death, though it be not immanent, as the eyes of the higher men look on.

Subsection 7. "deep is its woe." Apollonian reason (=day) cannot fathom the dark realities of the dionysian world (=night). What Zarathustra teaches is known only to those who have also experienced the deepest melancholy, the severest solitude, the darkest nihilism, the most taxing wanderings, the most nauseating insights into man. But many of those melancholy souls would seek Zarathustra as a mere substitute for god. Not even Zarathustra is the railing in the storm for this mishapen lot.

Sub-section 8. Only the dionysian man can withstand the trials of Zarathustra's type. When the terror of the "vision and riddle" turns to laughter, joy triumphs over the fear of death. In its ultimate sources, *"joy is deeper than agony."*

Sub-section 9. "Woe implores: go!" In dionysian mythology, the god resides in the grapevine (as indeed he resides throughout nature) as the very lifeforce of the plant. Harvest consequently becomes a celebration of the *suffering Dionysus*, friend of man and god of wine. Even in sorrow, life is worthwhile—this is the message Dionysus and Zarathustra share. All life wants to procreate beyond itself, and so vines yield grapes. Life is, according to II.12, a "longing for what is farther, higher, brighter." In the case of man, life wants to create the overman. In its process of creation, life suffers the birth pangs that signal her own continuation. Life suffers until it is completed, culminated, *perfected* in its creation. Thereafter, "what is ripe—wants to die." Thus the clock chimes Zarathustra's innermost thoughts and dreads and desires. Woe wants an end to itself: joy wants eternity for its object of desire.

Sub-section 10. "For all joy wants eternity—" Zarathustra's joyfulness returns, and in a drunken-like stupor experiences once again the completion and perfection of the world, as in IV.10.

Life is contrary in its nature; in all its complexities only opposites and contraries are found.[76] To affirm one moment, such as to desire its eternity, is to affirm all the sorrows of the world, for the universe is a complex substance of interrelated parts, whose ultimate being is inseperable from the existence of the whole. To desire one joy is thus to desire all the universe making that joy possible, i.e., "to *love* the world." For those who love the earth, time is eternity.[77]

Sub-section 11. Dionysian joy wants eternity for the world *exactly as it is*. In *Ecce Homo* Nietzsche writes,

> It is here and nowhere else that one must make a start to comprehend what Zarathustra wants: this type of man that he conceives, conceives reality *as it is*, being strong enough to do so; this type is not estranged or removed from reality but is reality itself and exemplifies all that is terrible and questionable in it—*only in that way can man attain greatness*.[78]

In contrast to joy narrowed to pleasure, dionysian joy affirms the pain of the world, as it does the world's pleasures, in the curses as well as the blessings, the midnights as well as the noons. Joy wants itself into all eternity and revels in the intoxication of existence. Dionysus is the celebrative, vitalist spirit whose divinity rests in the superhuman ability to bring great contraries together without resolving the tension created in his own spirit.[79]

All joy, then, seeks the eternity of the lowest and most terrible when it affirms the highest and most beautiful.

Life wants the higher man, because he is the means by which she bears his successor, the overman. His sorrows are the necessary pains for creation of the *first successes*, or "firstlings." When he wills the overman, the higher man wills the completion of a birth process and his own consequent "going under."

Sub-section 12. At deepest midnight the entire song is sung by the assembled higher men. Now Zarathustra has taught the eternal return in the form it occured to him in III.15. This poem, perhaps Nietzsche's finest, is a beautiful gem placed at the penultimate moment of his finest hour.

20. The Sign

In accord with the fundamental idea of the book, eternal return of the same, the first and final scenes are identical, closing a circle whose every point is at once beginning, middle and endpoint. It is a return with a difference, though, for Zarathustra is now very old and his ideas are in their maturest form. Further, his most critical problems solve themselves in this section, preparing his way for the third and final descent to man, thus fulfilling his own prophecy.

Like the sun, Zarathustra is compelled to, and repelled from, mankind by the needs of his innermost nature. Though he repeats the lament of Prologue 9—"I still lack the right men"—Zarathustra directly thereafter receives "the sign" prophesized at III.12 and IV.11, announcing the rightful heirs to his legacy. His emotional response, "The sign is at hand. My children are near, my children . . . " was prefigured often in the symbolism surrounding the Great Noon. And this is, at long last, the morning ending in the "Great Noon."

Still drunken from the heady experiences of the previous evening, the higher men sleep and dream while Zarathustra walks in the light of the world. Once they awaken and stumble onto the herald of the overman, they are routed. Their single cry of distress now vocalizes *the fear of the overman present in the higher man*. Pity for the higher man was the temptation set for Zarathustra by the Soothsayer in IV.2. In refraining from teaching the eternal return during the previous evening, Zarathustra succumbed to his temptation and *spared the higher man*. But now he is certain that the *overmen* are rising, and so *the higher men have now become expendible*.

As often noted, the impending *Untergang* connotes: 1) the *descent* of a star or *setting* of a sun, 2) the *decline* of a group or civilization, 3) the *end* or *destruction* of a world moral order, and 4) the *demise* or *downfall* or *death* of an individual. As this day dawns, Zarathustra prepares his descent (*Untergang*), sealing his own demise (*Untergang*) as he does so. In the chaos and nihilism following the great revolutions and wars Zarathustra foretells, mankind as a whole will undergo a decline (*Untergang*) in which all values devalue themselves. As mankind struggles against itself in class and nationalist wars of unprecedented proportion, the species will undergo a diremption into two types: the last man, who represents a *degenerative* path, and the overman, who represents the *rejuvenation* of man. Only the latter type could survive belief in the eternal return. And since the lower man is sterile in value creation, he has no truly rival ideas. Thus the central vision of the overman is the "scorching eye" that burns lower men without resorting to crude physical destruction of the weak.

This final exertion will spell death for Zarathustra, but his own happiness has long been secondary to providing the conditions of the overman (=my *work!*). Soon Zarathustra will descend for the last time to deliver his doctrine that will split mankind into two great counter-movements, the *last man* and the *overman*. As he summons the Great Noon, the book's imagery and language return to the opening scene, with minor variation. Thus rises the great day of self-evaluation for mankind which Nietzsche's unique brand of optimism meets confidently with a roaring laugh of Welcome!

Notes

1. See comments to Prologue 1, I.17, II.9, III.3, III.4, III.6 and especially I.22 concerning the connections between overman (=sun), love (=gold) and giving.

2. "What is happening to me, happens to every fruit when it grows ripe." But this is the symbol of "dying at the right time" from I.21.

3. " "That is what it will be, Zarathustra," answered the animals and nestled against him . . . . " Naumann (IV page 12) explains this differently.

4. As Hollinrake (page 274) notes, this "honey sacrifice" is an allusion to "the cave of Trophonius which supplicants entered with honey cakes to pacify the serpents." Nietzsche mentions this sacrifice at *KSA* I page 808 lines 31-32.

5. Naumann (IV page 12) identifies these animals as "pessimists and sceptics." But it is clear he alludes to the upcoming guests: the "growling bear" arrives in IV.2.

6. See Mark 1:17 and Matthew 4:19.

7. See comments to III.12.3 and III.16.

8. This image occurs at II.12 and III.12 and III.16.

9. See III.16 and IV.2.

10. The name *Hazar* comes from the historical zoroastrian religion, indicating the thousand-year rule of Zoroaster (or Zarathustra). (See page 295 of Peter Puetz' "Anmerkungen" to the Goldmann Klassiker edition of *Also sprach Zarathustra*.)

11. The original message was "All is empty, all is the same, all has been" (from II.19). It was slightly reworked in III.13: "All is the same, nothing is worthwhile, knowledge chokes." It is again reworked here as given.

12. This cry also occurs at III.3, with explanation. For further confirmation of my interpretation, see Zarathustra's own reflections at IV.20.

13. See Georg Brandes' *Friedrich Nietzsche* (London: 1914), translated by A. Chater. Nietzsche approved heartily of the phrase (see letter to Brandes 12.2.87).

14. See comments to III.12 (11, 12, 21, 22).

15. See comments to Prologue 6, I.10, I.11, I.12, I.22.2, II.18 and especially III.12 (11,12).

16. This melodramatic monologue was in fact a poem by Nietzsche, variously entitled "The Poet—The Source of Creation" "On the Seventh Solitude," "The Thought" and appeared as "Ariadne's Complaint" in the *Dionysian Dithyrambs*. By using his own poetry as a comical prop connected with wagnerian romanticism, Nietzsche laughs at himself and his mystical moments.

17. Compare with III.15.

18. There is one section announcing the death of god preceeding *Zarathustra*: see "Der tolle Mensch" in *Froehliche Wissenschaft* (*KSA* III pages 480-82). Other sections on the death of god: Prologue 2, II.3, III.8, IV.6, IV.7, IV.13.2, IV.14 and IV.18.

19. See II.2, II.3, II.4 and III.2. Schopenhauer esteemed pity and may also be a target here.

20. See II.3.

21. See e.g., III.11(2).

22. It seems strange to associate Zarathustra with redemption *from* atheism, but it is the basest (most nihilistic) forms of atheism discounted here. As well, Feuerbach did not think of himself as an atheist in the crude sense.

23. Compare Feuerbach's dictum, "What today is atheism, tomorrow is religion." Feuerbach replaced the concept of god (*Gottesbegriff*) with the species-being of man (*Gattungswesen des Menschen*), as had Strauss. Stirner replaced *das Uebermenschliche* with *das Ich* (the ego). Atheism in Nietzsche's lifetime tended toward communism or anarchy (Bruno Bauer, Eugene Duehring, Moses Hess, Karl Marx).

24. For other perpendicularity tropes, see II.7 and esp. II.1.

25. Yet see IV.17 for the Shadow's comment on this line.

26. See *KSA* page 250. Compare Feuerbach (*Wesen des Christentums*, Eliot translation, page 32): "What yesterday was still religion is no longer such to-day; and what today is atheism, tomorrow will be religion." Marx wrote a parallel parody of the Young Hegelians (Bauer, Feuerbach and Stirner) in *Die deutsche Ideologie* under the title "Leipziger Council".

27. See *KSA* pages 198-99.

28. Feuerbach's *Saemtliche Werke* VII pages 272-73 (my translation).

29. See *KSA* XIV page 334 and XI page 25. Translations are mine.

30. This section, along with III.1, completes the anticipation of the reunion of "the wanderer and his shadow" begun in II.18. The *zweite Abteilung* of *Menschliches, Allzumenschliches* II is entitled "The Wanderer and his Shadow." In general, the Shadow, to use Georgi Colli's description, "embodies an extreme and fatal aspect of his [Nietzsche's] radicalism." (My translation.)
     But in *Menschliches, Allzumenschliches* the Shadow is a more rational, impartial, scientific figure. Colli writes of Nietzsche during the *Menschliches Allzumenschliches* period, "Things do not excite him, and men have left him alone, so that the author may take more interest in himself—as the wanderer here, who is forced to speak with his own shadow. In conversation with him, one speaks easier with oneself." (My translation from the "Nachwort" to Band II of *KSA*.)

31. See *KSA* III pages 526-27.

32. See shadow image in II.19.

33. These cries of course are similar to those of the Soothsayer. For an explana-tion of the cry, "Nothing is true, all is permitted," see *Zur Genealogie der Moral* III section 2 (*KSA* V pages 398-401).

34. Source of Pan myth: Naumann IV page 99. There are a number of other noon times in *Zarathustra*, all signifying that the sun of man's knowledge stands at its highest point. (And when it does so, the shadow of nihilism is at its slimmest.) Yet this is not the "Great Noon," which is evoked in IV.20, but does not occur.

35. "My eyes he does not close, my soul he leaves awake."

36. See *KSA* I pages 30-31.

37. See comments to IV.2.

38. See comments to IV.2.

39. See comments to III.2, III.16 and IV.1.

40. Compare II.20: "I walk among men as among the fragments of the future—
    that future which I envisage. And this is all my creating and striving, that I
    create and carry together into One what is fragment and riddle and dreadful
    accident."

41. Naumann IV page 124.

42. See *Froehliche Wissenschaft* 285 (*KSA* III 527-28).

43. See *Froehliche Wissenschaft* 337 (*KSA* III pages 564-65) "The Future
    "Humanity"." Note the anti-*theological* sense, rather than the *political* impli-
    cations, of the "overman" doctrine in that aphorism.

44. See *KSA* VI 366.

45. See comments to Prologue 9.

46. Naumann IV, page 126. (My translation.)

47. See comments to III.12.21. (My translation.)

48. See *KSA* XIII 191.

49. See Schlechta III 911.

50. This creates a problem for Zarathustra. For he has previously commended
    willing greatness beyond one's own capacity in the slogan, "now *we* want the
    overman!" If the overman is beyond the capacities of higher man, then it
    would be difficult if not impossible to conceive of the overman, as Zarathus-
    tra's hints. Yet if the overman is beyond the higher man's conception, it seems
    meaningless indeed that one can "will" that the overman occur, nor is it any
    more conceivable to prepare his preconditions. If the overman is an ideal self
    to be striven after on an *individual* basis, then one could not know whether
    willing greatness in one's own self-legislated way be in vain or not until one
    attempts. But in that case, Zarathustra's message here seems vacuous.

51. See Prologue 5.

52. See *KSA* XIII 191.

53. Nietzsche parodies Luke 6:25. Aside from Matthew 19:14, this is the single most-alluded-to biblical passage in *Zarathustra*.

54. This song originates from the Fall of 1884 and was published under the title, "Only Fool! Only Poet!" in *Dionysian Dithyrambs*.

55. For the same image, with the schopenhauerian Soothsayer rather than the Magician, see III.12.18. The same image with the European nihilist as subject, see IV.16.

56. "For I seek more *security* .... "

57. Messer (page 161) writes: "The unknown appears to man as something threatening, dangerous .... "(My translation.) But clearly the spirit of science does not fear something threatening or dangerous: he has anxiety about error itself. He has a fear of being in ignorance or error, regardless of consequences.

58. See I.18 and II.10.

59. The song of sub-section 2 was originally written without the leading/finishing line, "Wilderness grows: woe to him that harbors wildernesses!" As in I.1, wilderness (or desert) represents nihilism which grows *and threatens to exceed all bounds* (see comments to I.1). "He who harbors wildernesses" is the lion in crisis, i.e., the rebel spirit in grave danger.

    Naumann (IV page 172) writes, ""The desert grows: woe to him, who harbors deserts," that means: the reproductive potential of mankind is stunted by the growth of culture and becomes sterile. The desert can be understood as that and also as chaos. The man who carries chaos within himself "goes under" willingly, indifferently, but not without the intention to give birth to a star at the same time. From the humanity doomed to the going under (*Untergang*) radiates the rays of hope for a birth of the overman, and thereby the principle of pessimism contained in this second meaning nevertheless finally turns optimistic." (My translation.)

60. See my comments to I.1. The phrase "crisis of the lion" has been used in my analyses of the Pale Criminal, youth on the mountainside, the apostates, et al..

61. As Montinari recognizes (*KSA* XIV page 343), Naumann has written the classic study of the ass litany (IV pages 178-91.) The ass festival originates in a medieval practice. Nietzsche's source, which is heavily marked in the margin

with notes (unusual for Nietzsche), was W.E.H. Leckey's *Geschichte des Ur-sprungs und Einflusses der Aufklaerung in Europa.*

62. His biblical allusions include Rev. 7:12, Psalms 68:19, Phillip 2:78, Number 14:18, Hebrews 12:6, Genesis 1:31 and 1:26, Matthew 19:14 and Proverbs 1:10.

63. The original title of this section was "The Old and New Faith," parodying David Friedrich Strauss' book of the same title. *Thus my previous identification of the Ugliest Man as Strauss is here confirmed.*

    The attentive reader will note that the title is more appropriate with the last section, and makes little sense here. Originally, IV.17 and 18 were a single section with the title "The Old and New Faith." This makes sense, as the two are united by their parody of Strauss. (See the first *Unzeitgemaesse Betrachtungen* "David Strauss als Bekenner und Schriftsteller.")

64. See II.17: "I am not one of those whom one may ask about their why."

65. See comments to IV.6. The figure may also parody Ludwig Feuerbach and his religion of man. Compare the Last Pope's answer "Better to adore god in this form than in no form at all!" with Feuerbach's "It is better to embrace with love even the most idle and unworthy object than to shut oneself up unlovingly in one's own self." (See *Saemtliche Werke* II page 372.)

66. Compare Feuerbach's *Wesen des Christentums*, Eliot translation, page 13.

67. It is becoming clear that there has been a general lack of appreciation of the Ugliest Man's importance in *Zarathustra*. He later plays the key role in IV.19.

68. There are passages galore against this point. (See e.g., IV.13, I.16 and III.12.)

69. Kaufmann denies that IV.7 parallels the Exodus story, but does not notice that this section does so. But his identification of the "Awakening" as the moment when the higher man *laughs* is wrong. The "Awakening" is that of *religious emotion in the Ugliest Man.*

70. The title to this section in the *Handexemplar* and *Grossoktav Ausgabe* was "Das trunkene Lied"—"The Drunken Song"—which Kaufmann retained. But Montinari uses the final title, *Das Nachtwandler Lied*—"The Night Wanderer's Song."

71. "I want to say to death . . . . " "Do you want to say to death . . . ?"

72. See comments to III.2.

73. The phrase, "the chroniclers," gives the impression that *Zarathustra* is one of several accounts of these events. The phrase "full of sweet wine" refers to the Book of Chronicles.

74. See comments to II.18, III.1, IV.1 and IV.20 concerning this cry.

75. See II.19 for a similar image.

76. See *Will to Power* number 1067.

77. See comments to I.20, III.16.

78. See *Ecce Homo* ("Warum ich ein Schicksal bin") section 5.

79. For the best descriptions of Dionysus in Nietzsche's own words, see *Ecce Homo* ("Why I write such good books") sections on *Die Geburt der Tragoedie* and *Zarathustra*.

Appendix I

Location and Major Action of the Speeches

Part	Section	Location	Major Action
Prologue	1	The Cave	Beginning of the *Untergang*
	2	Forest	Meets "most pious man"
	3-7	Market Place	Speech to the crowd
	8	Town and forest	Leaves city; gravediggers; meets Hermit
	9	Forest	Awakening; leaves the corpse behind
	10	Forest	Arrival of animals
Part I.	1-21	The Motley Cow	First series of speeches
	22	The Cave	Return to solitude
Part II.	1	The Cave	Dream of a child
	2-10	The Blessed Isles	Second series of speeches
	11	Isle of Tombs	Speech with former selves
	12-17	The Blessed Isles	More speeches
	18	Isle of Fire	Journey to Hell
	19-21	The Blessed Isles	More speeches
	22	Isles and Cave	Return to Cave
Part III.	1	The Blessed Isles	Preparations for the journey

Part	Section	Location	Major Action
	2	Open seas	Narration of vision/ riddle
	3-4	Open seas	Soliloquy
	5-6	Mainland	Arrival on land; speech
	7	Gates of Great City	Speech with his "Ape"
	8	The Motley Cow	Speech
	9	The Cave	Return to solitude
	10	The Cave	Dream; prophecy of the Great Noon
	11-12	The Cave	Speeches
	13	The Cave	Experience of waking sleep; calls himself "advocate of the circle"; falls into coma; once conscious, is silent for 7 days; animals give message of eternal return; he accepts it
	14	The Cave	Dionysian soliloquy
	15	The Cave	Speech to Life; gives message of eternal return
	16	The Cave	Yes and Amen Song
Part IV.	1	The Cave	Decision to descend
	2	The Cave	Soothsayer reappears
	3	Mountainside	Answers cry of distress; finds two Kings
	4	Mountainside	Another cry; finds the Scientific Spirit

Part	Section	Location	Major Action
	5	Mountainside	Finds the Magician
	6	Mountainside	Finds the Last Pope
	7	Mountainside	Finds Ugliest Man
	8	Mountainside	Finds the Voluntary Beggar
	9	Mountainside	Finds his own Shadow
	10	Mountainside	Perfection of the World; vision of Dionysus and Ariadne
	11	The Cave	Joins guests in Cave
	12	The Cave	Soothsayer demands dinner; Last Supper
	13	The Cave	Twenty speeches on and to the higher man
	14	Outside of Cave	Magician sings of the spirit of gravity
	15	Inside Cave	Scientific Man speaks of fear, courage
	16	The Cave	Shadow sings of Europe
	17	The Cave	Triumph over gravity; assinine litany
	18	The Cave	Zarathustra chastises guests for litany and rituals
	19	Outside of Cave	Ugliest Man affirms his entire life; Zarathustra teaches, actively, the message of eternal return
	20	Outside of Cave	Laughing lion and flock of doves appear

Appendix II

Audience or Addressee of the Speeches

Part/Section		Audience/Addressee of Speeches
Prologue	1	The sun
	2	The most pious man (first Hermit)
	3	Crowd
	4	Crowd
	5	Crowd
	6	Crowd
	7	Corpse, Self
	8	Second Hermit
	9	Corpse, Self
	10	Self
Part I	1	"My brothers"
	2	His "own heart"
	3	"My brothers"
	4	"Despisers of the body"
	5	"My brother"
	6	Judge and sacrificers
	7	Unspecified: presumably the reader
	8	A youth, his follower
	9	"All of you to whom furious work is dear"
	10	"My brothers in war"
	11	"My brothers, you great souls"
	12	"My brother"
	13	"You" (presumably the reader)
	14	"You men"

Part/Section		Audience/Addressee of Speeches
	15	"My brothers"
	16	"My brothers"
	17	"My brother"
	18	"My brother"
	19	Followers
	20	"My friends"
	21	"My friends"
	22	"Friends"
Part II	1	"His own heart"
	2	"My brothers"
	3	Friends
	4	Followers
	5	"My friends"
	6	"My brothers"
	7	"Preachers of equality"
	8	"Famous wise men"
	9	The stars
	10	Dancing girls and his own followers
	11	Dead friends/enemies (selves)
	12	"Wisest ones"
	13	Friends
	14	"Men of today"
	15	"Immaculate perceivers"
	16	disciple
	17	A follower
	18	Ship's crew
	19	Followers
	20	Cripple and followers
	21	"You who are good and just"
	22	"My friends"

Part/Section		Audience/Addressee of Speeches
Part III	1	"His own heart"
	2	Ship's crew
	3	"His jubilant conscience"
	4	The sky
	5	The small man (in absentia)
	6	Winter sky
	7	Zarathustra's "Ape"
	8	"He who has ears"
	9	Solitude
	10	Self
	11	"My own ears"
	12	Self, brothers (in absentia)
	13	The animals
	14	"His (own) soul"
	15	Life
	16	"O Eternity!"
Part IV	1	Self
	2	Soothsayer
	3	Two Kings
	4	The Scientific Man
	5	The Magician
	6	The Last Pope
	7	The Ugliest Man
	8	The Voluntary Beggar
	9	The Shadow
	10	"His own heart"
	11	Animals and higher men
	12	Animals and higher men
	13	Higher men
	14	Animals as witnesses; speaks to himself
	15	Higher men
	16	Higher men

Part/Section	Audience/Addressee of Speeches
17	Animals
18	Higher men
19	Higher men
20	Self, sun, animals

Appendix III
Thematic Structure of "Zarathustra"

Thanatos: I.2,3,4,9,21 II.4,10,19 III.12(2,13-18,20) IV.10

Eros (Ariadne): I.13,18,20 II.9,10 III.12(24),16 IV.10

The "superfluous," "all-too-many," "good and just": Prologue 3,4,5
    I.12 II.6 III.5 IV.13(2,3)

Crime, punishment, conscience: I.6,8,17,19 III.8,12(6-7) IV.7

"Great men," "great events" "famous wise men": Prologue 6 I.11,12
    II.8,18 III.12(11-12)

Followers/leaders: Prologue 7,8,9,10 I.21(3) II.1 III.7,8,9
    IV.1,9,11,13(1,6,10)

Isolation/Loneliness: Prologue 2,8 II.22 III.9 IV.13(13)

Friend/*Ueber-Mir*: Prologue 10 I.14,16,22 II.1, 12(30) IV.11

Giving/receiving: Prologue 1 I.21 II.3,9,15 III.14

Great Noon: I.21(2) II.19 III.5,7,12(25),16 IV.13,14,20

Uebermensch: Prologue 3,5 I.4,6,11,14,16,18,20,22
    II.2,4,7,9,17,19,20,21 III.2,3,12(3,30),13,14
    IV.10,13(2,3,5),19,20

The gods: I.3,15 II.2 III.8,12(2) IV.13(8)

Pity: II.2,3,4 III.2 IV.2,4,5,7

Virtue: Prologue 4 I.2,5,13,21 II.3,5 III.5,12(29) IV.13(11)

Ressentiment: II.6,7,20

Self-overcoming: II.12 IV.13(12)

Good and evil: I.8,15 II.12,21 III.10,11,12(8-10) IV.13(5)

Anti-romanticism: II.13,15,17 IV.2,4

Scholars: Prologue 8 II.14,16 IV.4,13(9)

Aristocratic radicalism: Prologue 6 I.11 II.6,7,18 IV.3,8,9

Nihilism: II.19 IV.2,9 (see also *thanatos*)

Prankishness/deception: II.9,21 III.4,6

Eternal return: Prologue 10 II.19,20,22 III.2,4,12(3), 13,14
    IV.10,19
Transfiguration: Prologue 1 I.1 III.2,1316 IV.10,19,20
Living dangerously/"crossing over": Prologue 6 Entirety of Part I,
    II.6,7,8,12,13,14,15,16,17,18, 19,20
Naturalism, physicalism, lamarckianism: I.4,21 II.17 III.1 IV.13
Will to power: I.15 II.19
Dionysus: I.7 II.10 III.12(19),13,14,15,16 IV.10,19
Rank and order: I.10 IV.3,12
Love of man: Prologue 2 I.3,21(2) IV.13(4)
Spirit of gravity: II.10 III.2,11 IV.13(10,17,18,19), 14 I.7
Values: II.11,12 III.12(21-23)
Militant atheism: I.16,17 III.5,12 IV.13(7)
Passing by: Prologue 9 II.4 III.7 IV.7
Death of god: Prologue 2 I.3,7 II.3 III.8,16(2)
    IV.6,7,13(2),14,17,18
Good Europeanism: IV.16
The higher man: Prologue 4,5,6,10 I.1,6,8 II.12,18,20 III.2,8,12
    IV.1-20,esp.IV.13
Overviews: III.1,3,9,12 IV.13,20

Appendix IV
"*Zarathustra*'s Plot Line"

SECTION IN TEXT	AMONG MANKIND	IN SOLITUDE AT THE CAVE
Prologue 1		Dawn at Cave
		Beginning of *Untergang*
Prologue 2	Meets Most Pious Man	
Prologue 9-10	Noon: arrival of animals	
Part I 21		First farewell speech
Part I 22		Promise of three returns
Part II 1		Dream: decision to return
Part II 2	First return to friends	
Part II 18	Journey to Hades: noon	
	Second return to friends	
Part II 21	Second farewell speech	
Part III 1		Near midnight, on a ridge
Part III 5	Arrival on Mainland, before sunrise	
Part III 9	Return to solitude	
Part IV 1		Honey sacrifice: decision to attract higher man
Part IV 3	Search for higher man begins	
Part IV 10	Search ends at noon; perfection of the world	
Part IV 11		Joins guests at cave
Part IV 20		Sign to begin third return, or the "Great Noon"

Appendix V
Partial or Complete Plans to
"Zarathustra"

For partial or complete plans for *Also sprach Zarathustra*, see *KSA* Band X 186, 377, 444, 470f, 481, 482, 588f, 591, 592, 593, 598, 619, 639f, 634.

Appendix VI
Sources for Nietzsche's Own Comments
on "Zarathustra"

1. Major Works
   Die Geburt der Tragoedie, "Versuch einer Selbst-Kritik"
   Froehliche Wissenschaft sections 342,381, 382
   Jenseits von Gut und Boese section 56
   Zur Genealogie der Moral Essay II section 25
   Der Fall Wagner Preface
   Der Antichrist "Vorwort" sections 53-54
   Goetzendaemmerung "Wie die "wahre Welt" endlich zur Fabel wurde"
   "Streifzuege eines Unzeitgemaessen" section 51
   "Was ich den alten verdanke" sections 4-5
   "Der Hammer Redet"
   Ecce Homo Nietzsche's Preface section 4
   "Warum ich so weise bin" sections 3,4,8
   "Warum ich so klug bin" section 4
   "Warum ich solche gute Buecher schreibe" sections 1,3,4,5
   Die Geburt der Tragoedie sub-sections 2,3,4
   Froehliche Wissenschaft
   Also sprach Zarathustra
   Jenseits von Gut und Boese
   Zur Genealogie der Moral
   Der Fall Wagner
   "Warum ich ein Schicksal bin" sections 2,3,4,5,8

2. Poems
   Zwischen Raubvoegeln
      Das Feuerzeichen
   Auf hohen Bergen
   Ruhm und Ewigkeit
   Von der Armut des Reichsten
   Sils-Maria

3. Letters
   To Deussen (26.11.88)(16.3.83)
   To Gast (20.9.84) (late August,Sils) (2.9.84) (19.2.83)
      (23.7.85) (30.10.88) (9.12.88) (16.12.88) (6.4.83)
   To Overbeck (5.8.86) (rec.24.3.83) (rec.28.8.83) (rec. 2.5.84
      Venice) (Summer '86, Sils) (22.2.83) (7.4.84) (5.8.86)
      (31.3.85 Nice)   (Spring '86 Nice) (24.3.87 Nice)
   To Burkhardt (June '83 Rome)(22.9.86)
   To Gersdorff (28.6.83)(12.2.85)
   To von Meysenbug (Very late April'84)(May '84 Venice)
   To von Salis (29.12.88 Turin)
   To von Stein (18.9.84)
   To von Seydlitz (12.2.88)
   To Foerster (April'85 Venice)
   To Rohde (22.2.84)
   To Brandes (10.4.88)
   To Fuchs (29.7.88)
   To Knortz (21.6.88 Sils)

4. Notebooks
   The notebooks containing the rough draft of *Zarathustra*
   are found in volumes 11 and 12 of *KSA* with the abbreviation
   "Z." (Thus volume 10 contains Z1, ZI2a, ZI3, Z14, ZII1a,
   ZII2, ZII3a and ZII4: and volume 11 contains ZII5a, ZII7b,
   ZII6a, ZII8, ZII9, ZII10 and ZI2c.)
   Notebooks before and after the creation of *Zarathustra*
   occasionally mention the work and related topics. The only
   organized index thereto is Schlechta's Index.

Appendix VII
Suggested Readings on Nietzsche's
Concept of Dionysus

Will to Power (edited by Walter Kaufmann): Sections 1003 to 1053 are given under the heading "Dionysus." Kaufmann is simply adopting Elizabeth Foerster's schema here. Especially important are sections 1003, 1009, 1038, 1041, 1041,1049, 1050, 1051, 1052.

Ecce Homo: There are a number of significant and lengthy passages developing the concept of Dionysus to be found here. From "Warum ich solche gute Buecher schreibe," see aphorisms 2,3 and 4 from *Die Geburt der Tragoedie* and aphorism 2 from *Jenseits von Gut und Boese*. From "Warum ich ein Schicksal bin," see aphorisms 2,5,8 and 9.

The critical passages, for our purposes, are to be found in "Warum ich solche gute Buecher schreibe": namely, aphorisms 2,6 and 8.

Appendix VIII
Remarks on Editions of
Nietzsche's Works

German

The appearance of the *Kritische Gesamtausgabe Werke, Kritische Gesamtausgabe Briefwechsel* and the *Kritische Studienausgabe in 15 Baenden*, edited by Giorgio Colli and Mazzino Montinari (de Gruyter Verlag, Berlin) now allows a standard reference edition spanning over Nietzsche's juvenalia, published works, notebooks and letters. Colli and Montinari have found the perfect solution to Nietzsche's problematic *Nachlass*: they have simply published the notebooks precisely as bound. No hypothetical tables of contents were taken from the *Nachlass* in order to organize the whole: what one reads thus approximates Nietzsche's original notebooks as closely as possible. The additional advantage of numbered lines, commentary and indices sets this edition far above either Schlechta, Musarion, *Historische-kritische Gesamtausgabe* and the *Grossoktav-Ausgabe* editions. In the near future, *Kritische-Studien Ausgabe* will be the only necessary German-language edition of Nietzsche's published works.

Unfortunately, there are few good concordances between German-language editions of Nietzsche's works, and this poses a particular problem for cross-referencing the *Nachlass*. At rare points in my commentary, I refer to Schlechta, *HKW* and the Musarionausgabe. Otherwise I have used only the *KSA* as a reference.

English

Although translation of *KSA* into a definitive English edition has begun, its completion cannot be expected for many years. The only existing complete edition of Nietzsche's works, edited by Oscar Levy, is totally unsatisfactory for the modern reader.

The best translations of *Gay Science, Birth of Tragedy, Genealogy of Morals, Beyond Good and Evil, Antichrist, Twilight of the Idols, Case of Wagner, Nietzsche contra Wagner, Will to Power, Ecce Homo* and *Also sprach Zarathustra* are by Walter Kaufmann. (I do not thereby imply that Kaufmann is a good Nietzsche scholar nor that I accept his *interpretations* of Nietzsche's meanings, which I often do not.) Good postwar translations of *Daybreak* (trans.R.J. Hollinrake), *Human, All Too Human* (trans.Marion Faber), *Philosophy in the Tragic Age of the Greeks* (trans. Marianne Cowan), *Use and Abuse of History* (trans. Adrian Collins) and *Schopenhauer as Educator* (trans. James Hillesheim) have appeared, making much of Nietzsche's work available to the English-only reader.

I generally give references to *KSA* in the footnotes, without an English reference. Where I believe the reader simply *must* have recourse to my source, I provide references to Kaufmann's translations whenever possible. Many translations from Nietzsche's *Zarathustra*-notebooks included in this commentary are my own translations, and many appear in English here for the first time.

Appendix IX
Remarks on Other "Zarathustra" Commentaries

German

The standard *Zarathustra* commentary in German both in terms of quantity and quality, is Gustav Naumann's *Zarathustra-Commentar* (4 volumes, 1905). Naumann and his uncle were not only Nietzsche's publishers and personal acquaintances, they also successfully blocked Elizabeth Foerster's attempt to suppress a paragraph of *Ecce Homo*. (This paragraph appears where it should in *Ecce Homo* in the *KSA*.) Naumann analyzes every major trope of *Zarathustra* and goes into great detail connecting *Zarathustra* and Nietzsche's other works.

The only other serious section-by-section commentary in German is August Messer's *Erlaeuterung zu Nietzsches Zarathustra* (Stuttgart, 1922). At critical points Messer relies on Naumann. At most points where a real difference occurs, Naumann's interpretations are superior.

Hans Weichelt's *Zarathustra-Kommentar* (Leipzig, 1922) is far too brief to be of use to the modern Nietzsche scholar.

Volume XIV of *KSA* contains a commentary to *Zarathustra* which is useful primarily as a resource for other commetaries.

English

Harold Alderman's work, *Nietzsche's Gift* (Athens: Ohio University Press, 1977), though not a commentary to *Zarathustra*, is an important interpretation of Nietzsche's masterpiece.

Kathleen Marie Higgins' recent *Nietzsche's "Zarathustra"* (Philadelphia: Temple University Press, 1987), while not claiming to be a commentary, and while containing some fine sections, still does not seem to establish a clear or purposive interpretation of *Zarathustra* as a whole.

Also very uneven is Roger Hollinrake's *Nietzsche, Wagner and the Philosophy of Pessimism* (London: Allen and Unwin, 1982):it is included here, as it concerns *Zarathustra* as its central focus.

Laurence Lampert's *Nietzsche's Teachings* (New Haven: Yale University Press, 1986) deserves to be called the first *section-by-section* commentary to *Zarathustra* in English. Lampert's work became known to me only during late stages in preparation of my commentary, and so I have been unable to date to read it.

Also very recent is a massive transcript of seminar discussions led by Carl Jung, entitled *Nietzsche's "Zarathustra"*. Still another very recent book is Gary Shapiro's *Nietzschean Narratives*, (Bloomington: Indiana University Press, 1989), which considers *Zarathustra* along with *Antichrist* and *EcceHomo*. It appeared only in late stages of preparation of this commentary, and so I am unable to render an evaluation of it.

Bibliography

Translations of Nietzsche's Works

Thus Spoke Zarathustra. Trans. Walter Kaufmann. New York: Viking Press, 1966.

Bsic Writings. Trans. Walter Kaufmann. New York: Modern Library, 1968.

Will to Power. Trans. Walter Kaufmann. New York: Vintage Books, 1968.

Gay Science. Trans. Walter Kaufmann. New York: Vintage Books, 1974.

The Portable Nietzsche. Trans. and Ed. Walter Kaufmann. New York: Viking Press, 1968.

Daybreak. Trans. R. J. Hollinrake. Cambridge: Cambridge University Press, 1982.

Human, All-too-Human. Trans. Marion Faber. Lincoln and London: University of Nebraska Press, 1984.

Philosophy in the Tragic Age of the Greeks. Trans. Marianne Cowan. Chicago: Regnery, 1962.

Use and Abuse of History. Trans. Adrian Collins. Indianapolis: Bobbs-Merill, 1977.

Schopenhauer as Educator. Trans. James Hillesheim. South Bend: Gateway, 1965.

Editions of Nietzsche's Works Employed in *Returning to Sils-Maria*

Coli, Giorgi and Montinari, Masino. *Kritsche Studienausgabe.* Berlin: De Gruyter, 1980.

Historische-kritische Gesammtausgabe. Munich: Beck, 1933-42.

Werke: Musarionausgabe. Munich: Musarion, 1920-29. Twenty-three volumes.

Werke. Ed. Karl Schlechta. Frankfurt am Mainz: Ullstein, 1979. Five volumes.

Works Referred to in *Returning to Sils-Maria*

Abegg, Emil. "Nietzsches Zarathustra und der Prophet des alten Iran." *Conferences prononcees a Geneve sous les auspices da la Fondation M. Gretler.* 1945.

Abrams, M. H.. *Natural Supernaturalism.* New York: Norton & Co. Press, 1971.

Alderman, Harold. *Nietzsche's Gift.* Athens: Ohio University Press, 1977.

Aristotle. *The Basic Works of Aristotle.* Ed. Richard McKeon. New York: Random House, 1941.

Augustine, Saint, Bishop of Hippo. *The Confessions of Augustine.* Ed. John Gibb and William Mongomery. New york: Garland Publishing, 1980.

Bennholdt-Thompson, Anke. *Nietzsches "Zarathustra" als literarisches Phaenomen.* Frankfurt: Athenseum, 1974.

Berlinger, Rudolf and Schrader, Wiebke (Editors). *Nietzsche kontrovers II*. Wuerzburg: Koenighausen and Neumann, 1982.

Brandes, George. *Friedrich Nietzsche*. Trans. A. Chater. London: Heinemann, 1914.

Cassirer, Ernst. *The Myth of the State*. New Haven: Yale University Press, 1946.

Deleuze, Giles. *Nietzsche and Philosophy*. Tran. Hugh Tomlinson. New York: Columbia University Press, 1983.

Derrida, Jacques. *Spurs*. Trans. Barbara Harlow. Chicago and London: University of Chicago Press, 1979.

Dostoyevski, Feodor. *Crime and Punishment*. Trans. Jessie Coulson and Ed. George Gibian. New York: Norton and Co., 1964.

Eliade, Mircea. *A History of Religious Ideas*. Trans. Willard R. Trask. Chicago: University of Chicago Press, 1978. Volume 1.

Feuerbach, Ludwig. *Saemmtliche Werke*. Ed. Wilhelm Bolin. Stuttgart: Fromanns Verlag, 1905.

Feuerbach, Ludwig, *Essence of Christianity*. Trans. George Eliot. New York: Harper Row, 1957.

Feuerbach, Ludwig. *The Fiery Brook: Selected Writings of Ludwig Feuerbach*. Ed. and Trans. Zawar Hanfi. New York: Doubleday, 1972.

Fichte, Johann Gottlieb. *Johann Gottlieb Fichte's Popular Works*. London: Truebner and Co., 1873.

Foerster-Nietzsche, Elizabeth. *Das Leben Friedrich Nietzsche.* Leipzig: Kroener, 1913. Two volumes.

Frenzl, Ivo. *Friedrich Nietzsche: An Illustrated Biography.* New York: Pegasus Publishers, 1967.

Goethe, Johann Wolfgang. *Der Briefwechsel zwischen Schiller und Goethe.* Ed. Hans Gerhard Graef and Albert Leitzmann. Leipzig: Insel, 1955. Three volumes.

Goethe, Johann Wolfgang. *Faust.* Trans. Walter Kaufmann. Garden City: Doubleday, 1963.

Green, David. (Trans.) *Greek Tragedies.* Chicago: University of Chicago Press, 1960.

Gregor-Dellin, Martin. *Wagner-Chronik.* Munich: Deutscher Taschenbuch Verlag, 1983.

Hegel, George Wilhelm Friedrich. *Phaenomenologie des Geistes.* Frankfurt am Mainz: Ullstein, 1973.

Higgins, Kathleen Marie. *Nietzsche's "Zarathustra".* Philadelphia: Temple University Press, 1987.

Hollinrake, Roger. *Nietzsche, Wagner and the Philosophy of Pessimism.* London: Allen and Unwin, 1982.

Holy Bible. New Schofield Reference Edition. New York: Oxford University Press, 1967.

Janz, Curt Paul. *Friedrich Nietzsche Biographie.* Munich: Carl Hanser, 1978. Volume 1.

Jung, Carl. *Psychiatric Studies.* Trans. R. F. C. Hull. Princeton: Princeton University Press, 1975 Second edition.

Kant, Immanuel. *Critique of Pure Reason*. Trans. F. Max Mueller. New York: Doubleday, 1966.

Kant, Immanuel. *Religion Within the Limits of Reason Alone*. Trans. Theodore M. Greene and Hoyt H. Hudson. LaSalle: Open Court, 1960. Second Edition.

Kant, Immanuel. *Foundations of the Metaphysics of Morals* and *What is Enlightenment?*. Trans. Lewis White Beck. New York: LIberal Arts Press, 1959.

Kant, Immanuel. *Philosophy of Kant*. Ed. Carl J. Friedrich. New York: Random House, 1949.

Kaufmann, Walter. *Nietzsche*. Princeton: Princeton Press, 1974. Fourth Edition.

Lampert, Laurence. *Nietzsche's Teachings*. New Haven: Yale University Press, 1986.

Leckey, W. E. H., *Geschichte des Ursprungs und Einflusses der Aufklaerung in Europe*. Leipzig: 1873. Second editions. Two volumes.

Loewith, Karl. *Nietzshces Philosophie der ewigen Wiederkehr*. Stuttgart: Kohlhammer, 1956. Revised Edition.

Macquarrie, John. "Pietism." *Encyclopedia of Philosophy*. Ed. Paul Edwards. New York: Macmillan Publishers, 1967. Volume VI.

Marx, Karl. *The German Ideology*. Moscow: Progress Publishers, 1976.

Messer, August. *Erklaerung zu Nietzsches Zarathustra*. Stuttgart: Strecker and Schroeder, 1922.

Middleton, Christopher. Trans. and Ed. *Selected Letters of Friedreich Nietzsche*. Chicago: University of Chicago Press, 1969.

Montinari, Masinio. *Nietzsche Lesen*. Berlin: De Gruyter, 1982.

Montinari, Masino et al (Editor). *Nietzsche-Studien. Ein internationales Jaahrbuch fuer die Nietzsche-Forschung.* Berlin: De Gruyter, 1977. Volumes I-IV (1972-75), VI (1977), VIII (1979) and XII (1983).

Mueller-Lauter, Wolfgang. *Nietzsche*. Berlin: De Gruyter, 1971.

Naumann, Gustav. *Zarathustra-Commentar*. Leipzig: Haeffel, 1899-1901). Four volumes.

Pasley, Malcolm (Editor). *Nietzsche: Imagery and Thought.* Berkeley: University of California Press, 1978.

Peters, H. F.. *Zarathustra's Sister*. New York: Crown Publishers, 1977.

Plato. *The Collected Dialogues of Plato Including the Letters*. Ed. Edith Hamilton and Huntington Cairns. Princeton: Princeton University Press, 1961.

Renan, Ernest. *The Life of Jesus*. Translation revised from the twenty-third French edition. Boston: Little, Brown & Co., 1926.

Ritschl, A. *Geschichte des Pietismus*. Bonn: 1880-86. Three volumes.

Schelling, Friedrich Wilhelm Joseph von. *Schellings Werke*. Ed. Manfred Schroeter. Munich: Beck, 1958-59.

Schiller, Friedrich. *Saemmtliche Schriften.* Historische-kritische Ausgabe. Ed. Karl Goedeke. Stuttgart: J. G. Cotta, 1867-76.

Schiller, Friedrich. *On the Sublime.* Trans. Julius A. Elias. New York: Ungar Publishing, 1966.

Shclechta, Karl. *Der grosse Mittag.* Frankfurt: Klostermann, 1954.

Schlechta, Karl. *Nietzsche-Chronik.* Muenchen: Carl Hanser, 1975.

Schleiermacher, Friedrich. *Ueber die Religion.* Stuttgart: Phillip Reclam, 1980.

Schlerath, Bernfried (Editor). *Zarathustra* Wege der Forschuung. Volume CLXIX. Darmstadt: Wissenschaftliche Buchgesellschaft, 1970.

Schopenhauer, Arthur. *Parerga und Paralipomena.* Zuerich: Diogenes Verlag, 1977. Two volumes.

Schopenhauer, Arthur. *Die Welt als Wille und Vorstellung* in *Arthur Schopenhauers saemmtliche Werke.* Ed. Paul Deussn. Munich: R. Piper and Co., 1911. Volumes 1 and 2.

Seydlitz, Reinhardt von. *Wann, warum, was und wie ich schrieb.* Gotha: 1900.

Shakespeare, William. *The Complete Works of William Shakespeare.* The Cambridge Text established by John Dover Wilson for Cambridge University Press. London: Octopus Books Limited, 1980.

Shapiro, Gary. *Nietzschean Narratives.* Bloomington: Indiana University Press, 1989.

Silk, M. S. and Stern, J. P.. *Nietzsche on Tragedy*. Cambridge: Cambridge University Press, 1983.

Solomon, Robert. "Hegel's Concept of *Geist*" in *Hegel: Collection of Critical Essays*. Ed. Alisdair MacIntyre. New York: Doubleday: 1972.

Solomon, Robert. *Nietzsche: A Collection of Critical Essays*. New York: Doubleday Press, 1973.

Strauss, David Friedrich. *The Life of Jesus, Critically Examined*. Ed. Peter C. Hodgson. Trans. George Eliot. Philadelphia: Fortress Press, 1973.

Stirner, Max. *Der Einzige und sein Eigentum*. Stuttgart: Phillip Reclam, 1981.

Strong, Tracey. *Nietzsche and the Politics of Transfiguration*. Berkeley: University of California Press, 1975.

Wagner, Richard. *Mein Denken*. Ed. Martin Gregor-Dellin. Munich: R. Piper and Co..

Wagner, Richard. *Das Rheingold*. Stuttgart: Phillip Reclam, 1981.

Wagner, Richard. *Die Walkuere*. Stuttgart: Phillip Reclam, 1981.

Wagner, Richard. *Siegfried*. Stuttgart: Phillip Reclam, 1981.

Wagner, Richard. Goetterdaemmerung. Stuttgart: Phillip Reclam, 1982.

Wagner, Richard. *Parsifal*. Stuttgart: Phillip Reclam, 1983.

Wartofsky, Marx. *Feuerbach*. Cambridge: Cambridge Press, 1977.

Waterhouse, E. S.. "Pietism." *Encyclopedia of Religion and Ethics* Ed. James Hastings. New York: T. & t. Clark Publishers, 1956. Volume X.

Weichelt, Hans. *Zarathustra-Kommentar*. Leipzig, 1922.

Wellek, Rene. *A History of Modern Criticism*. New Haven: yale Press, 1955. Volume 2.

Works On "Zarathustra," In Part Or As A Whole, Not Cited In *Returning To Sils-Maria*

Bemmelmen, Daniel J. van. *Zarathustra*. Stuttgart: 1975.

Bertallot, Hans-Werner. *Hoelderlin-Nietzsche. Untersuchungen zum hymnischen Stil in Prosa und Vers*. Berlin: 1967.

Bulhoff, Ilse Nina. *Apollos Wiederkehr*. Den Haag: Martinus Nijhoff, 1969.

Grille, Dietrich. "Der Uebermensch heisst neuer Mensch." *Deutsche Studien*. Volume 12. 1974. Pages 155-159.

Gramzow, Otto. *Kurzer Kommentar zum "Zarathustra"*. Berlin: 1907.

Harper, Ralph. *The Seventh Solitude*. Baltimore: John Hopkins University Press, 1965.

Heller, Erich. "Zarathustra's Three Metamorphoses," *Salmagundi*, no. 21 (Winter 1973): pages 63-80.

Heidegger, Martin. "Who is Nietzsche's Zarathustra?" *The New Nietzsche: Contemporary Styles of Interpretation*. Ed. D .B. Allison. New York: Dell, 1977.

Hinz, Walther. *Zarathustra*. Stuttgart: 1961.

Kaulhausen, Marie Hedi. *Nietzsches Sprachstil. Gedeutet aus seinem Lebensgefuehl und Weltverhaeltnis.* Muenchen: 1977.

Kleist, Heinrich von. "Gebiet der Zoroaster." *Saemmtliche Werke.* Muenchen: Knorr Verlag.

Krell, David. "Heidegger and Zarathustra." *Philosophy Today.* Volume 18, Winter, 1974.

Kunnas, Tarno. "Das Gute und das Boese in "Also sprach Zarathustra"." *Studia Neophilologica.* 48, 1976, pages 229-244.

Kunne-Ibsch. Elrud. "Textstruktur und Rezeptionsprozess am beispiel von Nietzsche's "Zarathustra"." *Comparative poetics, Poetique comparative, Vergleichende Poetik.* Ed. D. W. Fokkema et alia. Amsterdam: 1976. Pages 215-242.

Kunne-Ibsch, Elrud. *Die Stellung Nietzsches in der Entwicklung der modernen Literaturwissenschaft.* Tuebingen: 1972.

Leyen, Friedrich von der. "Friedrich Nietzsche: Die Sprach des "Zarathustra"." *Litteraturwissenschaftliches Jahrbuch.* Neus Folge 3, 1962, pages 209-238.

Mayroher, Manfred. "Zu einer Deutung des Zarathustra Namens in Nietzsches Korrespondenz." *Beitraege zur Alten Geschichte und deren Nachleben. Festschrift fuer Franz Altheim.* Ed. Ruth Stiehl and Hans Stier. Volume 2. Berlin 1970, pages 369-374.

Montinari, Masino et alia (Editors). *Nietzsche-Studien. Ein internationales Jahrbuch fuer die Nietzsche Forschung.*
——Stambaugh, Joan. "Thoughts on Pity and Revenge." Band I.
——Wein, H.. "Nietzsche ohne Zarathustra" Band I.

——Volkmann-Schluck, Karl Heinz. "Die Stufen der Selbstueberwindung des Lebens." Band II.

——Miller, C. A.. "Nietzsche's "Daughters of the Desert": A Reconsideration." Band II

——Masini, F. "Rhythmisch-metaphorische "Bedeutungs-felder" in "Also sprach Zarathustra"." Band II.

——Hollinrake, Roger and Ruter, M., "Nietzsche's Sketches for the Poem "Oh Mensch! Gibt Acht!" " Band IV.

——Neumann, H.. "Superman or Last Man? Nietzsche's Interpretation of Athens and Jerusalem." Band V.

——Thatcher, David S.. "Eagle and Serpent in "Zarathustra" " Band VI.

——Sterling, M. C.. "Recent Discussions of Eternal Recurrence: Some Critical Comments." Band VI.

——De Bleeckere, S.. " "Also sprach Zarathustra": Die Neugestaltung der "Geburt der Tragoedie"." Band VIII.

——Mehregan, H.. "Zarathustra im Awesta und bei Nietzsche—Eine vergleichende Gegenueberstellung." Band VIII.

——Lampert, Laurence. "Zarathustra and His Disciples." Band VIII.

——Soering, J.. "Incipit Zarathustra—Vom Abgrund der Zukunft." Band VIII.

——Magnus, Bernd. "Eternal Recurrence." Band VIII.

——Neckel, M.. "Der Weg Zarathustras als der Weg des Menschen. Zur Anthropologie Nietzsches im Kontext der Rede von Gott im "Also sprach Zarathustra"." Band IX.

——Mueller-Lauter, Wolfgang. "Das Willenswesen und der Uebermensch. Ein Beitrag zu Heideggers Nietzsche-interpretationen." Band X/XI.

——McGinn, Robert E.. "Verwandlungen von Nietzsches Uebermensch in der Literatur des Mittelmeerraumes: d'Annunzio, Marinetti und Kazantzakis." Band X/XI.

——Haase, M.-L.. "Der Uebermensch im "Also sprach Zarathustra" und im Zarathustra-Nachlass 1882-1885. Band XIII.

——Koch, M.. "Zarathustra ist kein decadent! Ueberlegung zu "Also sprach Zarathustra"." Band XIII.

——Naumann, B.. "Nietzsches Sprache "Aus der Natur." Ansaetze zu einer Sprachtheorie in den fruehen Schriften und ihre metaphorische Einloesung in "Also sprach Zarathustra"." Band XIV.

——Pangle, Thomas L.. "The "Warrior Spirit" as an Inlet into the Political Philosophy of Nietzsche's Zarathustra." Band XV

——Perkins, R.. "How the Ape Becomes a Superman." Band XV.

——Long, Thomas A.. "Nietzsche's Eternal Recurrence-Yet Again:" Band XVI.

Morawa, Hans. *Sprache und Stil von Nietzsches "Zarathustra"*. Berlin 1958.

Nelson, Donald F.. "Nietzsche, Zarathustra und Jesus Redivivus. The Unhloly Trinity." *The Germanic Review.* 48, 1973, pages 175-188.

Resenhoefft, Wilhelm. *Nietzsches Zarathustra-Wahn.* Bern 1972.

Salaquarda, Joerg. "Zarathustra und der Esel. Eine Untersuchung der Rolle des Esels im Vierten Teil von Nietzsches "Also sprach Zarathustra"." *Theologia Viatorum.* XI, 1973, pages 181-213.

Sonoda, Muneto. "Zwischen Denken und Dichten. Zur Weltstruktur des "Zarathustra"."

Taraba, Wolfgang. "Der schoepferische Einzelne und die Gesellschaft in Nietzches Zarathustra." *Literatur und Gesellschaft vom 19. ins 20. Jahrhundert.* Ed. H. J. Schrimpf. Bonn 1963, pages 196-228.

Wolfe, Peter. "Image and Meaning in "Also sprach Zarathustra"." *Modern Language Notes.* 79, 1964, pages 546-552.

Selected Major Studies of Nietzsche's Philosophy

Danto, Arthur C.. *Nietzsche as Philosopher. An Original Study.* New York: Columbia University Press, 1965.

Heidegger, Martin. *Nietzsche.* Trans. David Krell. San Francisco: Harper and Row, 1979. Four volumes.

Hollinrake, R. J.. *Nietzsche.* London: Routledge and Kegan Paul, 1973.

Jaspers, Karl. *Nietzsche. An Introduction to the Understanding of His Philosophical Activity.* Trans. Charles F. Walraff and Frederick J. Schmitz. Chicago: Regnery, 1965.

Norgan, George A.. *What Nietzsche Means.* New York: Harper, 1941.

Schacht, Richard *Nietzsche.* London: Routledge and Kegan Paul, 1983.

Index

214-215, 216, 218, 228, 231n9, 269, 273
Good and the Just, 11, 12, 41, 50, 75, 93, 134, 135, 136, 139, 141, 171, 181n56, 213, 217, 221, 222
Gravediggers, 26, 51-52, 79, 85, 108n39, 116n116, 156, 157, 189n136, 197, 238n81, 253
Great Events, xii, xiii, 18

Hegel, G. W. F., 68, 82, 109n51, 109n55, 110n58, 112n74, 117n129, 117n131, 165, 179n37, 186n109, 233n28
Hegelians, Young, 29n2, 111n67, 284n26
Heidegger, Martin, 111n67, 189
Heraclitus, 81, 240n108, 269
Hermit, 37, 86, 104n6, 138, 180n48; Hermit #1 (Most Pious Man), 39-40, 49, 64-65, 104n8, 132, 133, 251-252; Hermit #2, 52, 53, 65, 108n44, 161
Hess, Moses, 283n23
Higher Man, 250-268. *See also* Crossing Over and Lion
Hollinrake, Roger, 110n58, 186n108, 187n118, 188n126, 200, 232n20, 235n52, 239n94, 305
Homer, 111n70, 162, 185n107, 200
Hunchback, 169, 172, 173, 175, 189n138, 198

Jester, 47ff., 54, 56, 83, 91, 101, 107n33, 107n37, 109n50, 118n145, 119n156, 141, 156, 174, 189n141, 204, 209, 234n45, 273
Jesus. *See* Christ
Justice. *See* Good and the Just

Kant, Immanuel, 60, 68, 75, 105n18, 108-109n46, 126, 127, 158, 159, 160, 165, 176n5, 179n37, 183n87, 184n98

Kings, 249, *See also* Higher Man
Kundera, Milan, 267

Last Pope, 10, 27, 251-255, 287n65
Last Man, x, xiii, 17, 45-46, 52, 64, 75, 91, 106n26, 119n156, 122, 126, 155, 168-169, 205, 281
Laughter, 19, 168, 173, 190n145, 217, 259, 267-268, 271, 275, 278; laughing, 40, 52, 200, 249; laughing lion, 216; laughing god, 98, 251; laugh of welcome, 281; laughter forbidden by Jesus, 98, 214
Leech. *See* Scientific Spirit
Lion, 33, 49, 60-64, 73, 78, 80, 90, 93, 94, 96, 110n57, 110n63, 119n156, 120n168, 125-126, 142-144, 154, 232n25, 271; lion-in-crisis, 73, 78, 155, 160, 248, 286n59, 286n60
Luther, Martin, Lutheran, Luther Bible, 1, 2, 13, 106n24, 177n16, 177n19, 271

Magician, 10, 250ff., 268, 270ff., 275, 286n55
Marx, Karl, 76, 105n15, 107n38, 111nn66-67, 170, 188n125, 283n23, 284n26
Messer, August, 107n33, 107nn36-37, 108n39, 108n44, 109n50, 115n104, 115n114, 117n132, 117n137, 177n18, 177n20, 178n30, 178n32, 179n33, 179nn35-36, 180nn67-68, 187nn120-121, 188n126, 189n138, 190n143, 258, 286n57
Metaphysics, 26, 64, 66, 105n14, 150, 163, 164, 112n76
Metamorphoses. *See* Spirit
Mohammad, 121
Moses, 55, 61, 109n48, 216, 275

Naumann, Carl Gustav, 117n132, 117n137, 140, 177n18, 178n29,

184n91, 185n100, 187n118, 187nn120-121, 188n126, 190n143, 233n37, 234n48, 258, 282n3, 282n5, 284n34, 285n41, 285n46, 286n59, 286n61

Nihilism: Zarathustra not a nihilist, ix, 13, 196, 197, 208, presumption of nihilism, ix; future beyond nihilism, ix-x, xiii, 18, 97, 155, 202, 212; the coming of nihilism, x-xii, 166-167, 199, 205, 208-209, 216, 247-249, 269, 278, 284n59; concept of, 61; revulsion at, 62; lion as nihilist par excellence, 61, 62, 64, 143; and higher men, 93, 257, 278; idols create nihilism, 102, 211, 235n52, 269; or overman, 148; as spirit of gravity, 197; as test of human types, 220, 228; Magician as, 268; and Shadow, 284n34

Noon, Great Noon, 260

Oedipus, 255

Ormuzd. *See* Ahriman

Overman [*Uebermensch*]: riddle of the overman, ix, xvii, 16-17, 24ff., 56ff., 71, 73, 86, 99, 115n111, 125, 129, 145, 150, 164ff., 173, 175, 187n121, 190n145, 197, 199, 201, 208, 227, 2247, 268; type of the overman, x-xiii, xv, 17ff., 23, 25, 28, 33, 40ff., 47, 54, 64, 76, 81, 86-87, 89, 91-92, 97, 99, 101, 104n10, 1205n12, 105n18, 106n60, 118n144, 126, 131, 137, 140, 153ff., 156, 158, 160, 162, 179, 170, 173, 182n78, 183n84, 188n129, 188n130, 204, 207, 220, 222, 269, 282n1; birth of/diremption into the overman, 26, 119n56, 129, 134, 152-153, 168, 189n133, 253-254, 264-265, 278-279, 286n59; versus the last man, xiii, 17-18, 33, 45-46, 64, 106n126, 1222, 168, 205, 281;

contrast to the higher men, 45, 47, 49, 94, 128, 201, 212, 279, 280, 285n50; Zarathustra as overman, 146, 191, 195, 201, 222, 224-225, 239n92, 246, 247; Dionysus as overman, 19, 77, 212, 220, 225, 246, 269; dangers to the overman, xv, 182n74, 272; overman not a criminal, 74-75; overman not political, 83, 249, 261-262, 285n43; overman not the devil, 173, 190n143; overman not a god, 67, 71, 105n14, 126, 130, 163-164, 202; overman not a god, 67, 71, 105n14, 126, 130, 163-164, 202; overman, 141, 163-164, 216-217, 218, 280; overman and eternal return, 195, 200, 201, 203, 230n4, 276; synthesis of the overman, 170, 223, 228

Pan, 258, 284

Pathos of Distance, 39, 121

Philosophy: Nietzsche's philosophy untimely, viii; philsophical foundations of Nazism, 12; zarathustran philosophy, 18, 21, 216; characters in *Zarathustra* not individual philosophers, 236n60; idealists, 68; official state philosophy, 249; philosophical systems, 162; Nietzsche's philosphy of life, 75-76, 138, 216; western philosophy as disguised christianity, 165, 235n51; philosophers of the future, 67; philophy at the service of Zarathustra, 64

Most Pious Man. *See* Hermit

Plato, Platonism, 42, 82, 90, 184n89, 240n108, 269

Post-christian Era, x, xii, xiii, xv, 18, 82, 161, 247

Prometheus, 72, 99, 100, 102, 181n56, 211, 246, 253

DATE DUE
